Praise for *Book of Li*

'Deborah has been surprising me since she was 13. This brave and passionate book has done it yet again.' **Caroline Wilson**

'Deb is not just a talented wordsmith, she's a master storyteller. Her collected memories and ideas are so much more than the sum of their glorious parts. *Book of Life* is an enthralling, unputdownable read.' **Toni Collette**

'What it takes to live a life of independence, told with the infamous directness of one of our finest living songwriters . . . A witty, searingly honest testimony of what it really took to become one of Australia's most beloved storytellers.' **Clare Bowditch**

'It's a wild wind that blows through the pages of the *Book of Life*; full of movement, gusto, grit, creative struggle and love. Love of partners, love of family, and most of all, love of music. The text is spliced with songs I could almost hear. I appreciated every honest, emotional, human page. *Book of Life* reminded me life is messy, big, full of wonder and change as its heroine moves from the impetuous, passionate folly of youth to rich and textured maturity. I was utterly engrossed and deeply appreciative.' **Sofie Laguna**

'A wild ride! Candid and revealing, witty, wise and full of [the] wonder and grit of making glorious music.' **Brian Nankervis**

'Deborah Conway is ringmaster taking us on a wild ride through sex, love, birth, death, business, friendship, creativity and the magic of song. She is as sharp, honest, brave, funny and brazen on the page as she is on stage or at her table, offering nourishment for all comers.' **Ramona Koval**

About the Author

Deborah Conway has been a musician for over 40 years. Innovator, motivator, role model, facilitator and entrepreneur, Conway is fearless in her risk taking, has pushed and pulled existing boundaries and has always argued her cause with integrity and intelligence to pursue the highest standards of whatever is in her sights. For the last three decades, Willy Zygier, musician, songwriter and composer, has been her primary collaborator.

Aside from releasing a dozen studio albums and playing countless live shows, Conway has been a producer, festival director and actor.

In 2020 Conway was created a Member (AM) of the Order of Australia and received the Australia Council's Don Banks Award for outstanding contribution to music. In 2022 Conway was inducted into Music Victoria's Hall of Fame.

DEBORAH CONWAY

Book *of* Life

ALLEN&UNWIN
SYDNEY • MELBOURNE • AUCKLAND • LONDON

First published in 2023

Allen & Unwin
Cammeraygal Country
83 Alexander Street
Crows Nest NSW 2065
Australia
Phone: (61 2) 8425 0100
Email: info@allenandunwin.com
Web: www.allenandunwin.com

Allen & Unwin acknowledges the Traditional Owners of the Country on which we live and work. We pay our respects to all Aboriginal and Torres Strait Islander Elders, past and present.

NATIONAL LIBRARY OF AUSTRALIA

A catalogue record for this book is available from the National Library of Australia

ISBN 978 1 76106 938 3

Set in 12.25/18.25 pt Bembo Std by Midland Typesetters, Australia
Printed and bound in Australia by Opus Group

10 9 8 7 6 5 4 3 2 1

FSC www.fsc.org MIX Paper | Supporting responsible forestry FSC® C001695

The paper in this book is FSC® certified. FSC® promotes environmentally responsible, socially beneficial and economically viable management of the world's forests.

For Willy, everything.

Anyway, I have only lately determined to remember some of my early adventures. Till now I have always avoided them, even with a certain uneasiness. Now, when I am not only recalling them, but have actually decided to write an account of them, I want to try the experiment whether one can, even with oneself, be perfectly open and not take fright at the whole truth.

—Fyodor Dostoevsky, *Notes from the Underground*

To Charlotte I said that society columns should contain a shimmer of error.

—Vladimir Nabokov, *Lolita*

Contents

Foreword

We scratch out a life: some with grand ambitions and plans, some without care, some with rigour, some with hedonism; most with an unthinking combination of the above. If one can bear to write it down, maybe one can figure what they were trying to do with their allotment; come to some understanding of who, what, where and why they are.

My wife, my partner, Deborah Conway (Mrs Zygier—there're not too many of those in the world) is a fierce person; unafraid, incautious, loyal, loving and at times disagreeable, qualities that are valuable in a lover and a friend (especially when those are some of the qualities I could use more of). For thirty-two years at time of writing, we have been together, firstly as co-workers, then as lovers, then as parents, then as husband and wife—all of this is detailed in this book.

Most things we do together—finish each other's lyrics and musical phrases, share politics and ideas—but Deborah has taken on this book without me, though of course it too involves us as partners. There is much of my life I've had to relive and re-realise in these pages.

When our careers started, musicians were cultural heroes. Now, as we hurtle towards old age, we find that the popular musician is less a cultural fixture; less influential, but closer to the core truth of what we do, workers in song, curators of air.

In a sense, our songs have been an ongoing attempt at autobiography. The best of them get close—even if they're smothered in fiction and metaphor and poetry—still able to get at some primal, emotional truth about who we are, and I imagine that's the reason we've been compelled to write them. The song cries, 'This is me'. It stands as a little slice of revelation, an idea that, if it works, will stay, potentially after we are no longer able to croak out a note or have the strength to press down a string. But Deborah wanted to make her life explicit—to reckon with it. And thus this book.

Written mostly during the COVID-19 pandemic of 2020/2021, the volume got turned down at our place as she buried herself in the work. But of course, the music is there, each chapter connected either explicitly or obliquely to a song; and the poetry and the reality intertwine in strange ways. The music becomes life, and the life, music; and the writing, like the song, rings out into the air.

It is a sound that is strong, bouncing around, but as it and we inevitably must, will echo and reverberate, slowly but steadily, towards silence.

Willy Zygier, 2023

1

The Beginning

'Put an ad in the paper,' John said.

'Really, that's how I should find a band?'

'Sure: "Singer wants band" with your phone number. Put it in *Juke* magazine and see what happens.'

I got two responses. One from a three-piece band led by guitarist Sai Ferran-Lucas, a stylish fellow, rake-thin—dressed in black, of course—high cheekboned, dark eyes, restless energy. He had plans, he wanted me to be part of them. After my audition he came over to the large share house I was renting in Rockley Road, South Yarra. He paced around my bedroom and pitched his spiel. It was good: he was an earnest young man with bags of ambition.

The other interested party was guitar player Greg Thomas from rock outfit The Benders, whose singer had just departed. I carefully selected my wardrobe—tight black jumper, emerald-green suede miniskirt, blue tap shoes (without the taps)—and joined the queue of bearded men with established beer guts (I guessed the departed singer was the blueprint) outside a rehearsal studio in one of Melbourne's endless outer-eastern suburbs.

Four musicians all faced each other with space for a singer. I stood behind the microphone directly opposite the drummer, who was channelling Keith Moon, complete with stick twirls and a manic but strangely comforting smile. I was intrigued—every time I looked at him he grinned back. I was thinking, *better humour him, I might get the gig*. I got a call later that afternoon with an invitation to join.

Then it got confusing, I had been leaning towards 'man in black' Sai Ferran-Lucas until the stick-twirling drummer, a redhead called Dorland Bray, was dispatched with instructions to persuade me that The Benders were by far the better option. It was a tough choice, but the redhead sitting on my bed making me laugh felt like my new best friend.

I joined The Benders.

Patti Smith's album *Horses* was a regular spin on my stereo. I wanted to sing the opening track, her version of Van Morrison's 'Gloria', at our first gig. I rehearsed it along with a mountain of other pre-existing Benders material. But after weeks perfecting my version of Patti's version of Van Morrison's version, I decided it wasn't a different enough version and therefore it was cabaret—basically the worst thing you could be in the 1980s.

We didn't need 'Gloria' anyway. The London Tavern was packed, oversold even, with friends and family to witness my debut, which went off beyond anything I'd imagined. There were encores aplenty and a suitably sodden carpet. I loved it: being on stage was an incredible sensation, singing out front of that wall of sound, entirely in control. This was for me.

My abilities and my interests had just lined up. I was twenty.

2

Imperfect Words

'Imperfect Words', *Words of Men*, 2019

I might have been a teacher
A rabbi or a preacher then
But as the path got narrow
I understood I wasn't one of them

Not for me
The shepherd for a flock of lost souls
I sing I sing I sing
Imperfect words
They roll off my tongue
I got something for everyone

And as I've gotten older
I don't have the steady shoulder I would like

My framework is more fragile
It's true I'm less agile in a fight

Not for me
A pugilist scrapping on the kerbs
I sing I sing I sing
Imperfect words
They roll off my tongue
I got something for everyone

And when I was a dealer
I met people who were meaner than me
They stole my pot, my cash
You could say they let me down reliably
Not again
A merchant of magical herbs
I sing I sing I sing
Imperfect words
They roll off my tongue
I got something for everyone
They roll off my tongue
You know I got something for everyone

So gather round friends
Come listen to me
You cunts who thought
I lived the life of a devotee
Well I'm a big bad wolf
Breathing at your door

You let me in with these words I sing
You let me in once more

In a life that's full of choice
I got to use my voice, fate smiled
In my strange chosen profession
I got permission to stay a child

Not for me, responsibility
I'd rather be off with the birds
I sing I sing I sing
Imperfect words
They roll off my tongue
I got something for everyone
They roll off my tongue
You know I got something for everyone

I'd always liked singing. As a kid, I'd leap at any chance to sing in public. Singalongs at summer camps or parties, I'd be belting it out at any given opportunity; but apart from the junior school musical in Grade 6, where I scored the eponymous role in *The Tailor* (I can still sing the title song) in a hard-fought contest with Tania Hardy-Smith who became my understudy, I never sang at school. I didn't much like Miss Gibson, the music teacher at Lauriston Girls' School, who I thought was very bossy. I am perfectly prepared to admit she was probably only as bossy as she needed to be to keep thirty pre-pubescent girls in line and on task, but I arced up.

These days, I look back wistfully on those madrigal performances and wish I had been disciplined enough to take part;

they would have helped me immeasurably with harmony, blending and reading, all woefully undercooked skills for me.

As an adolescent, I begged for singing lessons. My mother thought I was too young but after much nagging she got a recommendation for a singing teacher. My younger sister and I both went along. My sister passed muster but the teacher told my mother I was at risk of getting nodules if I had lessons. And that was the end of it.

A few years later I got to sit in a circle around a piano in a dingy front parlour, with a ragtag bunch of eager pupils taking turns to sing exercises for Molly, the grandmotherly vocal coach who would critique us. I was initially enthusiastic but six months in, I stopped going. I'd learnt nothing.

When I was in Form 4, today's equivalent of Year 10, a company that assisted young people with career advice came to our school and gave us all a multi-page questionnaire to fill out. According to the boxes I'd ticked, I was destined to find job fulfilment as a travel agent. I had no notion of what I wanted to do, but becoming a travel agent—which I imagined involved caring about where people you didn't know went on their holidays—featured nowhere on my vocational wish list. Not only did I take no heed of the recommendation, it instilled in me a suspicion of experts.

It would have made my parents very happy if I had chosen to read law. My father, Carl, a barrister and solicitor, never openly stated this, but when I was around fourteen years old—roughly coinciding with my unrealised future travel agent designation—he took me to court in order to give me some insight into how the law worked. He was sensible, choosing a day of salacious cases, but I could barely stay awake during legal discussions about prostitution, drug heists and general vice, and concluded, sadly for him, the law was not for me.

At fifteen I took a summer job for two weeks in our family friend's jewellery store. I was supposed to look busy at all times, which meant that when I had dusted all the glass shelves, taken down the *tchotchkes* to polish, then put everything back exactly how it was—and there was still no one in the Bourke Street store to serve—I was not allowed to sit behind the counter and read a book. I tried and was roundly told off.

Who was I looking busy for? There was no one there! And what customer would be put off walking into a shop if they saw a salesperson using their time effectively while waiting for them? It was a completely senseless directive, and I quit before the fortnight was up.

At sixteen I did a stint in a Snoopy suit handing out chocolate bars in a supermarket car park. It was a pavement-melting-hot day and the kids were going crazy looking underneath my great furry head and trying to yank it off. I broke the cardinal rule and snarled out a warning: 'Rack off!' Though technically not a bark, it was enough to put me in the doghouse.

At seventeen I waitressed for a few weeks at The Lemon Tree in Carlton but got sacked for the harmless infraction of eating leftovers from the customers' plates while hiding behind a conveniently placed pillar. I realised with a diamond-focus singularity that I wasn't cut out to be an employee.

I was very keen on acting and was in all of the senior school drama productions. Lauriston, being an all-girl's school, cast the male roles with the taller girls, of which I was the tallest (apart from Margie Strom, but I can't remember whether Margie, who was an athletic type, was interested in the dramatic arts). At any rate I loved it, and was happy to stay back after school every day to rehearse with our drama teacher, Miss Val Heath, for even the smallest turn.

I remember being a dead person in Thornton Wilder's *Our Town* and relishing my role as Mr Billings in *The Happiest Days of Your Life*, a British farce that predates *St Trinian's*. I even snagged a couple of rare female parts: Louka, the saucy maid in George Bernard Shaw's *Arms and the Man*, and Nurse Brent in *Bonaventure*. But beyond junior school, Lauriston didn't stage musicals, so I didn't sing at school in all my middle and senior years. My mother likes to tell people that the most musical thing I did at high school was drop a cymbal down a set of metal stairs when classes were in and the school was silent. I'm almost sure I wouldn't have done that deliberately.

On our final day of Form 6, cooling our heels before the HSC exams, I was sitting in the empty assembly hall with a bunch of girls talking through our tertiary preferences. I was going to audition for NIDA—the National Institute of Dramatic Arts—and offered to perform the song I'd prepared, Barbra Streisand's version of 'Queen Bee'. I belted it out a cappella for the girls. They were amazed—or they said they were.

'You can sing!'

'Wow, I never knew!'

It was the kind of response that made me realise I could genuinely do this. I could connect. I'd always sung Liza Minnelli, Barbra Streisand and Judy Garland showstoppers in the shower, the ones most adolescents of that time liked to sing (these days it's Beyoncé and Idina Menzel). I thought I was pretty good, but once out of the shower, my mother would often observe aloud that my voice was a bit immature to do justice to those songs, in the kindest way she could. I was probably screeching, but to my ears I was terrific.

I turned up for my NIDA audition with my prepared Shakespeare and my Streisand song. I didn't get a call back. *C'est la vie.*

I moved on to my second preference, and enrolled in a Media Studies course at RMIT. The course was in its infancy, maybe even its first year of being offered, and the curriculum was loose. After three months of turning up to class to watch movies, I decided my heart wasn't in it and dropped out. I had no idea what I would do with a three-year Media Studies degree anyway. My parents were overseas at the time, so I had a couple of months to avoid facing whatever consequences would be forthcoming.

The following year I enrolled in a Bachelor of Arts degree at the University of Melbourne, majoring in history and philosophy. I managed to reduce eleven essential hours of tutorials and lectures down to one. The crunch was coming. In the middle of sitting the philosophy exam I had an overwhelming urge to wash my car, an urge I'd never had before, or indeed since; but sufficiently pressing for me to abandon my exam, leave the hall and attend to my red-with-white-roof Type 3 Karmann Ghia.

I passed my philosophy exam with honours, but knew with complete certainty that if I pushed my luck in Second Year with my otiose attitude, I would fail. My parents were again travelling overseas when I pulled the plug for the second time on a degree I knew I wouldn't know what to do with.

I had started modelling at eighteen, strictly for the dough. It was 1978, a few years before Claudia Schiffer, Naomi Campbell and Cindy Crawford turned models into supermodels. I never thought of it as a vocation but if I was going to be able to move out of home, I knew modelling had way superior earning capacity to retail and bar work, which paid a lousy $6 an hour while you put up with drunks until 2 am. I had been blessed with high cheekbones and height, so I took the money I'd saved from birthday gifts and had some photos taken, which I was told I would need if an agency was going to represent me. I arranged the photos in a nice black leather portfolio, brought them along to my appointment with Cameron's Modelling Agency, and they signed me up.

It was a gig I wasn't quite serious enough about. When I was still in Melbourne, I frequently turned up to jobs without a hairbrush for my extremely unruly mop. I thought it looked better unbrushed; when I brushed my hair it flattened out the curls and left frizz in its place. Nor did I like shaving my body hair; I occasionally got complaints about that too. I liked to think I was forging a different appreciation of feminine allure, but clearly I was ahead of my time (maybe I still am).

Despite my philosophical differences with the fashion industry, I figured if you were going to 'work for the man' you should maximise your hourly rate; I was very relaxed about exploiting my natural advantages posing for the camera or pacing up and down a catwalk to make $60 an hour. TV commercials paid a lot more. I was the 'Show us your smile' Macleans toothpaste girl, the 'Change the colour of your day' Crunchie chocolate bar girl, the 'Hot-Big-M-Eggflip' girl; I featured regularly on *Patons Knitting Patterns* as their cover girl and, lest we forget, my anonymous derriere, with the caption 'Get Yours into Bluegrass', was blown up to billboard size and infamously hung over the main traffic arteries of Melbourne—and possibly the rest of the country. I never asked.

As the controversy over the potential corruption of schoolchildren, not to mention the psychological damage of looking at an enormous bare bottom, was building on talkback radio stations,

I decided to reveal my identity. Along with my journalist pals Peter Wilmoth and Tony Heselev (brother of my friend John who had already suggested the aforementioned three-word ad in *Juke* magazine—they charged by the word), I sucked down a couple of bongs to ensure our quipping was on point and constructed an article full of double entendres like 'I had to get to the bottom of it', 'It's all behind me now' and 'I barely knew what I was doing'. Good, clean fun for young stoners.

The article appeared in *The Sun News Pictorial* the following day, accompanied by a photo of yours truly, eyes looking rather slitty, alongside the smoking-gun photo of the billboard. No doubt Bluegrass Jeans would have been delighted; my mother less so. She spied it early in the morning, dashed over to her mother's house and removed the offending page from the paper sitting on Nanna's doorstep. My mother was growing accustomed to protecting her loved ones from my depravities.

I had sung in local bands with friends, notably at a couple of the famous RMIT Architecture Reviews. There was a recording made of one, though I have no idea where that is now. But I listened to it at the time and the sound of my vocal was arresting, it encouraged me to chase the rabbit a bit harder. Hence the ad and the subsequent gig as lead singer with The Benders.

This was a worrying development for my father, who decided I needed to visit a psychiatrist. He was convinced that being in a band would lead to sex and drugs—and fair enough, it is rock 'n' roll's byline—and it was a questionable career path for a nice Jewish girl from a middle-class family.

Not unexpectedly, the psychiatrist concurred with me that I was the poster girl for sanity, and if my potential career choice (a highfalutin description) was not making my father happy, then that was my father's problem. At around the same time, my parents found out I was interested in getting a motorbike licence. I was sat down in the living room for an intervention and by the end I'd relented on the motorbike (probably for the best). But not rock 'n' roll!

The Benders played at the London Tavern a lot over our eight-month lifespan. In fact we played everywhere a lot. We had barely a night off, even though the crowd sizes didn't always justify us performing every Tuesday at the Market Hotel, Wednesdays at the Railway Hotel, Thursdays at the London Tavern, Fridays and Saturdays at Martini's or Macy's or wherever. No money exchanged hands. I wasn't doing it for the money; I was modelling to pay the rent and it hadn't occurred to me that being in a band might be a profit-turning exercise.

But over the long cold winter of 1980 when audiences were all staying home to watch TV, I began to crave a night in. The novel thrill of singing out front of The Benders' wall of sound had begun to pall. I had become weary on stage and started turning my back to the audience during the interminable guitar solos, pulling my singlet aside to flash my breasts at Dorland, both for my amusement and to register my growing ennui. He never dropped a beat.

And then we got a manager. I have no idea from whence he came, but he broke the news that despite our overactive gig diary we were in a considerable amount of debt, largely due to a recording, *Picnic at Oakleigh Rotunda*, that had been made and released before my involvement. The manager informed me that I would still have to shoulder an equal percentage of the financial obligation. Strangely, I didn't leave then.

Nor did I leave after the night we performed at Billboard, a gig where we would supposedly be paid . . . drum roll . . . $25 each. After struggling to find a car park, I turned up fifteen minutes late—forty-five minutes before show time instead of an hour—to be informed by our new manager that for my infraction I would be docked $10.

My irritation with that injustice was subsumed by the breaking news that John Lennon had just been gunned down outside his New York apartment block by Mark David Chapman. It was 8 December, 1980. The long cold winter had turned into a summer of dissatisfaction. Soon after, Dorland told me he'd had enough of the band and was leaving.

Dorland had an enviably straight-backed drummer's posture, slim hips, freckles, a thick thatch of red hair atop a classically pale, red-head complexion; red stubble if he hadn't shaved and lively blue eyes that danced with the inherent humour of life under his red bushy eyebrows. He was hilarious. He made me laugh and I made him laugh; he was silly and playful and unafraid to give expression to his feminine side. Consequently women loved his company and he loved women.

He loved music; we had long, passionate discussions about Talking Heads, Blondie, Randy Newman, Joni Mitchell, Tom Waits, David Bowie, a long list; and he loved wine. It was the hat-trick—wine, women and song! He was always good for a thorough postmortem bitch session—who doesn't love that?—and he liked gossip but he wasn't cruel (or, if he was cruel, he was fair).

A superb lyricist and a clever cartoonist, Dorland was brilliant in many ways. He felt his politics deeply, always coming out on the side of the underdog, but he was thoughtful, not reactive, and he fought fiercely against bullying tactics, be it from our industry or more broadly. He was the one making the set-up bearable for me; we'd shared our frustrations about the manager, the songs and the assembly line approach to gigs. We talked endlessly of the musical influences we'd rather be exploring; while The Benders sound was intense, dense, many, many notes crammed against each other, we were interested in the space between notes. Our new musical venture (at least in the early years) would be far more aligned to making music that was spare and direct.

When Dorland declared his intention to quit, I followed suit. He effectively persuaded me that we needed to establish our next musical venture in Sydney. I left my household, my friends, my family and my boyfriend (probably just before he left me) for the spirit of adventure. We were 'two drifters off to see the world'.

We packed our worldly possessions into my Honda Civic and drove north.

3

Cul de Sac

Leaving Melbourne felt like a breakout, even though I'd enjoyed living in my coming-of-age share house in Rockley Road, into which I had moved a year earlier with my childhood friend Caro Wilson. She had just started work as a cadet at the *Herald Sun* newspaper; Peter Wilmoth, another cadet journalist friend of hers, and Peter Capp, a panel operator friend of his, took two more rooms. Then there was Chris Hunter. He was a bit older and played bass in a band called the Cuban Heels.

We were a motley group, in an unrenovated 1920s Californian bungalow in an exclusive cul-de-sac in South Yarra when such things were possible. This place had a veritable lemon orchard out the back that not one of us knew how to take care of, though our dogs made good use of it. The population swelled to eight when one housemate's girlfriend and another housemate's sister moved in. One of them had a tendency to label items in the fridge 'NOT YOURS', and the other sometimes allowed her raging speed addiction to adversely modify her communications. I once found a note written in CAPITAL LETTERS stuck in my bedroom door with a kitchen knife; the contents of the note were secondary to their sobering delivery. It was a wonderful house to live in straight out of the family home.

I began life in Kew, before my parents built their own house in the early 1960s at 4 Ultimo Court, Toorak, a quiet cul-de-sac in a leafy corner of *Melway's* Map 58. We moved in when I turned three, and six months later my sister Shellie was born.

The house was a single-storey, pale-orange brick, three-sided building. The longest side faced north with floor-to-ceiling windows looking onto the crazy-paving patio, and a patch of grass where we had a swing set and plastic blow-up pool in the summer. Inside there were sliding decorative metal grilles to define areas in the large space.

Immediately to the right of the front door was the one room in this section of the house with a door, my father's den, an appropriate descriptor for that very dark room. The wallpaper was deep green, etched with a dull copper pattern; one window faced the front of the house, south, but in my memory the curtains were almost always drawn.

My mother tells me that as a toddler I upended her handbag, located and ate her lipstick which turned my poo hot pink; I also vomited after drinking too much red lemonade, which necessitated a doctor's visit to reassure my mother I wasn't throwing up blood. I was a sickly child with terrible lungs; a physiotherapist would come to our house daily, turn me upside-down and beat me on the back.

I was four when my tonsils and adenoids were removed, which resulted in at least a week of jelly and ice-cream for every meal and a more robust constitution. I was allergic to stone fruit but I loved apricots so much, I ate my way through the body rashes.

I remember my mother sitting on the floor of her dressing room to put on her stockings which were fastened with a garter belt.

One night Melbourne's notorious cat burglar paid us a visit. In the aftermath I peered through my mother's legs while two large men in navy uniforms surveyed her tumbled dressing room, the intimate contents of her drawers on the floor. The home invasion didn't scare me, but around the same time I was listening to a recording of the Pied Piper that amply supplied a rich dark vein of nightmare material for my imagination. The story is about a rat catcher who is employed by the village to rid them of a plague of rats, but once the job is done the fine upstanding citizens from the village refuse to acknowledge the payment owed. Revenge is brutal and immediate. The Pied Piper plays his magical flute and like the rats before them, all the little children follow the hypnotic sound into a cave and are never seen again. This terrified me so thoroughly that my parents gave the record away.

I remember turning seven and getting a long yellow feather quill and a globe of the world that spun on a metal axis. I get a warm glow when I think of that birthday haul. I still have the globe.

Toorak was a sedate neighbourhood, so we were allowed to wander outside the house freely, and in the warmer months with no clothes on. My darling mother tells me she could never understand why the neighbours criticised her for letting us out sans clothing.

I planted a tree in the front garden, a silver birch sapling, but we moved out of that house when I was nine and I missed seeing it grow to full size. I stopped by recently to look. The silver birch all these decades later is now a graceful adult.

The house had a wide entrance area, laid with pale marble floor tiles like the yellow brick road to the Emerald City. The visitor could follow it left to the lounge and dining room with its Arabian Night trompe l'œil but the view demanded a momentary pause while the new visitor's eyes were automatically drawn to the floor-to-ceiling windows framing the garden directly ahead. Imagine the surprise the unsuspecting guest experienced when they realised they were standing on top of a large in-ground fishpond. Despite the pond being covered in a layer of thick glass suitable for walking (or even jumping) on, people invariably found it disconcerting. The pond was almost as wide as the hallway itself, so a first-time visitor would look down and then take a few very quick steps forward, or attempt a small leap to the right followed by a tightrope-style walk along the edge to avoid stepping on it. It was a classic 1960s architectural feature but beyond the aesthetic, I suspect the primary reason my father had it built was that the unnerving provocation amused him.

The glass had to come off for cleaning fairly regularly.

One afternoon my father had arranged a business meeting at home, a rare event. Shortly before the appointed start time he looked at the fishpond and decided it had to be cleaned. My mother, his ever-patient helpmeet, gently reminded him he wasn't wearing fishpond-cleaning attire.

'Don't argue, just help me get the glass off,' he snapped, and then stormed outside to clean the filter. Moments later he stormed (there was a lot of storming) back inside, forgetting that he had just removed the glass cover. And right there is one of his truly magnificent gifts to me; the image, forever etched in my memory, of my father standing knee-deep in the fishpond, dressed in his best suit, screaming.

I once fell in too; I had been trying to paint the goldfish (in watercolours, of course) and lost my balance. I'm pretty sure Shellie also took a dip, but I can't recall if she had as good an excuse.

'Cul de Sac', *Half Man Half Woman*, 2010

I like this house
Your face
This place
I adore it
This room
My clothes
Our bed
I enjoy it
And all we should do is waltz right on through it
Our shack in our cul de sac

Everyday's fine
Like summer wine

We're love birds
We're drunk
On dreams and schemes
In the suburbs
This sedentary life
You're husband, I'm wife
We're on track in our cul de sac

We can pretend
We're rich
And spend
What we pleases
We'll buy
The sky
The birds and the breezes
And all they can do is fly right on through it
Out back of our cul de sac

Children grow up
Leave school
Leave home
Children get married
Have children of their own
The dog just died
He's under the daisies

Time drifts along
Our days
Stretch on

But lately
Each year
I'm here
Seems to take approximately
Half as much time as when I was nine
On Dad's back walking home
The twilight so long
The roses in bloom
While the moon led us on
Shining light on the path
We'd sing out at the dark
Coming back to our cul de sac

My father, though not a gambler per se, was heavily invested in the stock market. When the mining sector crashed in 1970 and all the fortunes that the mining company Poseidon had created were suddenly reduced to zeros on everyone's balance sheets, my parents sold our house and we moved into a flat. Carl decided it was time to go back to working as a salaryman, a barrister/solicitor in a government office. He relegated his toupee to weekends only.

The flat was in another cul-de-sac on *Melway's* Map 58 on the ground floor in a block of two with our landlord living upstairs. There was an empty block of land next door which was a good place to hunt for lizards and get lost in the long grass. The big house across from us was owned by a family whose three children were similar ages to us and who Shellie and I played with.

The family had a swimming pool that we were allowed to use whether they were in residence or not. I remember there seemed to be plenty of times when we had the joint to ourselves.

My father used to sunbake by the pool for hours wearing tiny Speedos, a tiny pair of opaque plastic goggles that barely covered his eyeballs and a bottle of coconut oil to encourage a sizzling tan. He only ever sunbaked lying on his back, so while his front was a deep roasted hazelnut, his back was as pale as a vanilla slice.

Every few hours he would come back across the road before staggering into our kitchen like a man who'd been wandering for weeks in the Sahara, screaming for a Tab with ice, which my mother would immediately rush around getting for him. There is so much wrong with all of this by today's standards that it's hard to know where to begin, but there was a lot wrong with it back then too.

One hot afternoon when we were all around the pool, Dad dived in and swam the length underwater before reappearing at the other end; well, almost all of him reappearing. His toupee remained free-floating, a strange sea creature surfacing for air.

I was nine when we moved into that flat, fourteen when we moved out, so I spent my formative years there. For the first time my sister and I were allowed to ride bikes, which I loved. Unfortunately, it all went pear-shaped when I ran my sister over (I seem to remember a tyre imprint on her forehead). In my defence, she did keep putting herself in my path in that taunting way little sisters have. *It was me or her, Your Honour.* In that same period, one of our playmates managed to fall off her bike and knock out all her front teeth. My mother rushed her to the hospital; there was a lot of blood.

The bikes disappeared after that, never to be seen again. But there will always be blood; like the time I was bouncing Shellie on the bed and she slipped and split her head on the pointy corner of our chest of drawers. There were tears and stitches. And blood.

We must have drawn inspiration from those hospital visits; we played lots of games of doctors and nurses with our neighbours. The thrill of being inspected naked was enhanced because we had included a hide-and-seek element into the game. Basically, if you were found you had to be examined. It was before Spin the Bottle or Truth or Dare, those more flirtatious games we played a bit later; nevertheless it was exciting in a primitive sexual way that is hard to completely understand from an older vantage point.

It was a game of resolve where you had to hide really well or endure embarrassment, tickling, and whatever else my eight- and nine-year-old neighbours decided to do to me. The giving up of autonomy was quite thrilling, some kind of primitive precursor to S&M, though I have never been tempted down that path; I must have satisfied those urges back in my pre-teens.

Our neighbours' father was enormously large and afflicted with dreadful psoriasis, that unfortunate skin condition that made his skin either dry and red raw or peeling off in white sheets. And he would often go on extreme diets to counter his psoriasis or obesity or both. I didn't really know him but we were in the family home a lot and of course I would open the fridge to check it out, maybe get a Coke, a staple in their fridge. Sometimes I'd open the fridge to find it completely stuffed with iceberg lettuce and nothing else. Maybe everybody was on the iceberg lettuce diet, I thought sadly.

Some years after we had moved out of that flat, it was revealed that it wasn't just lettuce being stored in the fridge. Apparently, we had been living across the road from one of Australia's most notorious counterfeiters, who'd been making enough 'lettuce' to stock a greengrocer for years.

I wasn't allowed a cat or a dog in the flat but I was allowed to keep terrapins. I had two—Terry and Tony (I don't actually remember their names)—in a glass aquarium in our back room. This was the sunniest room and I liked spending time in it. Along with the aquarium, my mother's desk, where she typed letters for my father on her typewriter, was set up there. There was a piano that Shellie and I played a little bit, though never enthusiastically; it was always scales in those days and I could never find the fun in that. My mother started writing a short story in that room, in longhand on a stenographer's pad, a bit Enid Blyton-like, after the fashion of *Famous Five* or *Secret Seven*. Maybe she was trying to encourage me to read; I didn't love reading until I hit twelve.

Two years after I discovered books were fun, we moved out of Martin Court and into Lansell Road (still on *Melway's* Map 58) with its capacious rooms, green walls, creepy basement, multiple bathrooms and dim light, the exception being my bedroom which had the only north-facing window in the house. I loved having my own room, being in there felt a bit like being in my own private treehouse, sticking out from the rest of the second floor at an odd angle, three big windows, one north, one south and one east, and surrounded by great gums. My father insisted on the room being wallpapered in a pattern of sepia vintage cars, which I hated, but I compensated by covering the walls with posters of Paul Newman, Free Love, and Prune Juice Will Set You Free, etc.

The privacy was an illusion of course, and after six years of living with all the iniquities that rub against young people needing independence, I was desperate to move out of the parental home.

Rockley Road meant liberation. Barely any rules! Coming home at whatever time I chose, or not coming home at all; not having to answer to anyone's concern or fury when I couldn't be located; playing a lot of loud music; smoking a lot of pot in the lounge room; being able to invite a lot of people around at whatever hour; having frequent and wild parties.

I knew nothing of how to cook, apart from bacon and eggs, which I lived on quite happily; coming from a kosher home, I was new to the taste of bacon and couldn't get enough of it. Eventually, I found an old French cookbook and taught myself how to produce some passable meals. I slept in until whenever, or until my mother rang at 10 am, always with the greeting, 'Oh darling, it's so late I can't believe I've woken you up!'

It wasn't that I didn't love my parents. I loved my mother without reservation; my relationship with my father was more complex. But being out in the world as an entirely autonomous person was so exhilarating it was years before the sensation of being grateful to come home to my own space wore off.

After six months, Caro moved back home to save money, and I was told about a drummer looking for a room. I went down to meet him at Hearts, in inner-city Carlton, where he was playing with his band The Checks. Paul Hester moved into Rockley Road and we became fast friends.

Paul had a great way of cutting through bullshit; he was an unerringly accurate mimic, he made me laugh 'til it hurt and, bonus, he was exceptionally domesticated (particularly fond of vacuuming). That is the lay-down misère of perfect housemates. He was my confidante, always good for a late-night chat, a pot of tea and a foot rub. I missed him when I moved to Sydney.

4

Standing on Wires

If moving out of home was exciting, moving to another state was freedom writ large. No one would know what I was doing. Like Joni Mitchell's Parisian traveller 'I felt unfettered and alive'.

Rob Hirst, Midnight Oil's drummer, was a good friend of Dorland's. He kindly opened his house in the northern Sydney suburb of Chatswood to us southern refugees, and we moved in with him and his long-time girlfriend Leslie Holland. Dorland stayed living there but I accepted an invitation to house-sit a tiny but *trés chic* apartment in Elizabeth Bay with a view of the harbour and Kings Cross.

Interstate calls were expensive and I didn't flippantly make them, definitely not to my parents. I'd never indulged in full-blown adolescent rebellion as a teenager, but it caught up with a vengeance now, and soon moved past eating *treif* and smoking pot and continued in an upward trajectory as I acquired more antisocial and frequently illegal behaviours. As the yoke of our hometown fell away, Dorland and I were getting wilder. I started shoplifting (though only from big department stores—I had scruples). Dorland was a leader in the field. He told me he'd once exited Myer with a queen-size doona under one arm and a sheet set under the other.

Dorland got a day job in a vitamin factory, leaving me to track down Helen Carter, a bass player Dorland had met while crawling around on a bar-room floor at the end of a boozy night when he'd last been in Sydney. She, having stumbled over his feet, or he, over her legs, the two had struck up a conversation about music, which led to both of them realising they should absolutely form a band together, geography be damned.

The minor obstacle of being too pissed to have exchanged phone numbers was overcome many months later when I, not having a day job, played detective. I had Helen Carter—not a supremely uncommon name—but the fact that she was a female bass player was unusual, so unearthing this mystery woman among inner-city Sydney's cool rock 'n' roll denizens turned out to be a single day's work.

I found her in an office, slowly going out of her under-stimulated mind with the tedium of typing up correspondence and photocopying. I felt like St George, come to slay the dragon and rescue the maiden from its lair. Helen dived enthusiastically into my open arms and I carried her across the threshold into our new musical collective. Helen's bass melodies became the backbone of our catalogue, those long sinuous riffs wove around the beat until she had conjured ear worms that crawled deep inside your brain.

Her left-field approach to the instrument carried the melody in almost all our songs and stamped the band with its unique style. Helen was a bundle of livewire energy, friendly and warm, though combative when necessary, not easily intimidated, smart and direct; all excellent qualities for the task of being a female bass player in a rock band in the '80s. We were sisters in our shared adventure, and in the youthful experimentation that occupied our downtime.

We three met regularly, first at the Darlinghurst flat that Helen shared with her guitarist boyfriend Stephen Philip, formerly of the seminal Sydney punk band Thought Criminals. Having decided we liked each other and shared similar tastes in music, alcohol and cheap pasta joints, we rented a budget rehearsal room in Kent Street to start working up our tunes, mostly penned by Dorland. We needed a guitar player, but for whatever reason, Stephen was playing hard-to-get. He did agree to sketch out parts for the multiple guitarists we were auditioning. The auditions were revealing, flaws in one guitarist after another: too jazzy, too folky, too many notes, too out of time, too many solos, or just too annoying. We knew it could only be Stephen.

Stephen was Goldilocks: just-right kooky sounds, no flashy solos, all funky riffs circling round Helen's complex melodic bass lines. A noisemaker of the best kind, his limitations were his strengths. We all knew it, including him. He threw his lot in with us and we adopted the name Do-Ré-Mi, the name lifted from the Jackson 5 song 'ABC', another Dorland idea. We were ready to put our first songs down on a four-track desk set-up in the rehearsal studio, get them out on an EP and release them to our 'waiting public'.

Roger Grierson and Stuart Coupe put out that first release in 1982 on their newly established label Green Records, through EMI. Helen knew Roger well, and Roger was an enthusiast. Roger loved music and he loved musicians, not all of either but luckily he loved us. Our new EP was called, imaginatively, *The Green EP*—green by label, green by cover and green by virtue of our inexperience.

'Standing on Wires', track one, side one, a biting if oblique protest song about the Cold War and Australia's subordinate relationship with US imperialism, became a minor hit on alternative radio stations around the country.

In the studio in 1982, Do-Ré-Mi recorded six more songs for our second EP to be released a few months after *The Green EP*, this one called *The Waiting Room*. Alternative radio was listening; it picked up track two, side two.

'Man Overboard', a speed punk thrash on gender politics, began with an angelic introduction sung a cappella before plunging headlong into something completely other. This twelve-inch piece of vinyl was meant to be played at 45 rpm—it said so on the label! Every time this instruction was ignored, I heard myself transmogrified into Nick Cave incanting as a solemn lament, 'Your pubic hairs are on my pillow'. It happened a lot. And yet 'Man Overboard' became an alternative radio high-rotation favourite, at both speeds. (We heard it enough at 33 ⅓ rpm to seed the idea of trying a slower, snakier version for the full-length album we would eventually record.)

We were having a lot of success with our modus operandi. Critics were reviewing our discs, some favourably, some less so, listeners were buying them, people were talking—who were we, why hadn't we played, when were we going to? Were we lazy? Dilettantes? Wankers? The other thing we weren't doing was talking to journalists, at least not without demanding a double-page spread sans ads and being able to choose the accompanying photos; *RAM* magazine acquiesced to our demands and other music journalists howled foul, and wrote about our obstreperous image. We were control freaks, but it wasn't doing us any harm. People were curious, incensed, irritated, intrigued; at least they were talking about us.

We had intended to release four EPs before we climbed on a stage, but after we'd released our second EP the building wave of interest was proving irresistible. Our first-ever live show was an invitation-only private function on 31 July, 1982, at an alternative performance space called Arts House. As it wasn't a music venue we had to organise a bar for the night, but it was worth the trouble. Dorland designed the flyers and a $1 donation was requested. Despite the exorbitant ticket price, the joint was packed and, according to the reviews, even from the very critical critics, we delivered.

'Standing on Wires' was the breath-holding song of the set; there was familiarity because of all the airplay but we'd also worked up an extended version, the four of us playing percussion in varying degrees of complexity; the effect was powerful and the room heaved with warm bodies pressed against each other, swaying and stomping along to the chorus. This was the polar opposite experience to the last time I'd played live music with The Benders. This was ownership. We all had serious skin in the game and we were all committed to the idea of the collective. Do-Ré-Mi was an indisputably tight unit every way you could interpret it. The positive feedback we got from playing our songs to real people in a room was addictive; we organised more shows in unusual venues, sticking with warehouses and galleries before succumbing to convention and playing pubs and clubs like everybody else. The unrecorded third and fourth EPs remained unrecorded.

5

Holes in the Road

Dorland and I had made the move north for music, but music still wasn't gonna pay the rent—not yet, at least. I remained signed to Cameron's Models, whose head office was in Sydney and where the adorable (but tough when she needed to be) Lydia Livingstone, Jane Cameron's business colleague, was working the phones.

Lydia was also working with fashion designer Linda Jackson and her work and life partner Fran Moore, helping them out with their expanding business. I became the office conduit for illegal herbal dry goods on a semi-regular basis, a service which transmogrified into my becoming Girl Friday for Linda Jackson Studios.

Linda, formerly in business with Jenny Kee in Flamingo Park, had opened her own fashion house very close to Radio Double or Triple J (whichever the handle was in 1981). It was a bright, sunny first-floor studio where lots of people created beautiful things in silk, silk taffeta, linen and chiffon; there were fabric printers, sewing mistresses stitching gorgeous frocks and others ornamenting outfits with mismatched and crazily inventive accessories. And there were plenty of visitors there to buy frocks.

Linda was like a rainbow of eccentric light waves, around 5 ft 4, impossible to miss and yet able to facilitate any number of activities without being domineering; hovering over everyone, and everything, like an eccentric good fairy, pinning, tucking, waving feathers and coloured cloth around, and making sure that all was done to her specifications while appearing entirely detached from it all. It was kind of miraculous to witness.

I wore Linda's beautiful clothes around the studio, got to play dress-ups when the clothes needed to be modelled for visiting clients, or strut the catwalk when a fashion show was scheduled. I would run to the post office as required, dressed in layers of black taffeta and Doc Martens. Back then Lydia was in a relationship with the talent agent Harry M. Miller, who was doing time At Her Majesty's Pleasure for defrauding investors in his bankrupt ticketing agency Computicket, and communications were being conducted via the post.

It was all pretty easygoing, and not really like a job at all. Linda and I would sometimes skive off to Bondi where she would take photos of me in her latest designs. It was perfect for me—the job you have when you don't like having a boss.

Renée Geyer was one of Linda's clients. One memorable day she popped into the studio for a fitting. She had a bottle of Johnny Walker with her, and was clearly quite fond of a drink. She'd been measured and was relaxing back on a chair when I was introduced to her as a singer. Her posture stiffened and immediately all her attention fixed on me. We started a conversation around playing live shows. Renée was of the opinion that you needed to play a lot of them to hone your craft, and in retrospect I would agree with her. However, at the time Dorland and I wanted our fledgling band to do things differently; we'd just escaped The Benders, playing five nights a week to not many people in some ghastly rock-dog venues, and we wanted a more refined aesthetic for Do-Ré-Mi, making each rare gig an art event.

As the level of whisky in the bottle sank, passions rose. I reminded Renée of this first encounter when we met again eleven years later in the recording studio across the road working on the soundtrack for the ABC TV series *Seven Deadly Sins*. She remembered it well, no hard feelings, no apologies! But back in Linda's studio in 1981, we were inadvertently cycling through pride, gluttony and envy as our discussion widened to a swag of other topics we disagreed on.

Suddenly, in the midst of 'working through our differences', Renée reached for wrath and took a swing at me. Being on the job, sober and agile enough to dodge her fist, I evaded contact but it was awkward, even with Linda there to soothe any ruffled tempers.

I learnt lots of things working for Linda, most importantly that dressing for fun, no matter what the occasion, is liberating; no clothing was so precious that a little scorch mark, rip or dirty patch could upset the equilibrium of your outfit. For years I wore black silk taffeta skirts and printed tie-dye rainbow singlets to the supermarket or gardening. (I lie—I was a shit gardener, but you get the idea.)

In 2019 the Powerhouse mounted an exhibition called 'Step Into Paradise', a retrospective of Jenny Kee's and Linda Jackson's inventive collaborations. Their auspicious meeting in 1972 had been not just the beginning of a lifelong friendship, but also the start of a new fashion enterprise. In 1973, Kee opened her Flamingo Park Frock Shop in Sydney's prestigious Strand Arcade. The shop was stocked with her famous Australian motif jumpers and frocks created by Linda.

Leo Schofield reviewed the Powerhouse exhibition in the paper and mentioned me. 'Everybody came. Lots of musicians, Deborah Conway, David Bowie, Billy Joel, Ringo Starr . . .' The quote is attributed to Jenny in the article and while it is terrific to be on the roll call with those names (it goes on to mention Lauren Bacall, Sophia Loren and George Harrison), the real truth is I wasn't so much a customer at Flamingo Park as the well-dressed delivery gal.

So there I was, living in Sydney, playing music with Do-Ré-Mi and still modelling. That year Cameron's was tasked with casting the role of Julie, a fashion model, in a feature film called *Running On Empty*, directed by John Clarke (not the comedian/writer/political satirist but the other one) and starring Terry Serio (the musician), Max Cullen, Richard Moir, Graeme Bond and Vangelis Mourikis (who afterwards left Australia for his native Greece and within a few years had established an award-winning career as a film star).

I read the script, a rev-head flick for car enthusiasts, and didn't much like it, but decided if I secured the part I could take advantage of the financial windfall, give modelling away for good and concentrate on what really absorbed me, making music.

I scored the part and was cast as the hero's love interest/occasional punching bag. I did have to dye my hair blonde, which I thought was pretty dreadful and didn't make me look better, but I guess they had some kind of cardinal rule about the leading lady having to be a blonde. On the upside I did get to drive a Corvette quite fast.

The shoot was all over Sydney: Botany was used for the first big race, Bondi was the location for Julie's fashion shoot with six lifesavers dressed for comic value in high-camp neck-to-knees; the photographer was played by Chris Haywood. We filmed in an apartment in Rushcutters Bay (Julie's pad) including the risqué shower scene, where Mike (Serio) and Julie get steamy.

We also filmed at The Rocks at the then largely neglected Hickson Road and the Goldsbrough Mort Building in Pyrmont. This was the location for all the scenes featuring The Aces Nightclub where the hook-up and shakedown action happened.

Named after wool importer Richard Goldsbrough and industrialist Thomas Sutcliffe Mort, the Goldsbrough Mort Building was a 'wool palace' in 1883, boasting a classic Victorian exterior and modern interior with hydraulic goods and passenger lifts, a sawtooth glazed roof and over 100 acres of floor space that accommodated 50,000 bales of wool. Ninety-nine years later, this five-storey structure had been out of use as a wool store for the best part of a decade and was growing increasingly decrepit.

Ageing, unloved, its glory days a distant memory and its future incarnation as luxury apartments as yet unrealised, the Goldsbrough Mort was a perfect film location. People could truly disappear in this cavernous space with all its hidey holes, sneaky corridors and dark corners to indulge in secret activities . . . and we did. At twenty-three I was a cat on a hot tin roof with an extremely overactive libido. This is not the kind of thing I want my mother (or daughters for that matter) to read about, but the rest of you, go crazy.

A quickie in a toilet cubicle on a floor that wasn't being used was par for the course (I'm sure I wasn't the only one), and who knew what other carnal, corrupting behaviour was going on. Film shoots consist of a small percentage of people doing the work while the rest sit around waiting to do theirs, and set-ups can take a long time, so the idle are frequently looking for distractions.

After the Sydney locations were done with, the production headed west to outback New South Wales, where a large chunk of the film was set. The location for most of these scenes was the red-earth desert area of Canbelego, around 50 clicks outside of Cobar, where our three intrepid adventurers, Mike, Julie and Mike's second, Tony (Mourikis), have gone to try and hustle up some racing action with the locals. It doesn't work out well for them and many cars are totalled in the ensuing scenes, adding to the car carnage that has already taken place in town. Lots of crash and burn here. After a particularly dramatic sequence involving petrol, fire, plunging off a cliff and water landings, Julie emerges from the vehicle and ascends a slag heap with Mike in hot pursuit.

I would note here that Julie is sporting a white mini dress that remains, despite all I have described, spectacularly white, probably her twentieth outfit thus far. And whilst there is no visible evidence of luggage, the reverse in fact since the car has been set ablaze, Julie continues to appear in a new saucy ensemble in every scene, sometimes inexplicably in the middle of one; we don't know a lot about Julie, but we do know she has an extensive wardrobe.

Around now is when we meet Rebel (Max Cullen), the blind(!) racing car driver/mechanic and rocker who likes nothing more than to drive his Blown Black '57 Chevy very fast across the salt flats at night without headlights (hey, what difference would it make, he's blind!), rebuilds Mike's car and coaches him in some fearless driving manoeuvres in one of those rapid-cut montages over a three-minute pop song (sung by Serio) that tells the audience there is a reckoning coming with an uncertain outcome.

The production was a happy one; we became a show-folk family, incestuous as that may have occasionally been. There was great camaraderie, from the stunt doubles to the make-up and continuity people, the caterers, focus puller, ADs and runners. It was an egalitarian set. I loved being part of a community of film-makers, but I hated the script, hated the story, hated the gratuitous costume changes, thought the entire enterprise was spectacularly corny, and was convinced the movie was destined to go straight to video.

I never thought of myself as an actress and had no illusions about being particularly good at it, but I got the gig because the filmmakers put acting skills aside and cast me as a clothes horse. I did it for the money, pure and simple. And since I was there, I experimented with an entirely different role. Up to this point I had been in two romantic relationships, both lasting a couple of years and ending in a stomach-churning entanglement of chaos.

But for those few weeks in the Australian outback where we were living in a cloistered bubble, promiscuous behaviour and consequence-free licentiousness were in the ascendancy. I became a female Lothario. I upped my partner quota by several hundred percentage points, sowing my wild oats until no clod of earth was left unsown, and exploring the principle of meaningless sex as thoroughly as if I were doing a PhD in the subject and graduating with first-class honours.

Running On Empty was released to reviews that ranged unsurprisingly from lukewarm to dreadful, though they didn't take into account the very particular audience the movie was making a play for. We had all missed the point—this was a film for car fanatics. The one time I watched it in a cinema the audience made not a peep during the shower scene but wolf-whistled every time another hotted-up vehicle zoomed across the screen.

And so an extraordinary thing happened: *Running On Empty* became a cult classic. It is these days considered a go-to picture in the pantheon of rev-head movies. *Running On Empty* was renamed *Fast Lane Fever* for a US release; in Germany it was retitled *Mike 3,8 auf 100* (Mike 3.8 on 100); in Italy they renamed it *Guerre Stradali* (*Road Wars*) and in France it was *Roues Sauvages* (*Wild Wheels*). All dubbed. Maybe that improved the acting, though I don't know; I never saw any of them.

A fan sent me a series of posters designed to promote the movie in all the various markets; they are sensational. I am rendered part-cartoon with glossy extra-long limbs and some marketing artist's fantasy idea of cleavage. None of it makes the film any better but a cult bad road movie is a significant improvement on a bad road movie.

Over the years a steady stream of men (always men) have presented me with a video or DVD release of *Running On Empty* for me to autograph. Once, at a festival just outside Bathurst (of course), I was asked to sign a car. They always tell me *Running On Empty* is their favourite movie, and that they're so happy to meet me. I used to think they were taking the piss but they are completely genuine.

I was invited a few years ago to a *Running On Empty* festival in Cobar, which I couldn't get to. I would have been honoured with an award had I fronted up, but what bigger honour than being smiled on with a cult hit movie from 1982 decades after the fact? That is a crazy plot twist.

As I had promised myself, I gave modelling away after *Running On Empty* and dedicated my time exclusively to music. Do-Ré-Mi was gathering steam, live and on radio. Martin Armiger, formerly the guitarist with The Sports and now a producer, contacted me after hearing the punk version of 'Man Overboard' and offered me the role of Tracey Mann's singing voice in a new TV series being made for the ABC called *Sweet and Sour*, tracking the exploits of a young inner-city band that were trying to make it in the business.

I ended up spending many months navigating the endless labyrinth of black-and-white linoleum-tiled corridors with the bathroom-green walls at the ABC's basement recording studios in Artarmon. They were great sessions. Martin was the epitome of encouragement and playfulness; he once described my dress sense as 'high dag', a description I embraced.

The work was intense. We recorded two volumes' worth of full-length soundtrack albums, and the show, which screened at 6 pm every weeknight, was a hit with the kids. I had requested not to be credited on the album because I thought the cognitive dissonance of being the voice of a kids' TV pop group and concurrently the front woman of a post-punk rock band wouldn't be helpful, so for a very long time my connection to *Sweet and Sour* was unknown.

It worked perfectly for the producers, who saw my anonymity as a way to smuggle in the idea of the TV band being authentic. My name, however, was inked unambiguously on the royalty cheques I received once the show and accompanying soundtrack albums became successful. Music was starting to earn me a living.

6

Man Overboard

It took a little while before what was implicit became explicit to me, before 'being in a band' became 'having a career as a musician', and acknowledging that it was the only thing I wanted to do. Playing, performing, recording, writing—I was good at it, people enjoyed my work, I didn't have a boss I had to please. I was my own boss, always; travelling and integrating work with leisure (I guess the career advisor got that part right), producing, directing, curating, discovering, commissioning. It has been an extended adolescence in some ways, not always pretty but always engrossing.

Dorland, too, poured his heart, his talent, his energy, his everything, into making this project his life's work. He was writing furious songs furiously while mentoring me as a songwriter. We spent a lot of time writing together, then working out the songs in a rehearsal room. We got airplay; airplay got punters to gigs; and sold-out gigs got the phones ringing and the suits visiting.

We acquired a serious manager from a serious agency, who got us serious record and publishing deals. Virgin Records had opened up shop in Australia and Do-Ré-Mi was one of its first three acquisitions, along with Samurai Trash and Bear Garden.

There was a celebratory gig at the Bondi Pavilion in September 1984. We decided to wear white to symbolically acknowledge our union; I went one step further and wore a slightly decrepit wedding dress I'd found in an op shop, which recalled Miss Havisham. It seemed like the rightly iconoclastic thing to appear in as one of Virgin's newly signed virgins. And, just like a wedding, the booze was free, the joint was full and the guests were all dancing. The bride was tripping on endless potential, her favourite stimulant.

Signing to Virgin was the watershed moment. Our experiments with art-space gigs and do-it-yourself recordings gave way to professional meetings with management to decide on our first producer, before jetting to the other side of the world to record our debut album with him and in due course, to embark on an endless tour. We'd evolved; now we were four 'drifters, off to see the world' together.

We played night after night, four or five shows a week for months on end, in smoke-filled venues with inadequate ventilation so that we'd all walk off stage smelling like ashtrays. I'd be singing, mouth wide, as punters blew smoke into my face, a recipe for losing your voice; both men and women thought they were flirting, thought it was sexy.

It wore us down. Dorland gasped between songs where the smoke and heat cooked up an evil-smelling cauldron at the back of the stage. It was an intense period of giving our all at every show for this serious music we were playing.

Do-Ré-Mi's first appearance on *Countdown* to perform 'Man Overboard' was captured in a series of candid dressing-room snaps of Dorland and Stephen doing inventive things with tampons. A way of loosening the nerves? Or maybe we needed to prove we weren't serious *all* the time. We found ways to let off steam, literally, lighting our farts backstage.

After intense writing or rehearsal sessions there were plenty of late-night drinking sessions, and sometimes we just fought, like warring siblings. Dorland was the brother I'd never had, and we didn't always get on.

In the early days the idea of air travel was beyond financial contemplation; we drove everywhere. We made the hellish fourteen-hour trip up the Pacific Highway to Brisbane, the four of us and our manager, the long-suffering Keith Welsh, in a beat-up white Valiant station wagon, probably driven by Stephen. Helen in the back trying to sleep next to the guitars, and me, sitting in the back seat scratching myself stupid due to an allergic reaction to flea bites.

The pests had invaded my Kings Cross flat and chowed down like an all-you-can-eat buffet. The heat, the itching and the smell of humanity, combined with the Pinetarsol I was smearing over my legs every half hour, made for a heady cocktail.

It was on that trip to Brisbane that we met and formed a close alliance with the 4ZZZ station manager Larry Ponting, who ended up moving to Sydney to become our tour manager; he did a good deal of the driving after that. Nothing much else has stayed with me from that first interminable trip other than the realisation that Brisbane to Sydney was too far a drive just to play a few gigs.

Our sound man, Geoff Watson, drove that same Valiant to Sydney, returning from our first shows in Melbourne up the

Hume Highway with Dorland, Helen and Stephen. It was the fastest route between the two cities, so despite earning the moniker 'the Deadly Hume' for the number of lives it claimed, it remained the most popular alternative.

I had opted to fly, which meant I could hang around in Melbourne for a few extra days, so I wasn't in the Valiant when it blew two tyres and rolled over a few times before landing in a ditch. Amazingly, no one was injured. On climbing out of the car, Helen looked up to see a priest standing atop the embankment. He'd seen it all unfold from his vantage point behind them and was now looking to render assistance (or maybe read last rites). He called down, 'Well, that could have ended badly.'

And for some musicians, it really did end very badly. The perils of touring, from self-inflicted misadventure, heroin, alcohol, thrill-seeking, to fatal illness and the road toll; so many gone too young. Recently, I watched a concert from 30 years ago called Australian Made, and four of the seven bands had lost their front persons—my peers and friends. It ended very badly for them.

Diary entry 2 December, 1986

> Overnight to Adelaide, Hay Plain. Rob [Rob Barnham, our tour manager] driving, Stephen, Helen, and me. The car is full of gas, the cargo is knackered, it's 11.45, calm, clear night, almost full moon. So bright I put sunglasses on over my smoke-sore eyes. Cruising along, the red wine long since retired to the floor empty and the even breathing of sleepers in the front and back seats. At 3.15, just after Robert has assured me that I will be lying asleep in bed by 5 am, the car putts

sickeningly to a halt by the side of the road. I, being the only one awake, am incredulous, but I am soon joined by my other band members who, now awake, are also incredulous . . . We know the next petrol station is around 15 kms. (Rob is telling us 5 but we know he's lying to keep our spirits up.) Personally I've gone hysterical. Helen and I can't stop laughing particularly when we realise no truck is going to stop and pick us up. I have even resorted to jumping up and down in the road lifting my top up and then throwing my hands together in a prayer pose as the trucks appear to gain speed as they whizz by. What kind of unfeeling bastards must be behind the wheels? Do they have mothers? Eventually a panel van pulls over. The cop driving has recently been dragged out of bed to go and arrest some guy who's gone berserk on a train; he's currently going berserk in the back of the panel van but Robert is long past caring. Away they go, with us none the wiser, we only find out the driver was a cop when Rob gets back.

We were mostly hysterical because we had gone through the same scenario on the same drive the year before. The Hay Plain. The very name was enough to frighten small children. It had a notorious reputation acquired a few years back, due to seven bodies discovered in and around Truro, a small town on the edge of the desert. The victims of the two male murderers were all young women and girls, and had been found in shallow graves in gruesome states. As you can imagine, with a reputation like that, hitching a ride in the middle of the night was always going to prove challenging, even standing on the highway with my top lifted.

Infamous South Australian mass murderers were a genre of their own. Aside from the tales of the Truro horrors there was the murderous cult known as 'The Family'; and still to come the bodies in the barrels at Snowtown. I did wonder, perhaps glibly, if it was something in the water; Adelaide was famously one of only two ports in the world where ships wouldn't take it on, the other being Aden in war-torn Yemen.

On the flipside, South Australia was the fourth place in the world to give women the vote; and the home of the two Dons—flamboyant pink hot-pants-wearing premier Don Dunstan and the greatest batsman on the cricket pitch, Don Bradman, fondly known as 'The Don'.

We were thinking none of this at the time.

Diary entry 2 December, 1986

In the meantime, as the moon continued its steady journey and the frost set in, the 3 of us ate my supply of stale bread, talked philosophically of the pros and cons of womanhood and listened to Van Morrison. Stephen was snoring on the back seat thru most of it while H and I tried to figure out when we should start worrying about axe-wielding maniacs coming to get us after they chopped up Robert.

Hours later Rob reappeared carrying the can. We cranked the heater and got the fuck out of there. It was dawn.

7

Yours, With Disgust

Before adopting the life of a permanently peripatetic musician, I had put down roots in my new home town. Once the owner of the *trés chic* Elizabeth Bay apartment returned, I found a share house to rent in Edward Street, North Sydney. It was a basic unrenovated four-bedroom place but the carpet was clean and a fresh coat of paint made it feel luxurious.

There was a grassy backyard where a Hills Hoist took pride of place, and the ducks living next door regularly invited themselves over through a conveniently misplaced fence plank to amuse themselves (and me) by waddling through the always-open back screen door and up the hallway; though it was less amusing having to clean off the duck poop.

I also had a dog. In fact I had two dogs, one I had gone to some trouble to acquire, driving up the coast to Nambucca Heads to pick up what I thought was a kelpie-blue heeler bitch but turned out to be a kelpie-Doberman cross. I called her Grace. Grace was a bundle of unfocused, hard-to-train id. (My dog-training experience was limited to being a volunteer puppy walker for six months for the Victorian Guide Dog Association. They charged me with the responsibility of puppy-sitting a massively oversized, dopey labrador, called Gambit. Still, what he lacked in brains he made up for in good nature and looks. After our time together, Gambit went back to fulfil his destiny but sadly, he failed Guide Dog School.)

Not long after Grace came to live with me, another bitch turned up at our doorstep: a blue heeler with a broken leg and no collar. I took her to the vet who fixed her up with a plaster cast, and then door-knocked around the neighbourhood to find an owner, to no avail. I called her Pearl and she came to join our household with Grace and the ducks from next door and all the other crazy rent-paying animals we were sharing with.

Pearl was a great dog, the breed I'd wanted all along, smart, obedient, affectionate, delightful company. I allowed my two bitches to roam the neighbourhood as they pleased. They never went far and were always home in time for tea and everyone was happy. It was a different time; the idea of allowing a dog to roam free would be unthinkable now but not in Sydney in 1982.

Still, two dogs started to become too much for someone who had only wanted one, so I put an ad in the local paper enumerating Grace's attributes and said she was 'free to a good home'. It felt like the right solution. The day the ad came out, there was an early phone call which sounded promising, but there was a hitch: Grace had disappeared. No amount of calling made her materialise and a search of the immediate vicinity didn't turn her up. The search was widened and Grace was found in a neighbour's front garden, foaming at the mouth and whining in pain.

I carried her gently to the car and drove straight to the vet in Neutral Bay, but Grace started writhing uncontrollably and furiously. Pulling to the kerb, I managed to rope in a dog lover who held the black-and-tan Doberman-kelpie-cross, squirming violently, in the backseat while I raced every amber light to the vet's. I had absolutely no idea what was wrong, but this was not how I imagined I would become the owner of one dog.

Once Grace had been taken into surgery I deposited the Good Samaritan where we had met, thanking her profusely; I had a huge day ahead of me and needed to get going.

It was during the weeks leading up to the AFI (Australian Film Industry) Awards and films released that year were being screened at a cinema in Double Bay on the other side of town. All members of the AFI eligible to cast a vote were invited to these screenings. Having been in *Running On Empty* the previous year, I had been sent invitations to attend all screenings in categories I was deemed qualified to judge. But if I missed a screening of any of the films, I forfeited my right to vote in that category. In principle, excellent reasoning.

In June 1981, the federal government had introduced an incentive for the Australian film industry in the form of the 10BA tax. It allowed anyone investing monies in an Australian film to claim a 150 per cent tax concession of whatever their investment was and to pay tax on only half of any income earned from their investment. The tax incentive had *almost* the desired effect; the years 1982–83 saw a marked increase in Australia's feature film output, tripling from the previous year.

I say 'almost' the desired effect because while it certainly upped the quantity, the rivers of tax-deductible gold meant that there were a number of films that should never have left the page. I can say this with some authority, having sat through every one of the 36 contenders for that year. It's difficult to recall most of them but *Turkey Shoot* was a clear standout for most appropriately titled.

I raced home for a shower and spruce-up after the emergency dash to the vet's and got out the door in record time. I was trying to squeeze in a visit to Grace Bros in Sydney's CBD, which was on the way to the cinema, and since I didn't get over there too often I was trying to optimise my time.

The previous week a badly stacked tea tray on the kitchen bench had tipped its contents to the floor, shattering all my favourite Cornishware blue teacups, and I was hoping to replace them before sitting in the dark in Double Bay for a few hours. I slid into a 30-minute park directly outside the department store on a very busy Market Street and mentally gave myself a round of applause.

After locating the Cornishware cups on the homewares floor among the more formal Wedgwood and Royal Doulton, with the insouciant nonchalance of someone who thinks that almost everything is working out quite well, I slipped a couple into my bag. Having saved some time, and in need of a warm cardigan for the chilly months, I had a look in the knitwear department. A good woollen cardigan for winter would be useful, and there were gorgeous new season colours in stock.

A dusky red one stuck to my fingers and I turned to leave, but then a rich bruised blue-purple caught my eye. Both of the cardigans were now in my bag along with the Cornishware cups as I made for the exit, passing but not stopping at any of the numerous cash registers on my way out.

Shoplifting had become a life-changing discovery for me. Why buy a thing when you could just take it? The thrill was addictive. I only stole from big department or chain stores and had justified my actions in some loose interpretation of Robin Hood stealing from the rich to give to myself. Only the previous month I had grabbed a couple of lamps from one of the big furniture stores, one under each arm, put them in my car and then gone back in to pick up the lampshades. When the household needed towels, I paid a visit to the manchester department, but didn't pay.

I felt like I was going for an Olympic Gold Medal for the Sheer Brazenness event, daring someone to catch me, each successful mission emboldening the next. I convinced myself I wore a cloak of invisibility while engaging in this rogue enterprise.

I had realised early on that casual abandon was the best cover: no furtive glancing over the shoulder. At most it was okay to look in the mirrors placed around the store to assess if there were store detectives at work; they were not usually difficult to spot and, once sighted, any further activity could be modified or abandoned. It was a game, albeit with unpleasant consequences I was yet to encounter.

But on this fateful autumn day I had become so emboldened as to be skating close to reckless; a self-evident inevitability, a natural reckoning, the pride/fall equation, basically a catastrophe waiting to happen. And thus my beeline for the Grace Bros exit was rudely curtailed by two hefty hands clamping down, one on each shoulder.

The adrenaline surge through my bloodstream in that nanosecond turned my legs gelatinous and my stomach to a fermented curdle, making any physical resistance a non-starter. Yet still my mind immediately turned to obfuscation.

What? Me? Why? How?

It was excruciating how I imagined I could squirm out of my predicament. The conversation was tediously predictable.

'Miss, did you not see the sales assistants behind our cash registers waiting to help you?'

'Help me with what?'

'Miss, you have items in your bag you haven't paid for.'

'No I haven't.'

'Oh yes you have . . . Miss, you're coming with us.'

'I can't, I have to be somewhere.'

'Miss, you should have thought of that before.'

'Miss,' repeated—the situation in a nutshell. *Oh, for heaven's sake.* I was led to the manager's office where I continued my charade of being wrongfully accused, all the way up until being asked to empty my bag on the table.

'Oh, you mean these Cornish blue mugs? These cardigans in dusky red and bruised purplish blue?'

Mask off, charade exposed. A call to the police was put in. And then the terrible realisation that this could suddenly get a whole lot worse than it already was. I remembered that in my purse I was not only carrying the entire month's rent in cash for the household, but also half-a-dozen small sachets of speed, which I had been hoping to offload later that day. Thinking on my feet, I asked to be excused to use the bathroom and went to grab my bag.

'You can't take that,' said the manager.

'But I need it,' I replied, slightly hysterical.

'Oh, well, okay then,' the chastened manager said, assuming no doubt that it was for some personal feminine hygiene requirement.

Once inside the toilet cubicle, with a female employee waiting outside the door in the dingy dark-wood-lined back service rooms of the Grace Bros offices, I retrieved the speed from my purse and pulled my pants down to have a wee; it was awfully good speed to flush down the toilet. Standing, I pulled up my knickers and tucked the speed sachets inside my underpants, nestled next to my crotch. I emerged from the toilet with my gambler's heart beating strong . . . just *maybe* I'd get away with it.

The police arrived and escorted me down to the station to be fingerprinted and photographed. And after all that, my remarkable and totally undeserved good luck held out a bit longer and mine was the last case to be heard before lunch. A very brief stint in the lock-up and then before the magistrate I went.

My defence was beyond appalling: 'Your honour, I'm an actor, but I haven't had any work for such a long while . . .' (violins playing softly, mournfully); '. . . The hundreds of dollars I was carrying in my wallet is not my money but the rent for our shared household that I have to pay today . . .' (violins escalating); '. . . I have no money, I am struggling to pay my share of the rent . . .'; (violins *accelerando*) '. . . Your Honour, I have never done this before and believe me I have learnt my lesson, I'll never do it again!' (For someone who couldn't act, it wasn't a bad performance.)

'Well, mind you don't, young lady; I don't want to see you in my courtroom ever again. This is a warning. You will pay a fine of $600 but next time don't expect any leniency—case dismissed.'

And with that I walked out of Sydney Central Local Court a free woman. What, no lift back to Grace Bros? I made my own way, my finely tuned schedule for the day in tatters and with a very good chance of missing the screening for the AFIs, which would render me ineligible to vote for anything. I found my car, which was now sporting an extravagant parking fine on the windscreen, which I pocketed resignedly and drove over to Double Bay. It was a beautiful Sydney early afternoon.

I had ten minutes to get there and park, very tight at the best of times. But amazingly my luck(!) held out and I arrived with seconds to spare after a lightning dash to the bathroom for (genuine) bladder relief. Relief, that is, until I realised (and in my defence, I laughed) that there, slowly sinking into the golden, limpid effluence at the bottom of the porcelain bowl, were my six sachets of high-quality methamphetamine.

I fished them out, dried them off in toilet paper, and slid them back into my bag, where they snuggled in with my parking fine, wallet stuffed with rent money and the capacious space not taken up with Cornishware teacups and warm winter cardigans in dusky-red and bruised bluish-purple.

Two codas to this tale: firstly, Grace didn't survive her ordeal, and not long after Pearl also succumbed to what we found out was an irate local deliberately poisoning the neighbourhood's pets. It would be many decades before I got another dog.

Secondly, I took the judge seriously, realising that I had skated as close as I wanted to a criminal record. It took a long time for me to recover my composure and invisible cloak of chutzpah. In short, shoplifting was off the table—until close to a year later when I tried to revive my skills on a bottle of pina colada and a pineapple juice mixer from a local Bottle-o, whereupon I immediately fell foul of the store detective. It was over and I knew it.

Yet my undeserved good luck again came to the fore. It was a Saturday afternoon, shortly before closing, and the manager had no desire to hang around waiting for the local constabulary for such a minor infraction. I was summarily dismissed from the store, sans goods of course, and really did change my wicked ways, learning the valuable lesson that most twelve-year-olds learn more rapidly—crime doesn't pay.

8

Bag of Sweets

Through the Edward Street years the drummers in my life were accumulating. John Lloyd, from Flowers/Icehouse, lived there, and John Bliss, the drummer for The Reels, found many excuses to drop in for cups of tea. I knew many drummers, they often moved in multiples—a tattoo of drummers?

When John Lloyd moved out of the North Sydney share house, Paul Hester took his place. The Checks, who had become Deckchairs Overboard, had moved to Sydney, and Paul and I took up where we had left off in Melbourne . . . until something strange happened and my dear housemate suddenly and without warning became my lover. It was a wild time; certainties drifted into uncertainties and lovely liminal spaces appeared beneath what the day before had been solid ground. Not unpredictably, drugs were involved.

I had started getting drunk at parties at fourteen. Cheap white wine was ubiquitous and I indulged enough that I was in my mid-twenties before I could drink a glass of white wine without being transported back to the nauseating memory of lying on a plastic sunlounge somewhere, calling for my mother between heaves into a bucket. When white wine had taken enough abuse I turned to Marsala, which I foolishly mixed with Fanta, so that I was no doubt intoxicated as much by sugar as by alcohol. Tequila was a room-spinning headache of punishing self-annihilation on a whole other level; it has ever since been a spirit I have handled with a great deal of respect.

I was also fourteen when I first smoked marijuana. I was staying with Jo at her parents' place on the Mornington Peninsula. A lot of the wild teenage parties I was getting drunk at took place down there over the summer. At the start of that school year, Jo had single-handedly delivered me from my debilitating social anxiety by being the first girl to befriend me after I stayed down in second form; she instantly became my best friend. Not only that, she introduced me to her best friend Caro, who instantly became my second best friend. That summer, Caro was staying with her family at her godmother's beach house next door to Jo. The three of us were a tight unit that holiday, apart from when Jo and I experimented with our first pot-smoking experience. Caro left us to it.

Jo and I took our little baggie, containing a couple of pre-rolled joints, back to her place. I was distinctly unimpressed with that first encounter. Getting high felt like nothing much had taken place. Was it in fact pot or just green tea? Despite my willingness to experience getting stoned, I felt entirely normal. But we still had to pay for our newfound drug habit, so the following day, Jo and I, like a couple of itinerant peddlers, went next door and asked Caro's mother if we could do her ironing for pocket money.

Unsurprisingly, Caro found that hilarious.

I fooled around with joints but ended up discovering what it really felt like to get stoned when I used a bong. For the uninitiated, a bong is a water pipe that you load with your tobacco-cannabis mix, light, then suck the smoke through the pipe, which, bubbling through the water at the base, seems to enhance the critical amount of tetrahydrocannabinol (THC) to your lungs and subsequently your bloodstream. No student house was complete without the bong on the coffee table. I made some critical missteps in the early days of mixing my drunk with my stoned but there's only so many times you want to make that mistake, which will take a rosy-hued world and turn the damn thing upside down and sideways until it is leering at you evilly from the bottom of the toilet bowl you're crouched and moaning over.

When I moved to Sydney, my trusty blue ceramic bong travelled with me. I was a firm believer in the wondrous properties of pot and had no desire to give it away. In fact, I recall thinking (which is remarkable because I don't recall that much from those days) that I would never grow out of getting high. Not only did I not give it up, but I became a purveyor of mood-altering substances for various clients.

I added new substances to my palette of experimentation. I tried diet pills, an amphetamine available over the counter, good for staying awake. Since I was driving up and down the Hume Highway almost weekly in the first few months of my moving to Sydney, to see the boyfriend I had left behind in Melbourne (despite the fact he was cheating on me), these little pep-me-ups would keep me going for the duration and then some. I finally got fed up with how jittery the pills made me and graduated to taking speed—methamphetamine.

I skipped cocaine (fondly referred to in some circles as Bolivian marching powder) as too expensive and frankly, after speed, way too subtle. I wanted my drug of choice to hit me square in the face with unavoidable psychotropic cues. Speed was perfect, and practical if you had a lot on.

I tried opium, which made me feel like the world was grinding down in slow motion to a half-lit stop on the way to Death Valley. The other opioid, heroin, was a ghastly, landscape-shrinking encounter with which I went ten rounds to outwit the urge to vomit, an inevitably fruitless contest. Hooray for me and my natural revulsion for the most highly addictive substances. I was lucky.

There was LSD—lysergic acid diethylamide—aka acid, an entirely other entree to a brave new world. I had eaten magic mushrooms in Bali when I was twenty and on holiday with my first boyfriend. Despite making me nauseous and a little paranoid, I quite enjoyed it. But acid was fully glorious. I adored everything about it and while it still made me want to throw up, strangely that didn't feel like an unnatural or even unpleasant thing to do—just part of the ride.

There were captivating adventures to be had without leaving my bedroom. I couldn't drag my eyes away from my Van Gogh prints on the wall, marvelling at 3D animations flying from Vincent's sunflowers, his cherry blossom orchards in Arles waving in the breeze, the branches growing in front of my eyes, his fishing boats at Saintes-Maries-de-la-Mer sailing in and out of the frame. And the exquisite *Starry Night* pulsing, swirling with lunar activity; all of it convincing me that Vincent must have been taking some kind of hallucinogen when he was painting.

Taking acid was an exercise of being fully in the moment; like every New Age therapist, yogi or meditation guru would tell their devotees, there is no future, there is no past, there is only here and now, an enviable state of mind but very hard to achieve. Tripping was the shortcut, a way of being so completely absorbed with the current moment that engaging in any other activity, like leaving the room to use the bathroom or grab a sandwich, could seem almost impossible.

Having summoned the wherewithal to complete the task, it would then feel like the only place that you should be was on the toilet or in the kitchen making that sandwich, which then became engrossing. Nothing was too inconsequential to be fascinating; the clock ticking, the rain thrumming on my tin roof, the whorls on my fingertips, the blue tributaries of blood lacing under the pale skin of my thighs.

I spent many weekends of my twenty-third year dropping acid. I had plenty of co-travellers in these consciousness-altering excursions, which generally took place after dark. One time we climbed the Sydney Harbour Bridge (many years before it was a legitimate tourist attraction), throwing ourselves around the barbed wire fence that surrounded the locked gate three metres above the traffic on the north-west corner guarding the ascent, arriving at the red-lit pinnacle shortly before dawn.

Curiously, my two companions (one of whom is now my doctor) and I weren't the only trespassers that night. Two other intrepid adventurers companionably offered to share a joint one of them had extracted from his sock. And just to be social, we did.

They were wild days. One Sunday night after Paul's band (Deckchairs Overboard) and Do-Ré-Mi had finished our respective sets at Stranded, a venue in the basement of the Strand Arcade in Sydney's CBD, we partied until dawn and then I drove Paul home north over the Harbour Bridge. I was probably still a little high, though it had been many hours since we'd ingested the drug and I'd forgotten that peak-hour traffic on Monday morning meant all lanes bar one across the bridge were designated as city-bound. I pulled my little blue Honda out to overtake the car in front, only to find a stream of commuters driving directly at me. I pulled back in fast and we survived, crazily laughing, as one does when one has just had a near-death experience following an all-night marathon shindig.

There were other, more sedate activities, like Paul and I walking the beaches in the moonlight or staying home to eat and make love. When we travelled the world together, we explored Tokyo, Italy, London, Greece and France with our trusty little swag of mind-expanding accoutrements. From Shinjuku to the Eiffel Tower, the Tuscan Hills to the Parthenon, we were enhanced. Paul started to suffer monumental headaches post our uber-sybarite stimulations, which put a stop to them, and probably for the best.

A year ago I heard a podcast that mentioned, in passing, experiments that were conducted on smokers to assist them in giving up their habit with the aid of LSD. It brought to mind a moment after I'd been up all night tripping. I was sitting in my North Sydney back garden in a sunny spot smoking a cigarette, feeling equal parts fascination and revulsion at the colour of my skin in the glare of a bright morning. Purple, white, bluish-red; it was like I could see the nicotine travelling through my arteries, slowly ruining my circulation. I thought, *I should not be smoking*. I have never smoked a cigarette again. Psychedelics are wild, unmapped territory. In my mind I wrote and wrote in this state, discovering hidden rooms of delights, hidden floors, glory holes stuffed with sacred secrets. In need of exegesis, I swam in muddied allegorical swamps, dived into my subterraneous conscious. Until eventually, in need of sleep,

I would take Rohypnol and let consciousness fade into a soft patina of lavender bed clothes stained with the creamy misfires of future generations never to be. In my mind I wrote and wrote again but in the end I used nothing but the milky white marks left in my foggy head; the palimpsest of the most vivid hallucinations.

I used drugs in part to explore facets of consciousness that were otherwise hard to attain. But I was not successful in incorporating the resultant mind ramblings into cogent work. The trip was psychedelic, but the postcards I sent home were merely a penumbra of the journey.

Paul and I were a couple for the next four years, living together in different houses, playing music, travelling, experimenting with life's adventures. Paul was headhunted by Rob Hirst to join Split Enz—yes, Rob was in Midnight Oil, but everyone was connected. Paul left Deckchairs and moved back to Melbourne to formalise the arrangement.

Eventually Split Enz split up and Paul joined Neil Finn as a founding member of The Mullanes, soon to be Crowded House. By then, our long-distance relationship was revealing irreconcilable schisms: I was happy when I was with him, and content when I wasn't; he missed me when I wasn't there and found me suffocating when I was. We called it a day while we could still stay friends.

'Bag of Sweets', *My Third Husband*, 1997

It's my bag of sweets
Melting in my hot hand

Sticky little treats
Taste so good but they're so bad
I'd devour you anytime
Anywhere
I don't care
If the lights are on
If I'm fiddling in the dark
I will wait alone
'Til the gates of your sweet park
Sugar me as they spring wide
Close behind
I'm inside . . .
(You might think it's nothing—
What I'd do for my bag of sweets
Hang around learn something
Tell me what's in your bag of sweets)
. . . my own mouth my lips
Forming words I've never heard
Every switch is switched
This is fun in a brave new world
Listen to me while I sigh
I cry
I die
It's my bag of sweets
Melting in my hot hand
Sticky little treats
Taste so good but they're so bad
Listen to me while I sigh
I cry
I die

9

Writing's on the Wall

Do-Ré-Mi was off on a big adventure. Our first album, *Domestic Harmony*, was to be recorded in London at Virgin's Townhouse 3 Studio in the shadow of the Battersea Power Station with producer Gavin MacKillop. We landed on Dorland's birthday, 2 January, 1985.

London was covered in white powdery snow that was falling steadily. The black cab dropped us at our accommodation, a mansion house apartment block off the Edgeware Road. We were told later that Gabriel Byrne was upstairs filming a BBC program and they had discovered a dead body on the set. It was that kind of place: dark furniture, dark corners, dark, hidden nooks, the perfect place to spend a wintery three months.

In 1985 the Australian dollar and the British pound were at parity, an absolute boon for the keen shopper, which Helen and I most definitely were. I bought myself a 1964 blonde Epiphone guitar with white scratch plate and whammy bar for under £2000. It was gorgeous. It still is.

Daylight hours were limited in the depths of a northern winter but it wasn't a problem: there are no windows in a studio. Gavin liked working at night, often all night. We'd begin our sessions in the afternoon and work through to the early hours of the morning, the empty bottles of red wine accumulating in a corner. We were loose. My vocals were all scheduled after midnight with only Gavin in attendance. We were soon having a steamy affair, more steamy because it was secret, which lasted exactly as long as the recording sessions. We stayed friends and went on a Mexican holiday together some years later—separate bedrooms.

The three months went fast—studio time does that. We were back in Australia playing shows by early April with our contentious single 'Man Overboard' with its *pubic hair, penis envy* and *anal humour*-laden lyric (quite provocative back then) and, far more controversially, no chorus. Virgin was convinced it would be a hit and they were right: the song shot to Top 5 on the *Countdown* charts and was played on commercial as well as alternative radio. We were the latest 'darlings', the 'it' things.

For the first time I was being recognised in the street, lauded just for doing my job, and sought out for my opinions on entirely unrelated matters. It was strange and I felt cautious. I was not a babe in the woods but I made big mistakes, like being invited to breakfast with a journalist and actually eating breakfast. The writer reported my order and, problematically, how I ate; that was the last time I had a meal in front of a journalist.

There were other lessons. I had strips torn off me for having the temerity to tell *The Sun* newspaper's Paul Stewart (we're friends these days), when he asked me if I felt lucky about recording overseas, that I didn't think we were lucky, just well-organised. He went to town accusing me of hubris and an arrogance I hadn't thought I was projecting. I was getting valuable lessons on how to be wary; the press could be vipers.

But we were also taken seriously. There was a lot more music journalism around then and high standards were being set in certain quarters, even though others couldn't stoop low enough. Some of the British music press were ruthless in their critical analysis. There was a review of a new Eurogliders single in *Melody Maker* in which the journalist described Grace Knight as sounding like a 'mallard stuffed up a vacuum cleaner', which was hilarious, unutterably cruel and obviously speculative (who knew what a mallard stuffed up a vacuum cleaner would sound like?). *NME* and *Melody Maker* were like that, competing with each other for who might write the more scathing review. The press could be appalling, but the good journalists kept the pressure on us to be better. From being interview-shy we had become tireless publicity seekers, blitzing print and airwaves with our constant presence. There are scrapbooks crammed with articles, reviews, interviews, photo opportunities, opinion pieces, surrealist opinion pieces . . . there was a lot of copy to write, a lot of pages to fill and a lot of gigs to play.

After the long fallow periods between our first gigs, we had suddenly changed gear and played more than 250 shows in nine months. We were tight, professional, respected, popular. We were innovators, coming up with the idea that anyone unemployed could buy a half-price ticket to our shows on our Beat The Dole Drums Tour of 1985.

Dirty Pool Management, Virgin Records and EMI Publishing were all very happy having signed us. 'Man Overboard' was a big hit. We followed it with single and video releases for 'Warnings Moving Clockwise' and 'Idiot Grin'. But we were doing so much television that it was like every album track had been released as a single.

The press was by turns fawning and scathing. It is a curious thing to look back now and see how many journalists were bet-hedging with their descriptors like 'formidably impressive', 'intelligently danceable' or 'dull and worthy' and 'derivative and unoriginal', sometimes in the same article.

We finally stopped performing and headed to Amsterdam for six months at the start of 1986 to write a second album. Helen and Stephen had an apartment in the exclusive suburb of Vondelpark, while Dorland and I shared a housing commission-style flat on the tram line in a semi-industrial area with Anita, who worked for Dirty Pool and was given the task of ensuring we didn't get into, or cause, any trouble.

The three of us crammed into a two-and-a-half bedroom, no-frills flat (I got the half). It was poxy, overwhelmingly beige, noisy and crowded, and while I loved Amsterdam I don't think we made better work living there than we would have made at home.

I read *The Master and Margarita*, watched reruns of *Green Acres*, ate a lot of cheese (the Dutch national cuisine), ran up and down the many canals in the summer shooting water pistols at the tourists (can't imagine how that would go down now) and ignored the ubiquitous and legal coffee shop franchises, like Happy Families, that specialised in cannabis baked goods, because in 1986 I decided to give pot away. The currency was colourful, the prostitutes were a tourist attraction, the authorities were unerringly chill, the liquorice was salty, the women were exceptionally beautiful and the men exceptionally not.

As soon as we'd written a batch of tunes we were shipped across to London and put up at another of Virgin's many fabulous properties, this one in Oxfordshire, called The Manor. It was a *Trading Places* scenario: one minute we were slumming it in Amsterdam, the next, living it up in a stately home with staff, an indoor heated pool, grounds full of manicured topiary and an extensive wine cellar. Oh yes, and a studio, which, to be honest, I can barely remember. After months of deprivation we were very distracted by luxury and creature comforts and felt the need, like starved creatures, to gorge before being thrust back into the wilderness again.

There were other distractions; the Americans had launched a bombing raid on Libya a week or so before we arrived and there was the expectation of imminent reprisals. We searched the perfectly blue, clear spring skies for any signs of warcraft, to no avail. Within a few days of that skirmish, the core of Chernobyl's nuclear plant in the USSR melted down, resulting in death and catastrophe for the town, which remains, all these decades later, abandoned and condemned.

The rest of Europe was measuring elevated atmospheric radiation, the ferocity dependent on whichever way the wind blew. The UK press were issuing daily warnings as they tracked the fallout, the skies darkened to deep purples and the press headlines screamed 'Oxfordshire Has Worst Radiation Levels in the World!' but in the end the actual readings were insignificant.

With all that as the backdrop, including our clean sweep of the *Countdown* Awards that month—Best Female Vocalist, Best Debut Band, Best Album and Best Single—and the subsequent celebrations, the recording of demos was relegated to a sideshow. Ten days and multiple vintage bottles of red later, we were banished back to our squalid accommodation and a dingy rehearsal room in Amsterdam to prepare ourselves for our upcoming European support tour with the Red Guitars.

The Red Guitars were an indie pop band from Hull who also had a female bass player and sounded not dissimilar to us; they'd had success on the indie pop charts though they didn't make it much past our tour together, breaking up in August 1986.

We performed in the Netherlands, including Amsterdam at Cafe Paradiso; in the Hague, Manchester, the Town & Country in London; Glasgow, Vienna and a number of towns in Germany. Do-Ré-Mi was virtually unknown but there was enough curiosity for a small crowd's worth at each whistlestop. Everyone on this tour, it seemed, were big drinkers and there was a generous rider being supplied and consumed at every show.

My memories of that time are fragmented, but Manchester distinguishes itself because I tried to get the heater going in my room by jiggling a fork into the workings just before I was thrown violently to the other side of the room.

I remember Glasgow being very grim, with not a lot of Red Guitar fans in attendance and zero fans for us. But the German leg was a category apart. I felt strange crossing into Germany for the first time; the Holocaust cast a long, dark shadow. My Jewish parents had never bought a German car or, despite their extensive travelling, had never set foot on German soil. It was not exactly the feeling of collective trauma, more a perception drilled into me from an early age that Germans were not to be trusted. Going to Germany made me feel like an outlaw. That feeling of being a stranger in a strange land was front of mind the entire time we were on German soil. We played shows in Hamburg, Frankfurt, Cologne, Bavaria and Munich, all flying visits, but we paused in West Berlin to take in the sights for a couple of days. Three years before the fall of the Berlin Wall, driving to Berlin meant driving through East Germany.

We took the Autobahn via the East German Corridor and like everyone, we were stopped at the border leaving the West and entering the East. Helen made the mistake of pulling out her Canon and snapping off a few shots, whereupon the guard, unsmiling, stuck his hand into the open car window, yanked the camera out of her hands, opened the back of it and pulled out the film.

It was fast, brutal and non-negotiable—the reality of serious rubbing up against the unserious—unlike us, these people were not mucking around. Helen was given a very stern talking-to. Shortly before the Autobahn crossed back into West Berlin we pulled off the road into a duty-free liquor store and bought up big on the different kinds of vodka that the Russians were so skilled at producing; Bison Juice was one of them, the vodka equivalent of tequila with the worm. We all took a slug from the bottle after that nerve-rattling border stop.

West Berlin was like nowhere I had ever been. It was the living, breathing manifestation of capitalism, propped up by the Allied Powers—the US, the French and the British, all pumping rivers of gold into this shining example of the other side of the ideological coin: capitalism on steroids, a punch in the nose for the other team.

I spent hours wandering around this extraordinary city that gleamed with good fortune, bristled with designer goods, ran with countless fountains in beautiful public squares, whose boulevards were lined with department stores full of luxury items. In Melbourne we had one of those, Georges in Collins Street, but in West Berlin Georges was like Target. Just one of these shopping palaces, the KaDeWe, held seven floors of the most expensive merchandise that could be procured. The effect was dazzling, as if the very streets were diamond-studded.

And then, abruptly, we were all operating inside an absurdly clumsy metaphor—there was the Wall. Cutting a brutalist concrete slash topped with barbed wire across the once grand city of Berlin that had fallen so utterly, so abominably to the unspeakable atrocities wrought by Hitler and his many, many willing accomplices, here was the unintended consequence of the National Socialists' enduring legacy—the rise and rise of the other kind of socialism. An inescapable reminder of cause and effect.

The following day, the four of us applied for a visa, which cost us DM5, and entered East Berlin via the heavily guarded Checkpoint Charlie. We had had to exchange DM25 into East German currency at the exchange rate of 1:1, outrageous because the East German currency was worth a fraction of that; we were warned that we were forbidden to leave East Berlin with any East German marks in our possession. The contrast between East and West was mind-blowing. We walked through Checkpoint Charlie and it was like we had travelled back in time to 1946.

The walls were covered in pock marks from World War II bullets; we wandered around decrepit streetscapes of ruined, collapsing buildings, waiting for an earthmover to put them out of their misery, everyone walking past us grimly wrapped in a grey overcoat, no billposters, no advertising of any sort. Apart from the red insignia on the many uniformed guards we saw on the streets, we had entered a world drained of colour.

We had a map and tried to work out where we might eat lunch, or look at a shop, and eventually found a cafeteria, expansive but empty. The food we ordered from the uninterested waitress was as colourless as everything we had seen, boiled cabbage and some grey meat, most of which I left on my plate. There were no pictures on the walls, but the windows onto the street were large and we could see the grey clouds darkening the skies, draining the light to complete the perfect greyness.

The DM25 we had exchanged put a lot of East German marks in our pockets but aside from lunch we could find nowhere to spend them. There were no museums or galleries. We looked for a shop, but aside from a single display window that appeared to be selling recorders, but with no visible entrance, we eventually gave up.

And so, with our allotted few hours spent, the four intrepid band members, who all identified so strongly with the Left and its promises of the good and the kind, headed back to Checkpoint Charlie to cross freely with our Australian passports back into the West. But we had a problem—our wallets were stuffed with East German marks which we'd been cautioned we had to spend before we attempted to leave, and failure to do so would result in unpleasant consequences, the details of which we had no desire to flesh out.

I tried to give mine to a man passing by but he looked at me in horror and walked rapidly away. I thought about giving them to the border guard but sensed this would have been deeply frowned on, as a bribe implying guilt of some kind. I opted to discreetly deposit the notes into a bin, the first and last time I have literally thrown my money away. There was distrust from everyone we encountered. I felt no romance, no sense of justice, no intrigue, just a blunt feeling of threat.

Red Guitars was popular in Berlin and Do-Ré-Mi had fans there too. The show that night was in a grungy art space—the kind that Berlin had in abundance—and the venue was packed with young hipsters; Nick Cave had relocated there in 1985 and his guitar player Blixa Bargeld turned up at the gig. Afterwards some of us blew off steam from our culturally dissonant day with a bar crawl around the funkiest joints in West Berlin until dawn was breaking and the traffic was ramping up.

There was an English couple with us I didn't know, friends of the Red Guitars who were either living in Berlin or just happened to be visiting. Fatefully, the young woman decided that that night would be her last: and as we spilled out onto the footpath, she kept walking, onto the road, in front of a truck. I remember being overwhelmed as much by the theatre as the tragedy.

This was a place where drama happened; the backdrop heightened everything and commanded a response. I have no idea of her motivations, but from a deep place I felt that Berlin was somehow implicated; the responsibility of living atop a razor wire between two warring ideologies would have to play a role in dictating a state of mind, intimately entwining sanity and insanity.

I would like to say that 1986 was the beginning of the end of my unquestioning (if less than full-throated) allegiance to the ideology I'd signed onto. As a band we thought of ourselves as a collective, as anti-capitalist, but our visit to East Berlin didn't instigate a conversation about whether what we'd decided we were against was so very bad, and what we imagined we were for was so very good. We were deeply invested in our worldview, in which the far Right produced egregious evil—and fair enough, it did.

But why did we stop there? Why didn't we interrogate the far Left's responsibility for unimaginable horrors? I'd heard of the Khmer Rouge and Pol Pot's Killing Fields, about The Great Leap Forward, about the Gulags and the Stasi, but still I clung to misplaced trust in the 'goodness' of the Left versus the problematic Right. It took me way too long to work out that the apparent polar opposites are close cousins.

The European tour was done and dusted. I had learnt a few useful German phrases from the Red Guitars' crew on our long car rides; for example, 'Where are your beautiful red trousers?' We were returning home to release 'Guns & Butter', a standalone single, which along with the shows we were going to play would serve to remind audiences we still existed.

Back in Australia, Virgin still hadn't given us the green light to make the second album.

We needed to write more songs.

We needed to demo more songs.

We needed to play more gigs to refill the coffers.

And I needed somewhere else to live.

'The Writing's on the Wall', *Stories of Ghosts*, 2013

Throw them overboard
Loose the safety cord

All my deep beliefs my ballast in this life
Has weighed me like a chain and ball & kept me pinned to certainties long gone
And the writing's on the wall

Sold my soul today
Got a pocketful of change
Almost what it's worth
On current currency exchange
My prayer went up to g-d
Where's my love, my fame, my talent that should have come from up above
All I get is writing on the wall

It's started getting cold
I can see my breath like smoke
It reminds me of New York
When you used to love me back
And we'd walk and talk for hours
Through those graffitied streets
And the giant holes that once were world trade towers
We never saw the writing on the wall

I am numbered, I am weighed, I am found to be wanting—in the balance I am lame, and insensitive to other people's pain

Back in 6BC
There was a conqueror's feast

Where Belshazzar held court amongst 1000 lords
They drank from stolen cups toasting their false gods
'Til the disembodied claw
Put the writing on the wall
He thought he had it all
Just pride before the fall . . .

10

Accidents Happen in the Home

I had been looking forward to going home and moving back into my one-bedroom flat at the leafy end of Kings Cross, Macleay Street, Potts Point. (Not the flat with the fleas I mentioned earlier.) I enjoyed getting home after gigs and traversing the seamy Kings Cross red-light district late at night. I'd developed a way of gliding through, oblivious to the male gaze and the commentary to the point where I simply disappeared.

I loved living alone, a reprieve after a bunch of share houses I'd moved through in the early '80s. But with Do-Ré-Mi busy on the other side of the world drinking Virgin studio's cellars dry, I had had to sublet my apartment—with its parquetry floors and perfect view over the back of Elizabeth Bay House and out to the Heads—to pay the rent. I came back to find I'd been unceremoniously thrown out, white-anted by my sub-lettee to the body corporate. There was some spurious rumour being circulated that

I was a 'working girl' because I got home late at night, sometimes with a fellow in tow. I was homeless.

(That same flat had featured briefly in the film clip of 'Man Overboard' with director Geoff Crosby—one-time synthesiser player for Hunters & Collectors—smoking a cigarette while wearing my blue towelling dressing gown. It is from a distance but nevertheless, for the sake of rock trivia, you may be interested to pick that out if you happen to see the clip.)

After my unceremonious ousting by the body corporate from my Potts Point eyrie, I asked my friend Jackie Dennis if she would move with me into a flat in Elizabeth Bay—specifically Gotham City, as it was affectionately known by the locals due to its forbidding aesthetic. Jackie worked as a publisher for Mushroom. We had met in Melbourne but reconnected after we'd moved to Sydney to pursue our careers.

Jackie was the perfect housemate with her infectious optimism and ability to radiate competence in the face of chaos. Her wide-mouthed grin with overbite and gap between her front teeth, of the kind that all the top models now sport was on display often, whether we were hanging out making each other laugh, swinging wildly on the squash court or bemoaning our single status between drinks.

To celebrate our new digs, we invited friends for dinner and cooked up Thai prawn lemongrass soup and green fish curry. I asked Dorland. He brought along his current girlfriend, who'd been working on a fishing trawler. She wouldn't touch the food and, in solidarity, he wouldn't either. Jackie was unimpressed. They met again, a year or so later, after I'd bought a house in Sydney with a small inheritance from my grandmother and asked Dorland if I could pay him to paint it for me. He said 'sure thing' and then called me to say he'd saved money buying heavily discounted salmon-pink paint.

I was living in Los Angeles at the time so I asked Jackie to check what he'd done, to see just how appalling it was. I never did find out, but their second meeting was a vast improvement on the first: they fell in love, got married and shared me as their best man.

Jackie had an extensive record collection. Shortly after we'd moved into Gotham, I started looking through her albums to see if I could find myself a date. I dug out Paul Kelly's debut solo album *Post* and played it on repeat all afternoon. I fell in love with the songs, and Paul looked damn good on that front cover.

We already knew each other; Paul Kelly and The Coloured Girls and Do-Ré-Mi had been thrown together on a few different tours, and we'd become friendly over shared war stories. I went to a Coloured Girls gig that night and afterwards I took him to bed.

We were a fine couple for a minute, and then he introduced me to his cousin Alex McGregor, and as though it was a plan, I fell into bed with Alex. The morning after, Alex stood gazing out of the generously proportioned windows at Rushcutters Bay. I was still in the secret phase of this affair and told him, 'Don't stand so close to the window.'

Alex said, 'Hey, good line, could be a song title, I'll tell Paul'. And that was the end of the secret phase.

The day he introduced me to Alex, Paul produced a cassette out of his top pocket and announced he'd just written a new song. Did we want to hear it? Alex fished a cassette deck from under the piles of papers on his desk and Paul inserted the tape, pressed play and cranked up the demo for 'Dumb Things'. It was an unquestionable hit; we tapped our feet. When his album *Under the Sun* came out at the following year, 'Dumb Things' was the opening track and 'To Her Door' was track eight. Neither song made the Top 10.

A couple of years later, Paul, Kaarin Fairfax (who would soon be Paul's second wife and mother of his two daughters), Alex and I were in Washington DC spending Christmas 1988 with Paul's brother John Kelly, his wife Lyn and their family. Paul played us the song he'd been working on, 'Everything's Turning to White', his elegiac homage to Raymond Carver's short story. It came out the following year on the album *So Much Water So Close to Home*, but like previous albums none of the singles went Top 40.

Paul was releasing a record every two years, sometimes more, and they all included memorable songs, but serious chart success was not forthcoming. The pressure was building like a blocked gas line; this thing was gonna blow. In 1997 *Songs from the South*, a greatest hits double album, came out and reached number two on the ARIA charts. By 2017 *Songs from the South* had sold seven times platinum, those twenty songs instantly becoming part of the Australian oeuvre and catapulting Paul Kelly beyond a household name into national living legend status. Paul's is the story of Aesop's tortoise: slow, steady, methodical, diligent, resulting in the surprise victory lap. I have witnessed my gifted friend's rise and rise and have never seen him succumb to vanity or hubris.

During our brief affair, he would send me postcards when he was away; a line of poetry, a dream fragment, a puzzle or an incantation of love. They were romantic, adult, illicit and collectable. Sadly, most of them drowned in the steamer trunk I'd left in my parents' waterlogged basement.

I've witnessed Paul's complicated personal life in close-up, juggling roles as father, grandfather, husband, ex-husband, lover and ex-lover. He is in love with love, with the beginnings, the middles and the ends; swinging from committed serial monogamist to Lothario; it fuels his restless songwriter's curiosity to test himself, to push the explorations of desire and discomfort, of lust and loss.

His course of life includes the other addiction, flirtation with the demon opioids. I have been shocked at his inability when caught in that honey trap to see the extent of his indiscretions. I've seen him pull back and shield the people he loves from his worst proclivities, but the shield doesn't always extend to the people who love him.

I don't like everything he's written—in fact there are quite a few stinkers in his catalogue, he'd barely be human otherwise—but his strike rate is remarkably good. Seniority has given Paul a gravitas that he has parlayed into curating a bespoke collection of poetry, an unarguable good for all. I love that he has done this, and that he keeps on challenging himself and taking his increasing circle of ardent fans into places they probably never imagined going.

My friend is a very human hedonist who loves sensual pleasures, a beautiful painting, a beautiful body, good food, a cold beer, an aged whisky, a swim in the ocean, sex, gossip, laughing; he belongs equally to the machinations of Shakespeare as he does to the cricket stats.

His cousin Alex was an unconventionally handsome man. I thought he looked a bit like Philip Roth, or maybe the less Jewish version, John Updike, an author whose work Alex had introduced me to. Alex was the eldest in a large Catholic family, full of high achievers; he had a long aquiline nose, blue-green eyes, the physique of someone who writes for a living but likes swimming and plays tennis on a daily basis; not built but not scrawny either. Alex was that person in the room who, when he spoke, everyone would quieten down to listen to; maybe that comes with being the eldest of eight. He was always interesting.

He'll be appalled at this description probably, but in my observation this was how people responded to his probing curiosity, his humour, his reading of most situations with perspicacity, his very impressive memory (sometimes to his own detriment, he would tell me), his uncanny ability to be relaxed in all company and across so many topics.

Paul, Alex and I made for a free and easy threesome in the middle of those heady 1980s. Paul and I would be a couple in Sydney, but when he went back on the road, what he did was his business and what happened in Sydney when he was away was my business, though at that point it was Alex's business too. Our cosy triangle lasted several months before Alex said, loosely paraphrased, 'Enough: I'm not participating in this hedonistic, bohemian indulgence anymore, I'm the one getting shafted. Deborah, you have to choose.'

It was easy. I loved both, but I knew it had to be Alex. Paul wasn't unhappy, and I later ended up covering 'You Can Put Your Shoes Under My Bed' as an homage to the period. If you can manage to conduct matters of the heart without dishonesty you have a fighting chance of remaining on civil terms with all involved.

I adored Alex, he felt like the future, stability to my chaos. We would be a couple for five years, living in Sydney, London and Los Angeles. He had front row seats to the disintegration of my band and my attempts to construct myself as a solo artist. It was Alex who would become a bulwark against some of the madness that was about to follow.

11

(Not) The Happiest Place in Town

Do-Ré-Mi was working towards going back to the studio to record our second album in 1987, which as it transpired meant going back to the UK. Alex and I had been together for less than a year when I was on a plane for England to make *The Happiest Place in Town* with producer Martin Rushent in a studio near Hastings in the town of Battle.

Battle was aptly named (and not just for 1066); there were some extremely regrettable incidents during those recording sessions. One night when I was trying to sleep, kept awake by the drunken revelries of the other three, I lost my temper, stormed downstairs and screamed at them, which was bad enough, but far worse, when they laughed at my tantrum. I grabbed Helen by a breast and gave it a swift twist, which elicited Shock and Awe. And bruising. I ran back upstairs with Dorland in hot pursuit, and slammed and locked my door with him banging and yelling on the other side.

In the cold light of the following day, many heartfelt apologies were issued and eventually accepted; we still had an album to record. But it was the start of a lingering tear in our trust. The causes were not so easy to ameliorate. I was feeling left out, superfluous to the proceedings. Whether that was a problem aggravated by the publicity/record company machine always needing to feature the lead singer (which all of us tried to counter), or whether it was more to do with how and who we spent time with when we weren't working, it came to a head that night and a new sense of tribalism within our very intimate and delicately balanced interplay was now in the ascendant.

Martin Rushent oversaw the production of the best album we could make; there were a number of songs released as singles—'Adultery', 'King of Moomba', 'Haunt You' and the title track, all with accompanying film clips. Back in Australia we toured, spoke to the press, and posed with a man in a giant koala suit to launch *The Happiest Place in Town* at Dreamworld—a truly dreadful idea that we should have kiboshed, but for some reason didn't.

Maybe we were just tired. There had been a lot of work and very little time to recover from any of it, including the intensity of our collective group dynamic. We played support to the Simple Minds' national tour and the press turned on us. They decreed that we'd become too much a part of the stadium-rock establishment, no longer fresh, no longer new, apparently going through the motions with new material that wasn't as good as our old.

We didn't take a lot of notice, but 'Adultery' didn't set the charts on fire; it was a long way from the success of 'Man Overboard'. Basically, we delivered until we didn't. The problem with playing perpetually and cramming in as much publicity as you can is the loss of space to sit and contemplate the blank page, the most important component in the generation of new material. Time was something we no longer had much of.

Compared to *Domestic Harmony* there were far fewer reviews for *The Happiest Place in Town*. The reviews we did get were mostly good, though a notable exception was Clinton Walker's rather savage piece in a column in *RAM* titled 'Joy Kill': 'Few albums these days offer the listener more than a few favourite tracks and *The Happiest Place in Town* is no exception.' And, 'To me songs like "Valentine's Day", "Heads Will Roll", "Friends Like You" and "That Hanging Business" . . . sink into a morass of colourless breast-beating.' Ouch! *The Happiest Place in Town* was released in Europe with minimal record company support.

Within a few short months we were back on a plane to the UK to write and record demos for our third album. This was punishing; for our music, our publicity, our stamina and our relationships. Still, we soldiered on, and launched the spring offensive of 1988, the four of us holed up with Martin Rushent again, in his studio Genetic. We were living in simple, light-filled cottage accommodation, surrounded by trees and meadows full of wildflowers in the pastoral English countryside, a perfect setting to be at each other's throats.

We had been a collective for eight years but, as is often the case with bands, there was a bubbling undercurrent of jealousies, rivalries and attempts at manipulation. We could all rub each other the wrong way; we could all be obnoxious, but in hindsight, more than any personality trait, I think an unfounded suspicion nursed by the others that I had undeclared ambitions to become a solo artist had the unintended consequence of driving that exact outcome.

Added to the mix were tensions between Virgin and Martin, who had just been taken on salary by Virgin Records working as an in-house A&R (Artist & Repertoire) man, which effectively meant our producer was compromised. We were producing material in quantity but not of a quality that either the company or Martin or even our manager Keith Welsh was bowled over by.

Maybe we'd run out of ideas, but more likely we weren't able to do this creative thing to a record company schedule; we needed more time and less pressure to allow songs that actually said something to emerge. Unquestionably we were floundering, but none of the four of us recognised it or at least was prepared to admit it. Without any live shows to supplement our income we were slowly becoming becalmed in treacherous financial straits, completely dependent on Virgin for our ever-more-precarious per diem.

Dorland was steadfast in his enthusiasm for the band, while I was beginning to feel estranged, suspecting that our live performances had crossed a line; our extended pub touring had started to flatten the nuances and left us in bludgeoning pub rock territory. I was starting to prickle under Dorland's deep-seated need to micromanage everything, and was wearying of the upside-down version of democracy that we practised: if three of us wanted something and one didn't, the one who didn't won. Friction arising from living so closely together had escalated, and the centre would not hold.

Alex, who was staying with us, became persona non grata, our very own Yoko Ono. Keith, who'd been at our helm for a good clutch of years, even while desperately attempting to avert the approaching derailment, was also in the bad books. A letter to our lawyer Ian Philip, Stephen's brother, written and signed by

Dorland, Helen and Stephen, complaining about Keith's handling of the various difficulties they/we were working through, along with some more personal invective, ended up being faxed through to the wrong number. All was revealed (including to me) when Keith, not Ian, responded to the letter. An excruciating error with days of toxic fallout, it heralded the end of the empire. Do-Ré-Mi never recorded a third album.

Virgin ended the relationship in a sly fashion, claiming a hiatus rather than a conclusion. For them the current situation was untenable and there was no more money to spend on us. They told us that no one was waiting for a third Do-Ré-Mi album, but that if I were to make a solo record they would be happy to revisit the Do-Ré-Mi project after its release. Understandably there was legitimate grumbling at the capricious nature of record company edicts, but Keith advised us to take the directive at face value.

Virgin had quietly calculated that recruiting me as a solo artist could be a way to salvage something from the significant funds they'd outlaid. The upshot was that despite never having nursed ambitions to go it alone, I took Virgin's offer as a chance to get away from the band politics before they turned even more poisonous. I was launching my solo career for all the wrong reasons.

Dorland was the first person I told. He was sad, he was understanding, he wasn't angry and I don't think he was shocked. After we separated there was a period of mourning, a forsaken feeling in varying degrees for all of us, but the directive from management was that we make no announcements about our disbanding. Possibly they were hoping for a different outcome, but it was not to be. And so, eight years after we began, we ended, with just a few ripples emanating from where our collective stone had sunk.

There are meticulous archives, diligently collated by Helen, which hold a lot of this story. They end quite suddenly in May 1988, with a page of favourable reviews of the new album and single 'King of Moomba' from the English music press and an article called 'Living in Harmony' from UK music magazine *Sounds*.

In those archives is a 1988 Toby Creswell article in *Rolling Stone*, in which he interviews me.

> 'Do-Ré-Mi isn't always fun,' says Conway. 'That was a real shock to the system when I realised there was going to be some incredibly hard work. I discovered this after we released *Domestic Harmony* and just did two hundred and fifty-six shows in nine months. It's backbreaking but there's always the possibility you're going to have the best gig of your life—it happens . . .'

Until it doesn't.

12

Someday

There was just one hitch with the brand-new plan: I had no idea what I would do. Going solo had not crossed my mind before Virgin made the offer. That should have been a very good reason to turn it down. But to my eternal detriment, I am persuasively credible at appearing to know what I'm doing; as a stalling tactic it works well, but as a life guide it almost always ends in tears.

I threw around some ideas, sold them convincingly, and almost convinced myself. 'I'm going to make a dance album but with a rock edge,' I said, vague enough to give me plenty of wriggle room, throwing in Neneh Cherry as a style reference. I was a fan. She was quirky, danceable, on the charts and on Virgin. It got me and them over the line. And there was my first mistake. If I had really meant what I was saying, if I'd listened and learnt about what making a record like that might entail, I may have avoided the expensive calamity that the next two years became.

The spring wildflowers were making way for the summer performers as we vacated Genetic and disengaged from each other. The clear air was welcome. Alex and I went exploring over the next few weeks, in England and on the Continent, locations both exotic and agreeable.

We found shelter and succour in the homes of various friends and relations, including a flying three-day visit to Paris to stay with Shellie during her residency at the Cité Internationale des Arts, falling in love with Paris; the architecture, the galleries, the bakeries with their trays of almond and chocolate pastries; and the African Quarter Barbès–Rochechouart, full of tiny shops crammed with heavy reams of bright waxed fabric, and delicious smells from the nearby market stalls. Back in London my friend, the actress Greta Scacchi, invited us to stay for a few weeks at her terrace house in Kennington, close to the famous Oval cricket ground.

At the height of summer I landed alone in Rome on a sweltering night at 2 am and took a taxi to a cheap pensione somewhere near the Colosseum, where Alex would meet me the next day. The driver drove around that majestic ancient amphitheatre, quietly defying time, earthquakes and the Fall of Rome, now in the dying moments of the Second Millennium and lit up with golden lights. It was so still, so eerily beautiful. I wound down the windows and gulped lungfuls of hot Roman air.

The weather turned cooler and Alex and I visited Spain, first to Madrid and the Prado to stare transfixed at the saturnine figures of Goya. I bought myself a luscious tomato-red coat for the coming northern winter, ate tapas and drank flagons of tempranillo. We caught the train to Seville to hang out in the Moorish-inspired public gardens full of mosaic tiles and fragrant orange trees laden with fruit; and lastly, to Cadiz, the port town Columbus sailed from to discover the New World and the town where I discovered churros and empanadas and couldn't eat enough of them. But I never wrote a song about any of it.

After our long languid summer of no fixed address, Alex continued travelling while I returned to London to knuckle down and write, holed up in an uninspiring beige bedsit in Earl's Court. It was a locale made famous for being the gathering ground of badly behaved Australian expats in the 1970s film *The Adventures of Barry McKenzie.* The shortening days, the severe grey stone buildings indistinguishable from the leaden skies; the dour encounters I was having daily around my neighbourhood; ordering a salad which would get you a slice of tomato, a limp lettuce leaf, some tasteless cucumber sliced transparently thin with a bit of chopped cheddar and an accompanying scowl. It was all light years away from the European cities I'd been falling in love with.

Dorland had stayed in London and, with our wounds sufficiently licked, we had started writing together again. He would catch the train to Earl's Court from where he was living in Stamford Hill, usually toting a bag of vegetarian sausage rolls he'd picked up at his local kosher bakery. We sat around my flat drinking tea or wine, eating flaky pastry and writing songs. We had the chance to repair the frayed edges of our previous fraught months.

We wrote 'Someday', the lyric covered in the fingerprints of that period: English like *Postman Pat*, toast and marmalade, and heavy drizzling skies. And we wrote 'White Roses', a deconstruction of Al Green's romantic 'Let's Stay Together' reconstructed as a country lament about the end of a relationship—prescient, as it turned out, though neither Dorland nor I knew quite how prescient it was at the time.

Songwriting aside, I couldn't shake the notion that life was happening elsewhere; like a version of pins-and-needles or restless legs; no matter how fiercely I bit into life, the impression that more of it was happening just beyond my frame, a tastier, more compelling, better-attended version, was inescapable. The dissatisfaction of the grass being greener on the other side skulked beneath the surface; who knew where the other side was, though I did suspect getting there might bring disappointment.

Luckily for me, America was in the offing. Virgin Records and my publisher EMI wanted me to go there to meet professional songwriters and work with them. Keith Welsh's final task as my manager was to organise a trip to the US in October 1988 for a practice encounter. We took meetings in New York, LA and a side trip to Boston where the fall colours were dazzling, the songwriting less so. After two days in someone's studio apparently recording something, I had nothing to show for it. Keith remembers the fellow I worked with as patient, friendly but so deeply frustrated with the process that he asked Keith if he could play guitar on the song.

Keith doesn't play guitar.

I returned to the low skies and povvo conditions of my Earl's Court bolthole and dreamt of living off the fat of the record company in America. Directly following that trip, Keith stepped aside to accommodate Virgin's request that my manager live in the same hemisphere as me; however, because the job came without the offer of an income, Virgin UK A&R man Jeremy Lascelles (great-grandson of King George V and therefore in line for the throne under exceptionally unlikely circumstances) took on the task of my personal management himself. It wasn't ideal. Lack of skills and conflict of interest spring to mind, but at the time, like so much else, I didn't think about it all that much.

Alex returned from his European travels and met me in London; he was aiming to find work as a freelance stringer covering American cultural areas of interest for English and Australian publications, and LA was his preferred option both for the work and the lifestyle. Having been in New York for a few days in November, I had fallen deeply in love with the place, but figured all the shiny distractions would be less shiny in LA. It all aligned nicely into a win/win sum, whichever option we chose. So as London atrophied to an oppressive, damp splodge we hauled ourselves and our meagre belongings across the Atlantic.

We spent a whirlwind long weekend in New York staying with friends in the freezing depths of a January winter, where I got so cold walking the downtown streets I had to duck into a photocopy shop and pretend to browse (you try browsing at a photocopier shop) so I could regain the feeling in my toes and fingers before I lost them to frostbite; and then to our final destination, La La Land, where winter was a temperate low of 12° Celsius, high of 20° Celsius and sunny.

13

For All the Wrong Reasons

Alex and I landed on 19 January, 1989, spending our first night in a no-frills serviced apartment in Sherman Oaks where, in the early evening—6.53 GMT precisely—we felt the earth move, a 5.0 earthquake, its epicentre under Santa Monica Bay. The next day's *Los Angeles Times* confirmed that 'the main shock epicentre was 10.5 miles west of Los Angeles International Airport and about 8 miles south of Malibu. The earthquake was felt from northern San Diego County to Santa Barbara and as far east as San Bernardino . . ..'

Alex was in the bath watching the water ripple up into waves and calmly, with the merest hint of consternation, telling me to stand in a door frame. I found the rattling exciting in the way people do when they know very little about earthquakes and their destructive power; from my origins of topographically stable continents, earthquakes were exotic, more akin to a carnival ride, a moment of recognition that we're not in Kansas anymore.

At some stage between my first and second tremor, we visited the California Science Center, aka the Earthquake Museum, which meant that by the time I was living through my second earthquake I'd undergone an initiation and come to develop a more advanced toolkit, which included awe, respect and fear, far more useful if you're working out how to survive one.

That second earthquake we experienced in our semi-detached two-bedroom house on North Ogden Drive, a short walk (perish the thought, no one walks in LA) to Fairfax, very close to the famous Canter's Deli which had been there since 1931 and served chicken soup with giant matzoh balls at 3 am if you so required. And occasionally I did require comfort that could catapult me back to my childhood.

I stood beneath the doorframe and watched all the *tchotchkes* on our shelves do a shimmy. The stereo turned backwards; the plants leapt like rams, the books like young lambs. Now I felt awe. It's a very strange feeling when the Earth moves beneath you, when everything that was dependable and solid becomes custard. Not a bad metaphor for the making of the album I was ostensibly there to work on.

Apart from the earthquakes and the smog, Los Angeles really was a great place to live, with myriad pleasant distractions; the beach, the mountains, the high desert blue skies and starry nights, if you could get far enough out of town to see them. And as long as you could drive, everything was very easy to access—shops, cinemas, regular supermarkets, supermarkets dedicated to health food (of course, it's California!), cafes, bars, pools, gyms, tennis courts, plenty of parking when you got there, or valet parking should the mood take you.

As they say in LA, nothing was more than a 20-minute drive away. If you wanted to work, this was a work town: the producers, studios, writers and record companies were all here too, and working and playing became indivisible activities.

Meetings over margaritas and Mexican and Everyone wanted to make the moment work so Everyone was telling you exactly what you wanted to hear. The bad news would be delivered after your wonderful meeting was finished and you could be let down gently by your manager. These were cultural lessons to be learnt over time, in the interim I was enjoying all the rides.

We had a small circle of friends, mostly Australian—some passing through, some permanently relocated, or like us, temporarily so. We were all trying our hand at breaking into the American showbiz dream in one way or another. The roll call was telling.

Paul Kelly was there to write and record; Paul's girlfriend, the actress Kaarin Fairfax, was auditioning for roles; Colin Hay had just moved to Topanga Canyon and was recording his second solo album—we would write a song together that he recorded, 'She Keeps Me Dreaming'; Steve Kearney, post-Los Trios Ringbarkus, was working on a script while his American actress girlfriend Claire headed off to auditions.

Actress Sigrid Thornton and her director husband Tom Burstall were living in a bohemian palace befitting their established status, warmly welcoming all and sundry to their parties, where we got high and then got in the hot tub. Claudia Castle, the filmmaker, was feeling out possibilities, and Toby Creswell, the writer, was always working the room. John Clifforth was trying to establish a new musical entity after the demise of Deckchairs Overboard; while his wife Lisa Dethridge sailed through life in her curiously detached yet impassioned way. Lisa had just got her driver's licence when shortly afterwards I was in the passenger seat and she was using both feet in an automatic car, one on the accelerator and one on the brake!

We were all caught in the stop-start, most of us less literally than Lisa—the ones who were digging in and the ones who were floating above, all circling *something*, which some of us found and some of us never did.

Garth Murphy, long, rangy, a quietly spoken relaxed Californian, reminiscent of Sam Shepard to look at, and his petite, vivacious wife Euva Anderson, who was possibly Brazilian but that was never confirmed, owned a rambling mansion with many bedrooms, painted pink and festooned with climbing roses in the Hollywood Hills, a kind of prototype for Airbnb.

Garth and Euva were mysteriously elegant, seeming never to work at anything apart from being endlessly hospitable and available when required, to distract their ceaseless turnover of short- and long-stay visitors, actors, writers, directors and producers.

Garth had co-owned a house in Sydney's Palm Beach with Australian filmmaker David Elfick, and there were many well-known Australians on the guest lists. Parties in the pink house on the hill were frequent, wild and unsupervised. There was a decadence about the place that chimed well with the times, including rooms containing gothic, strangely sexual artefacts—whether to be used, or not, and how, was left to the imagination.

In my memory the house was a destination for hedonism, the guests happy to take a break from the rigours of movie business networking. I found myself going there often, no invitation required. Alex wasn't interested; he found what solace he needed almost exclusively in his work, while I was looking for distractions. The pink house was always open. I could swim in the pool, get lost in the view and there was usually someone interesting to talk to. It's the kind of house that appears in my dreams now, like a setting from a David Lynch movie.

It was a dreamlike year—maybe all years are like that when you're this far away from them—but there was something Faustian about the perpetual encouragement to immerse in fantasy and put off concrete decisions; it wasn't conducive to the knuckle-down, the hard yards that had to be carefully thought through. Maybe this was why I was so drawn to the place, ducking and weaving around the looming final denouement, for all the wrong reasons.

As 1989 slid by I sat on the couch in our front room with the big windows facing onto our relatively quiet suburban street. Not too many distractions there; the almost indistinguishable Californian winter turned to unnoticeable Californian spring while I kept my head bowed to the songcraft, always struggling with the bridge, the damned bridge. There were a lot of tears, according to Alex. Three decades later I have forgotten them, but he remembers; he quoted Audrey Hepburn at me a couple of days ago: 'The secret of a happy life is good health and a bad memory.' I looked it up; she said she *wished* that she'd invented that aphorism.

Whether or not I remember the tears, I have a visceral memory of the maddening frustration. I was battling a fog of indecision and, absent a clear purpose, I had no chance of getting anywhere. It makes complete sense: if you want to get somewhere you need to know where the hell you're going! I floundered without a guiding principle. I was furious with myself that songwriting didn't come more easily; I struggled to write words I didn't think were banal, and melodies that were either not original enough or so original they defied being remembered.

At the same time EMI were hard at work setting up appointments for me with professional songwriters, of which there were many. I endured a few dismal non-productive encounters but the first successful one was a banger.

Scott Cutler was dark featured, slightly abrasive, forthright, playful and Jewish, we got on immediately. His credentials included being a grand nephew of Irving Berlin. Rusty Anderson, a gangly, sweet, long-haired hippy with twinkling blue eyes, was a guitarist, songwriter and producer who knew Scott, which is why we were introduced. Rusty and I spent a few lovely entertaining but unproductive days together. A few years later Scott and Rusty co-wrote 'Torn', which Natalie Imbruglia had a multi-platinum hit with. Rusty then went on to work with pretty much every big name in the business including Paul McCartney, Elton John, Stewart Copeland, Miley Cyrus and k.d. lang to name but a few, just not me. Win some lose some.

I have a photograph album full of snaps: in some of them the locations are easy to place, others more opaque. Dorland and I cavorting in Disneyland with a young Declan Kelly (Paul's son). Dorland and I at Joshua Tree with guitars. Paul and I sitting cross-legged, poring over a guitar and pages of notes with an abundance of drinks in attendance (maybe London, maybe LA). Scott reclining in a studio chair between takes. Rusty, hair swinging in guitar-hero stance, me lying on the couch laughing among the reams of looseleaf lyrics definitely in Silverlake where Rusty lived and worked. Ollie Leiber (son of Jerry, as in Jerry Leiber and Mike Stoller) in the studio in Minneapolis, me lying on a couch behind him. On the couch at Ogden Drive with various props, guitar, Walkman, notebooks, cat (which belonged to the neighbours but liked to visit) and even me on the couch, constructing the photo album that all these photos are collected in (are you sensing a theme here?).

The photos are faded but I've cut them up and pasted them over each other to better tell a visual story of the moment. Page after plastic-covered page, it is a cavalcade of the living and the dead. Steve Connelly, Michael Hutchence, Lian Lunson, Nick Cave, Colin Hay, Ollie Olsen, John Hillcoat, Evan English, Polly Borland and the beautiful and brilliant Wertheim twins, Margaret and Christine. There are photos of my birthday, celebrated with dear friends over afternoon tea in the Huntington Botanical Gardens in Pasadena; photos of Alex and me during that white Christmas in Washington with the Kelly cousins, in Mexico and New Mexico.

We got around, we did a lot of stuff. Alex was a rock, and our year in LA was a coming-of-age adventure, a faintly absurd, slightly embarrassing description considering I turned thirty in 1989; nevertheless my coming of age is what it was, the start of shucking off the perpetual adolescence that being in the bosom of a band, especially one with a manager, not only made possible but encouraged.

So many of my generation had enjoyed an extended childhood; we never had to fight a war, live through a depression, or, in Australia, worry about starving when unemployed since the safety net was so comprehensive. Join a rock band, and that phenomenon was exacerbated many times over. Our every need was mostly taken care of, and in return we didn't ask questions about where all our money was going or how it was being spent.

Well, I didn't anyway. The relinquishing of basic autonomy kept us in an absurdly naive state. We had no idea of our finances and we didn't care. I look back now with incredulity; we were so easy to take advantage of.

I was beginning to confront reality, but not soon enough for what was at stake. We pushed the work–play balance around. The pleasure principle was in the mix, but the work was a constant—a constant frustration.

I thought a songwriting relationship should be personal, intimate and raw; an exercise in trust, in which I had to be able to show my vulnerabilities to another person who would take me seriously. Thus far, I wasn't practised in the corporate attitude of, 'Hello, pleased to meet you, let's sit in a room and I'll show you mine if you show me yours'. I held back. And mostly I didn't like the outcomes beyond the initial feeling of, 'Hey, look, we wrote a song' kind of like riding a bicycle with no hands and announcing it just before you fall off.

A song wasn't something I could just whip up—more's the pity. It's not to say that the kind of song you might write when it's not a personal knock-'em-down, drag-'em-out tussle is inferior to the ones where you give a little piece of your heart; it was just how I approached it. Unsurprisingly, this attitude set me up for a lot of failure.

Dorland came to LA pretty soon after we'd settled in and we picked our relationship up from where we'd left off in London, writing songs. Most we rejected, but some squeaked through quality control. Two we wrote I ended up recording in Minneapolis with Ollie Leiber. Ollie was up-and-coming, having been instrumental in turning a Lakers cheerleader into an International Dance Queen. Paula Abdul was topping the charts all over the known universe thanks to talent, hard work, good timing and Gemma Corfield, the A&R powerhouse that we shared at Virgin Records' US office.

Naturally, since Gemma was also scouting out opportunities for me, Ollie and I ended up together recording a couple of tracks in his studio in Minneapolis and mixing them down the road at Paisley Park. (While there I glimpsed the late great 'artist formerly known as . . .' in all his purpleness, dressed like he was about to walk on stage; there might have even been a cape.)

The finished tracks were the authentic Minneapolis Sound, even down to the same backing singers who sang on Prince's single 'Kiss', but there was a cognitive dissonance between the production and the song—square peg, round hole. I tried to keep an open mind, but my open mind was openly screaming, 'Do not put these on a record!' Ollie was a sweet young man doing what he had already successfully done but he too knew this was a fail.

There were two significant obstacles: the songs I was writing were nothing like dance songs, and I was not anything remotely like a dancer. I had cited Neneh Cherry as my blueprint—fragmented chunks of rap, rhythms, dirty sounds, slight words, alternating soft and hard rhymes, sexual provocations that slide over the brainpan, memorable enough to sing but not distracting the listener from the core business of getting down on a dance floor—but instead had co-written songs that were throwbacks to

Tin Pan Alley, maybe even Gilbert & Sullivan. How did I imagine I could sing the word 'cornucopian' in a dance song and make it work?

> Two hearts get tangled up in a cornucopian loving cup
> Her own reaches after them, if she could drink she wouldn't say when

Honestly, I have no idea why I had gone so far down this path without the emergency brakes being applied. But they weren't; not by the record company, not by the producer, not by my English manager or my A&R man (who were one and the same person, as you may recall); and, most importantly, not by me.

When I was a pre-teen, I occasionally decided that I needed a day home from school and pulled a sickie. My mother would call the family doctor, and sure enough the doctor always found something wrong with me. I'd ask myself afterwards—was it that I was so convincing, or were they truly just that gullible?

Now the joke was on me. I had engineered myself to be the smartest, stupidest person on this project, and all I was doing was screwing myself over. I had made a basic error of imagining I could repurpose any old song into a dance track. That is not how it works.

The Ollie Leiber–Minneapolis exercise left me no nearer to where I musically wanted to aim—only where I didn't. There were more recording sessions with other producers—long hair, short hair, The Valley, West Hollywood. Patrick Leonard, Madonna's producer, was among the meetings I took. (I met Madge lolling around on a couch with Sandra Bernhard, playing up for all the people in the room. There was the crackle of healthy ego jousting between us, but when she found out I was an Aussie she dropped her guard and spoke warmly of Molly Meldrum.)

And all the while big things were happening in other parts of the world in 1989. A 7.1 magnitude earthquake shook San Francisco to the core on 17 October, destroying a section of the Bay Bridge and killing sixty-three people, a terrible day. We watched the news footage in horror. Three weeks later, 9 November, our TV news brought scenes of the Berlin Wall falling, an end to the Cold War, resulting in jubilation for all enemies of tyranny and the dawn of a whole new world (just not the one Tim Rice was talking about); back in Australia my best friends were getting married but I couldn't go, I was stuck in an endlessly repeating Californian dream.

Finally, I found myself in a room with producer Ian Ritchie, a saxophone player and loops aficionado. I had declared I was going to make a dance album, and weirdly, stubbornly, despite the obstacles, I was still wedded to that idea. Accordingly, all the rhythm tracks were sequenced and most of what ended up going down was coming out of a box. I convinced myself I liked the recordings, at least while we were making them.

Ian chimed in, in his lilting Scottish brogue: 'The difference between starting an album from loops and starting with live instruments is that everything you add to the former improves the sound but everything you add to the latter diminishes it.'

I believed it at the time.

14

Release Me

The record was in the can and so was I, flying back across the Atlantic at the start of 1990 to relocate to London in preparation for the release of my first solo album. Many a slip twixt the cup and the lip. There was still so much more money to be spent. Firstly, Jeremy Lascelles stated that there was no obvious single—'It's Only the Beginning' rendered as a dance track with an angsty lyric just wasn't cutting it—and announced that we'd have to head back to the studio.

It was Scott Cutler's idea to record a dance version of the Bad Company song 'Feel Like Makin' Love'. He arrived in London to produce it and immediately hated what we had wrought. He wasn't the only one. Here's a review from one of the British music mags:

> Deborah Conway—*Feel Like Makin' Love* (Virgin) [1990]
> Christ Almighty, another one of the bastards! This one borders

on madness. Deborah, a very, very pretty girl indeed, has chosen or, more likely, been chosen to sing over a Housified 'Feel Like Makin' Love', the old Bad Company cock rock anthem. Why? Since it's perfectly obvious she's only in it for the spondoolies, why Housify? Why didn't Deborah, looking the way she does and singing the song she's been chosen to sing, having seen the success of Alannah Myles, why didn't she play it straight? Why not thrust and grind and pout? In short, why not do it like Bad Company did it? It could've sold a million, it could've had a million lascivious inadequates following their raging erections down to Our Price. But no, they just had to Housify. Deborah, you poor hip bitch. You're gonna be one bitter old woman.

Despite Scott's and my sense of impending doom, the additional track appeared to answer all Virgin's needs, and so a 12-inch mix of the single (with a rap) was ordered up—two, in fact. The 'Unity Mix' and the 'Inspiration Mix', were, needless to say, deeply lacking in inspiration. I was promptly dispatched to Barcelona to get my photo taken for the album, the single, and any promotional shots that were required.

Sometime shortly after they were taken, I was prancing about the Brixton Academy, dressed in a vintage red swimsuit with black fishnet tights and Doc Martens looking (apart from the Docs) like a EuroTrash Dance Queen to mime 'Feel Like Makin' Love' for a Channel 4 TV show called *Dance Daze*, to be screened in October.

I have blocked out the memory but I know it happened because I have written proof, a letter to my sister describing my ensemble and bemoaning all the decisions that got me there. I needn't have worried; the enterprise was done and dusted well before October.

Virgin left me sitting in the little flat off the Portobello Road for which they were paying the rent, the phone bill and a per diem, like maintenance for a high-class courtesan. I was living in an eternal waiting room. They pay, I wait. They pay, I remain ready to put out. They pay, I deliver.

Alex stayed in LA working; we had a tacit agreement that our relationship would be open while we were apart. I wasted no time. I had an affair with a Jewish Englishman I'd met in Los Angeles who looked me up when he got to London; he then introduced me to his friend, another Jewish Englishman, a sculptor. There's a pattern.

Like all good doomed affairs, my brief time with the sculptor was full of memorable, never-to-be-repeated moments, heightened by the fact that we took months before embarking on a physical relationship. We rode 64 kilometres on bicycles to and from Chartwell, Winston Churchill's house in Kent, slogging up the hills and flying down the other side, and when we arrived back at his flat we rubbed ice cubes over each other to cool down, which of course only made us heat up even more. We visited multitudes of churches, and sketched life-drawings of each other on his red couch; I read Hermann Hesse's *Siddhartha* to him on long drives. He made a bust of me. We tortured each other with restraint which only made the lovemaking, when it happened, more intense.

Nevertheless, it *was* doomed. My life was too complicated, and I was too indecisive, juggling too many big loves, ambitions and men, not to mention countries, with a heart not big enough to embrace it all without aching. I was undeniably attracted to the drama of the star-crossed affair and I had an open-ended diary to indulge myself. As the months passed I divided my time between these clandestine, overwhelming love affairs and tinkering around on my guitar.

'Somewhere between the swamp and the mountains. Somewhere between fear and sex. Somewhere between God and the Devil passion is and the way there is sudden and the way back is worse.' Jeanette Winterson summed it up in *The Passion*. That passage hit me with the force of recognition. So I stole it and attempted to write a path out of my present, out of my eternal waiting room.

'For All the Wrong Reasons', *String of Pearls*, 1991

For all the wrong reasons
I took you to bed
Seduced you so gently
And made you my captive
For all the wrong reasons I took you to bed
For all the wrong reasons
I threw you aside
I severed you quickly
I answered no questions
For all the wrong reasons I threw you aside
For all the wrong reasons
I married another
I carried six children
I bore him no grudges
For all the wrong reasons I married another

Somewhere between the swamp and the mountain
Somewhere between sex and fear
Somewhere between God and the Devil passion lurks
The way there is sudden the way back is worse
Maybe I could walk on water
Maybe I could swim on sand
Maybe I could forget all about you my burning heart
But right now I'm drowning in the tide
Right now I'm sinking in the mud
And so my tears keep falling just like autumn skies
Seems I don't learn anything and I don't know why
For all the wrong reasons

How is it that one day life's so simple?
How come the next day life's so strange?
How did I stumble through this twilight deaf and blind?
To be delivered by your voice
To be devoured by your eyes
I must gather up my senses
I must rally the full force
Put away this misery and madness from my soul
Start taking care of what is mine and make amends for what
I sold
For what I stole

Songs were spilling out of me now, plopping out, oozing out. I was writing to express the frustration and I recognised it was a more honest representation of me than anything on the record awaiting release.

'Buried Treasure', 'Release Me' and 'String of Pearls' were written during this period; inspiration, coming at me from all quarters.

As a child, my favourite Friday night outing was to sleep at my paternal grandmother Hettie's flat, where she lived with her sister, my Auntie Lottie. Sometimes our other aunties would be there too. There were lots of them, all spinsters or widows, they'd alternate their chatter between their broad Yorkshire accents and Yiddish when they didn't want us to understand.

There was the great cook auntie, the cheek-pinching auntie, the slip-you-a-dollar-or-two auntie, the sterner auntie who wasn't impressed with my dungarees, the adorable dimpled always laughing auntie, the smothering-hug auntie, the aunties who lost all their marbles by the end and thought I was a little boy; and my favourite, Auntie Dolly.

At ninety-one years old, Great Auntie Dolly, who by then had outlived all the other great aunts, decided, without telling any of us, to uproot her life in Melbourne and move to the other side of the country. I asked her years later if she was happy in Perth. In her Yorkshire brogue, undiminished through seven decades she said, 'Well, nooo, I don't like it so much, but you know I don't have to stay here forever.'

They are some big bold genes to fill. I wrote 'Buried Treasure' thinking about 'all my great aunts who never got married and lived to a hundred'.

As time stretched on, Virgin tried to work out the right moment to release the dance album. Each fresh expenditure to salvage the money already spent mounted, and every new decision only exacerbated the previous bad decision. The waiting was a physical weight, I wrote 'Release Me'—'I believed for a while you believing in me'.

I'd been listening to Syd Straw's debut album *Surprise*, on which one of the songs, a Michael Stipe co-write, is called 'Future 40s (String of Pearls)'. Clearly it made an impression, though definitely not one that led to a conscious decision. *Surprise* was released on Virgin Records in 1989. I got a copy and spent the first six months of 1990 listening to it. Syd had handed in her membership of cult band The Golden Palominos to do her own thing and *Surprise* was the first fruit of the harvest.

I fell in love with Syd's throaty drawl, which conjured a mischievous, care-less cut-through, the sound of Americana openness, the sound of driving far and farther—all particularly appealing when you're stuck in a one-bedroom flat, waiting for the pause button that someone else has pressed to be released.

Plans were coming and going, deadlines being pushed back. It was beginning to dawn on me that I hated my record. I'd been pursuing a trail of fool's gold, and had led myself down the wrong musical path. I held no one more responsible for this misguided direction than myself, but the consequences are the same whether you have the luxury of blaming someone else or not.

I had enough time on my hands to write songs for the record I wasn't making and also to write songs I thought Syd could sing, my fevered fantasy born of searching for worthwhile distractions. And then, some kind of magic.

One sunny afternoon, checking out coffee joints in my neighbourhood (which should be noted was a particularly groovy one), I noticed a woman looking remarkably like Syd Straw. I approached her for a better look and blow me down, there she was, the person I hadn't been able to get out of my head for months, just sitting there waiting for a friend. I may have been a little breathless, a little puppy-like as I introduced myself and told her I was obsessed with her music, that in fact I'd just written a song for her. She responded in her laconic Californian accent, tinged with a slight southern twang, that she was pleased to meet me and that she'd love to hear the song.

I gave her a few salient bio markers—Australian, musician, signed to Virgin, waiting for a release date—her ears pricked, she recognised the common ground. We exchanged phone numbers, and over the course of some months we spent time together. She played me hers, I played her mine, we tossed around new song ideas and shared our record company woes. (Syd ended up taking the song I'd written with her in mind, 'I'm Not the Toughest Girl in the World', dropping the 'I'm Not' and recording it on her follow-up album [not through Virgin] *War and Peace* [now there's a title with a message]).

Syd was in a similar situation to me. Virgin had brought her across to London, put her up in a flat and was matchmaking her with other songwriters hoping for that second album with which they could turn her into a superstar. She seemed further along the path of scepticism than I was. She told me a prescient story of her friend who'd worked for years completing an album only to be unceremoniously dumped by the record company; and the next thought I had was, *Well, that could be good.*

Back at the desk in my Portobello Road flat I went autobiographical and wrote 'String of Pearls'. My fairly rudimentary guitar skills were enough to give me a solid folky backing. Farmer's chords G C G D verse; a C D chorus; and an Em and Am thrown in for the bridge, all played lyrically over a loping 3/4 time.

I whipped the song out in one day-long writing session, singing it over and over as I honed it. The day wore on and I started hearing pounding from somewhere close by. I finally worked out that it was my neighbours from the downstairs flat beating on their ceiling, my floor, with a broom I supposed, to indicate I was making too much noise.

I checked my volume but kept working. I was absorbed, it was easy; that's what happens when you write about what you know. I had my opening—'A long time ago when my mother's hands were all my world'—and off I went from there; she provided that solid base.

The last chorus has a cute lyrical switch: after repeating 'Some wear' four times, I dropped in 'Somewhere over the rainbow' over the musical climax. It gave me goosebumps at the time, a) because 'Somewhere Over the Rainbow' is one of those songs that gives me goosebumps and b) because I thought it was clever and I was pretty happy with myself for coming up with it.

'String of Pearls', *String of Pearls,* 1991

A long time ago when my mother's hands were all my world
She taught me everything there was to know about holding
 and being held
Like a grain of sand in an oyster shell
The seed of knowledge grows
The small thing becomes a pearl
At the tender age when everything is unfamiliar
I can remember all the rough play princess and the wild
 crusader

Never too shy for a mission of discovery
I learned about the well of my curiosity

Some wear their heart on their sleeve
Some wear the patience of saints
Some wear the weight of the world on their shoulders
I just wear my string of pearls
My string of pearls

The first time that I really fell in love
I gave half my heart away and taking care of half of his
Proved we were old enough
All of those teenage radio songs
About romance that lasts forever
Well I found out they'd got it wrong

Some wear their heart on their sleeve
Some wear the patience of saints
Some wear the weight of the world on their shoulders
I just wear my string of pearls
My string of pearls

Waiting for gurus or gypsies or gods
Under these burning clouds
Searching for comfort above

When I joined a band to be a rock 'n' roll star
I tasted how sweet it was to be the girl that everybody wanted
Playing in their bar

Spotlights shine on me
'Cos when the party's over
You're just a waste of electricity

Some wear their heart on their sleeve
Some wear the patience of saints
Some wear the weight of the world on their shoulders
I just wear my string of pearls
My string of pearls

I got a life
I guess it suits me pretty well
I gotta crawl down narrow alleyways to Heaven or stroll
boulevards to Hell
Bead by bead of wisdom and poetry
All the blind paths and avenues
Dimly lit by my rosary

Some wear their heart on their sleeve
Some wear the patience of saints
Some wear the weight of the world on their shoulders
Some wear a crown of thorns
Some wear out their welcome
But somewhere over the rainbow
I will wear my string of pearls, my string of pearls

And then it happened: the record and I were dropped. We had spent the best part of two years and countless pounds to have my big solo dance adventure implode with barely a bump or grind.

While Virgin had been trying to rescue some of the money they'd outlaid on the Do-Ré-Mi project, they still had their second prize, a nice fat tax offset to balance Phil Collins's enormous chart-topping successes. It was an exemplary display of decadent *fin de siècle* music business resource squandering. In the end Do-Ré-Mi and I were just a side column in Virgin's account books.

It was the northern summer of 1990. Everything certain had been thrown carelessly away; I had no record company, no band, no manager. But I had something else. Finally, I knew what I wanted to say and how I wanted to say it. I had found the key. I had unlocked the music.

15

Last to Know

I'd known Amanda Pelman since we were around fifteen years old. We didn't go to the same school, but we had so many mutual friends we may as well have. We'd lost touch, but I remembered her as being the most grown-up person in the room, so it didn't surprise me, when we bumped into each other in LA in 1989, that Amanda had become a very successful artist manager, currently steering young pop act Indecent Obsession to the top of the charts.

Amanda had been one of the guiding lights in Kylie Minogue's success, signing her to a deal with Mushroom Records and mentoring her down the yellow brick road from television soap to pop-music icon. Decades later, Kylie remains the most successful solo female artist Australia has produced. Her intriguing musical journey began with a cover of Carole King's and Gerry Goffin's classic, 'Loco-Motion'. It had been a massive number 1 hit in the US for Little Eva in 1962, ditto for Grand Funk Railroad in 1974, and in 1988 it was Kylie's turn to hit number 3 on the US charts. (Three decades, three top ten US hits, that's a song with pedigree.)

Kylie's nickname from that first chart success on was, affectionately, or in some cases dismissively, The Singing Budgie. But she was no dumb bird and from her first forays into this pop world Kylie flew above the stereotype to confound her critics and enjoy an extraordinarily successful, stadium-filling international career with a string of #1 hits in thirty-seven countries, including in the US, British and Australian charts. And just as she was about to be pigeonholed again Kylie polished her cool credentials with a number of dark dance pieces and a dirty bird (sorry, I can't help myself) duet with Nick Cave which only enriched the mystique and shone both of their crowns to a platinum finish.

Amanda Pelman was entrenched in Melbourne's music scene and both of us sensed a good opportunity to work together. On my way home from London I sojourned in LA and played her my songs. We talked about what I wanted career-wise, which by then I understood much more clearly, and worked out a strategy to achieve it. We agreed to work together to secure a record deal for my debut solo album.

Before I had even set foot back in Australia, Amanda was hot on the trail of a deal for me with Mushroom. I quizzed her about other companies; my knowledge of Michael Gudinski was the scuttlebutt from the half of the music business he *hadn't* charmed. It wasn't that I was uninterested, but I did want to know that we'd explored all the options. Amanda assured me that Mushroom was offering the best deal.

Michael Gudinski, founder and head of Mushroom Records, now Mushroom Group, was often, either mockingly, fondly or resentfully, referred to as 'God'. As one of the most powerful players in the small music business in Australia—Michael's fiefdom of Melbourne was even smaller—it was an apt name.

Once upon a time he could lift a bunch of musicians from obscurity to a moment in the sun with a flick of his pen.

Of course the musicians didn't reap much of a financial benefit, but in return for that signature on a Mushroom record contract, the bright glare of publicity enabled many a young hopeful, who had been lingering in the musical badlands of being barely known outside their local bar, to launch a fully formed national profile; sign a publishing deal (also with Mushroom), get a song on high rotation on commercial radio, a publicity tour, an album on the charts, a support with an overseas act touring Australia (probably booked by Michael's co-owned international touring company, Frontier Touring) and a national live tour (most likely booked by Frank Stivala, Michael's partner in the booking agency, Premier).

Whether the act had a brief shining moment of glory and then fizzled again into obscurity, or went on to enjoy a long-term career was not something Michael could completely control, but it was something he could influence.

On returning to Australia, I'd decided to live, not in Sydney, but back in Melbourne. It was a decision that surprised me a bit, but I felt strongly that as I had run away from it at 21, I should give living in Melbourne as an adult a shot. My family was there, as was Mushroom. I called Do-Ré-Mi's old manager Keith Welsh to discuss my plans. He recommended I get together with Richard Pleasance, who had just left Boom Crash Opera, a band that Keith also managed. Richard had decided playing bass in a loud rock band was exacerbating his tinnitus and wanted a change of pace.

Keith let Richard know I was looking for a collaborator and suggested we meet in Melbourne.

Keith tells me now that both of us expressed reluctance to work together. We had a history, often being on the same bill and passing time in the band room before our slots. Richard could be charming and funny and equally curt and antisocial. It was potluck which Richard would be backstage when you got there; that was the source of my reluctance, I don't know what his trepidation about me was.

Whatever it was, he got over his and I got over mine, and we formed a relationship that resulted in Richard producing half the tracks on the *String of Pearls* album including 'It's Only the Beginning'. He would have produced the rest, but he was also releasing a solo album that year, so I got to sing on his album and of course he sang and played all over mine. Grumpy Richard made a few appearances, but Charming Richard and I enjoyed the recording experience a lot.

Richard's record, full of lilting, catchy tunes, was named after Carlisle Street cafe the Galleon, which was steps away from the St Kilda seaside, and very popular with the natives. I had joined their ranks, moving into a small block of flats in St Kilda East right next to the Sandringham line. My romantic flat by the train tracks had no heating, a bathtub that had been painted instead of enamelled—every time I took a bath I'd have to peel off the oily white film that clung to me—and no insulation. I could hear my downstairs neighbour talking on the phone in her ordinary speaking voice.

My windows were so close to the rail line that every time the train whooshed past, either slowing down towards or speeding up away from Ripponlea Station, I had a perfect view of the commuters. On the occasions I was watching television, the static would overwhelm the broadcast and turn my screen into black-and-white fuzz. But I loved it. My view was limited enough to enhance the great mystery of where those steel parallel lines were heading, enticing me to imagine what lay beyond my wooden-framed, double-hung rattling windows, to envisage rolling meadows full of wildflowers instead of the backside of East St Kilda's low-slung housing and power poles.

I knuckled down and wrote the remainder of the songs that would eventually become *String of Pearls*, including 'Last to Know', a love song to Melbourne, to St Kilda, to my room on the rail line, so site-specific that it became a musical portrait of my desk. I played the song to Paul Kelly after dinner one night at his sister's place and he suggested the haunting B-minor section at the end. I got a heart running wild. I really did.

'Last to Know', *String of Pearls*, 1991

I might be the last to know
What comes so easy to all my friends
I'm so good at letting go
Regrets go belly up towards the end
Said goodbye so many times
It seems a miracle that I'm still sitting here
Staring at these parallel lines
Stretching out and going somewhere

I got a jar of shells by my bedside
I got a silver train running outside
I got a heart running wild, running wild

Love is such a temporary thing
It comes and goes a thousand times a day
No hard feelings in the songs I sing
Just another town to blow my heart away

I got a yellow rose from my garden
And a faded photo of my father
He's still keeping one eye on the weather
I got a heart running wild, running wild

Make believe you're somewhere else
It's a game I've learned to play a lot lately
Driving 'round here by myself
With the dog palms and the sunsets and the sea

I got a jar of shells by my bedside
I got a silver train running outside
I got a bird that sings in the morning
Shadows on the floor slowly shifting
I got a box of paints but the lid's gone
I got a string of pearls from my last song
I got a heart running wild

At the same time I was writing the last songs for *String of Pearls*, I was playing live with different groups of musicians. Every Tuesday night I was singing at the Cherry Tree in Richmond with Rose Amongst Thorns, a four-piece with Dror Erez on piano, the roaringly talented Chris Wilson and either Paul Hester or Peter Jones on drums, depending on who was in town. We liked each other and enjoyed playing good songs together; it was no more complicated than that. Peter was drumming on the album we were making and would join me on tour for years to come while Chris and Dror both made guest appearances.

It is very hard to reconcile our youthful insouciance and the bristling exuberant life we all generated on stage, in the studio and around town with the tragically shortened lives of Peter, Paul and Chris. It's the compact. We are born and in due course we will die. But in the case of my three absent friends, it happened far too soon.

Eventually I was ready to record, and Metropolis studio in Bank Street, South Melbourne was booked. It was hot—the north winds were ferocious that summer, I rode my second-hand bike—a 28-inch-wheel, pale-green-enamelled beauty with a triple-sprung Brooks leather seat to the 'office'—buffeted by the desert blasts, but the studio was cool and it was easy to spend long hours in a dark room musically sculpting what had taken me such an inordinately long time to figure out.

Before the album had been released or the tour confirmed, we had a publicity poster made picturing a black-and-white Brett Hilder photograph of me holding a guitar, my eyes soft and gazing left beyond the frame. I liked to call it the 'I have a dream' shot. Self-mocking as I could be, I lay in bed staring at the poster I had just Blu-Tacked to my wall and had an epiphany; I was about to be very successful. I felt plugged in to the zeitgeist; it was electric.

String of Pearls was released in October 1991, and I hit the touring trail hard for a solid ten months or more of gigs, with a five-piece band and four-piece road crew replete with PA, lighting rig and truck. I was surrounded by all the accoutrements of success, with a single on high rotation on multiple radio stations, a charting album, and audiences of 700 nightly. After the previous three years of foundering in an arid decision-free zone, wasting a lot of time, it felt amazing to be on stage fully owning every decision and every performance.

But a portion of that ownership was illusory. I'm not sure exactly when I figured out that Amanda's management company, MAP Management Co., was co-owned by 'God'inski, but when I did I was taken aback. *Last to know, me.* Why the hell hadn't I realised? How appallingly naive I was.

Amanda's office was on the ground floor of Mushroom's Dundas Lane building, and she and Michael had a long history of working together; but the fact was, Amanda's potential conflict of interest in signing me to a record company with financial ties to her management company had never been spelled out. Her loyalty was, at the very least, split. Had any other record company been approached? Or interested? Had they offered a similar, or even perhaps slightly more favourable deal? I would never know for sure.

The tour finished up; we had filled hundreds of venues nationally with thousands of punters over many, many months and had sold 70,000-odd albums. What's more, *String of Pearls* held the record of most shoplifted CD during that period! But when it was all done and dusted and the books were being balanced, Amanda discovered a $20,000 shortfall I owed her in commissions.

I am not imputing wrongdoing; people make mistakes. But it was quite a learning curve to find out after such an intense period of work, generating fabulous income—though clearly spending it extravagantly on the aforementioned touring expenses to which I was patently not paying enough attention to and should have been—I was seriously out of pocket.

I have learnt the hard way to be vigilant, to know and be across my business, and I am grateful to everyone who taught me that. Amanda and I continued to work together through the recording and release of *Bitch Epic*. We've had our disagreements but we're still good friends; her continuing support and enthusiasm for me over many projects have more than made up for her early non-disclosure.

16

It's Only the Beginning

'It's Only the Beginning', *String of Pearls*, 1991

I like the way that you took advantage
Stayed at my party 'til everyone went home
A perfect stranger
Need a place to lay your hat
The lone ranger couldn't saddle me with that
But you were right on track

It's only the beginning
But I've already gone and lost my mind
I feel like making daisy chains
And playing hide 'n' seek
When it's only the beginning
The fairy dust is still in flight

And this could be the love of a lifetime even if it lasts a week
Or maybe just a daydream

When we go walking along the river
Watch the old men fishing the sunny side of the pier
It's like a movie and you're my leading man
The way you woo me just like Cary Grant
You wanna hold my hand
It's only the beginning
But I've already gone and lost my mind
I feel like breaking windowpanes all up and down my street

When it's only the beginning
We can bring the house down every night
And this could be the love of a lifetime even if it lasts a week
Or just the sweetest daydream

And do you ever feel the passion
To jump from a speeding train
I'd like to be the wheels beneath you
I'd like to be the rain
That could wash away your pain
It's only . . .

So hold me closer
Let me feel you sigh
My Spanish butterfly

It's only the beginning
But I've already gone and lost my mind

I feel like breaking windowpanes all up and down my street
Any day now I will hear you call
And this could be the love of a lifetime even if it lasts a week

I wrote 'It's Only the Beginning' in 1989 in Los Angeles with Scott Cutler, after he told me about a date he'd been on the night before. I used an amalgam of sources as inspiration, some fictional, some lived, some wildly exaggerated.

When I demoed the song the following year in London, I freaked myself out with the unadulterated happiness of it, unaccustomed as I was to exploring such themes in my serious post-punk band. So I rewrote the lyric with Dorland, giving the song a more sinister slant and recorded it for the ill-fated dance album we were making.

'It's Only the Beginning', *Unreleased*, 1990

I wouldn't say that she was the kind to
Hide her affections behind a heart of stone
Is what I'm saying
Enough to ring a bell
For all her praying
She's still waking up in hell
As if she couldn't tell

It's only the beginning
And she's already gone and lost her mind
She's got 'em breaking windowpanes all up and down her street

Any day now
I know she will fall
She gonna find the love of a lifetime even if it lasts a week
Her Valentino so to speak

Cry on my shoulder that could help her
Lose her desire to need the bruising kind
Her reputation
Is really nothing new
But this situation
Is tearing her in two
I only wish she knew

It's only the beginning
And she's already gone and lost her mind
She's got 'em breaking windowpanes all up and down her street
Any day now
I know she will fall
She gonna find the love of a lifetime even if it lasts a week
Her Valentino so to speak

And does she ever feel the passion
Or is it just a game
I suppose she's got her reasons
But none that I could name
She's a human hurricane

Please forgive me
For saying what I do
I just see myself in you

Dorothy Mendes, my nanna, 1957.
Check out her hat.

Young Hettie Garb, my grandma, 1920.
It seems I have her mouth.

My grandfather Solly, grandmother Hettie and Carl Cohen, my father, strolling on Blackpool boardwalk, circa 1940.

Elizabeth Mendes—my mum, aged 21.

Carl Cohen; aka Carl Conway (he changed his name to avoid antisemitism); aka Carl Carmichael, the stage name he adopted to tread the boards, aged 36.

Liz and Carl; young love, New Year's Eve, Melbourne, 1956.

Me as a smiley baby, 1960.

Me, my mother's hands and the car
I didn't push my sister out of, 1964.

My sister Shellie and me, 1966.

Me on holiday with Mum and Shellie, Surfers Paradise, 1969.

Father–daughter bonding, 1973.

The Conways in Israel, 1974, sporting our iconic tembel hats.

My favourite great auntie Dolly: life is serious, 1990.

The laughing great aunts—(from left to right): Annie, Lottie and Rosie—with Grandma Hettie, late 1960s.

Modelling for Big M. I was the 'Hot-Big-M-Eggflip' girl for their TV campaign. Here I'm the September pin-up, Miss Caramel, in Big M's 1979 calendar.

This image was the Bluegrass billboard ad, a deep dive to the bottom of the concept 'sex sells'.

Pushing Patons, 1979.

Dressed, daubed and photographed at Bondi Beach by Linda Jackson, 1982; part of my wide-ranging job description as 'girl Friday'.

My first gig with The Benders at the London Tavern, Melbourne, 1979.

Sitting for professional photographer Brett Hilder in his Surry Hills studio, just for fun, 1981.
Brett Hilder

Running On Empty, Italian poster, circa 1983. I played Julie the love interest/clothes horse.

Do-Ré-Mi: Helen Carter, Dorland Bray, me and Stephen Philip. *Domestic Harmony*, our debut album, is rising on the charts. The pic is from a *Juke Magazine* photo shoot for their front cover story, 1985.

Do-Ré-Mi in London, 1986. Goofing around in a local park with hangovers after our triumph at the *Countdown* Awards the night before. Tony Mott

Do-Ré-Mi up on the roof. **Brett Hilder**

Big mouth. In a green velvet frock Stephen Galloway designed and made for me, 1988. Tony Mott

With my boyfriend Paul Hester in London, 1982. We stayed on a couch in a council flat rented by people he knew, feeding coins into the meter so the heat would stay on through that cold winter.

Me with Alex McGregor and Paul Kelly at El Alamein Fountain, Kings Cross, 1986.

I have a dream. Just before the release of *String of Pearls*, 1991. **Brett Hilder**

I have an ARIA. 1992.
Tony Mott

String of Pearls album launch, 1991, me centre with (left to right): Molly Meldrum, Sue and Michael Gudinski, and my manager Amanda Pelman.

My *String of Pearls* touring band, The Mothers of Pearl at play (left to right): Willy Zygier, Bill McDonald, me, Peter Jones, Al Harding. Photo courtesy of Al Harding

Willy, me and Al jamming on Sydney Harbour, 1992. Photo courtesy of Al Harding

With Willy Zygier backstage at a festival somewhere, 1992.

Willy and me on set for the 'Alive and Brilliant' video clip, 1993.

Marie Claire magazine photoshoot for the ABC series *The Seven Deadly Sins* with me representing 'Gluttony'. The image was repurposed for the cover of *Bitch Epic*.

Epic Theatre band in our bold-coloured matching suits designed by Sally Mill (left to right): Michael Barker, Al, Paul Edsel, Willy, Bill, me and Tina Kopa.

Ultrasound rehearsal with (clockwise from bottom left): Willy, Paul Hester, me and Bill McDonald—daughter Syd is asleep in the guitar case, 1995. Mardi Sommerfeld

Exhausted in London, 1996.

My Third Husband tour, with my second child and bass player Jackie Orszaczky, 1997.

Multitasking with daughter Hettie, at the launch of Rock Chefs for Mirabel, a fundraising initiative for the Mirabel Foundation, 2002.

Our first recording session with daughters Syd and Alma for *The Songs of Patsy Cline*, in our Williamstown bathroom, 2001.

Wide awake in Williamstown (left to right): Alma, Syd and Hettie, 2002.

Cards and carrots: Hettie, Syd and Alma, in our living room in Williamstown.

Always, Patsy Cline, 2001. I played the role of Patsy in eight shows a week for six months and loved every minute of it. **Ross Bird**

Through the looking glass: recording *Summertown* in Studio 1971 (aka my parent's house) with (left to right): James Black, Willy, Gerry Hale, me and Shannon Birchall, 2003.

Summerware party on Goat Island, Sydney Harbour. We played Summerware parties in barns, bedrooms, offices and islands.

Birthday dinner with Dad, Mum and Shellie, circa 2009.

Hitched, 2007. Pierre Baroni

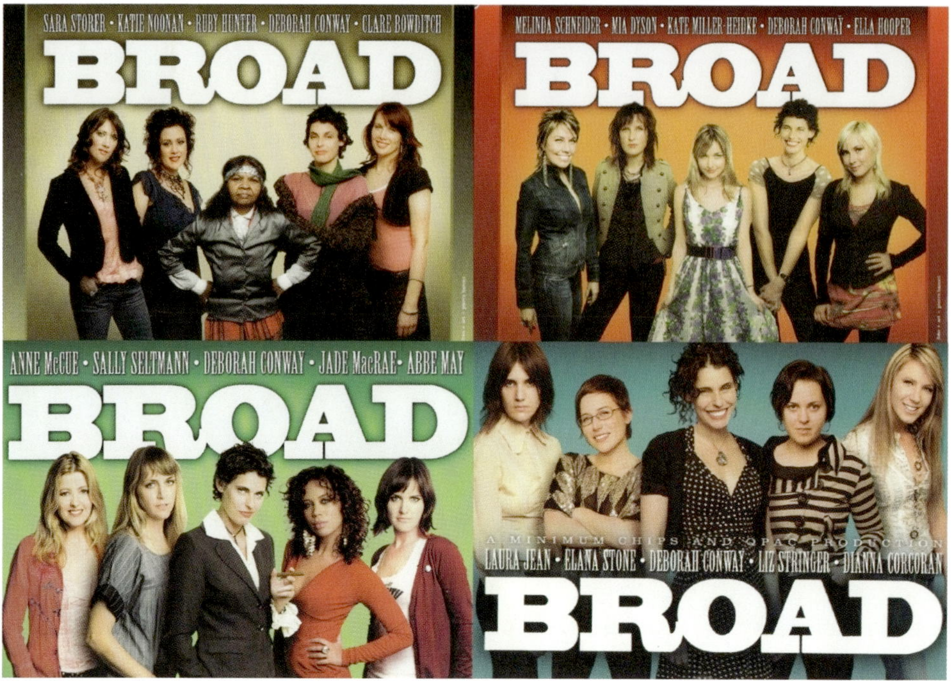

Posters for the BROAD shows over the years (clockwise from top left): 2005, 2006, 2007, 2008. Pierre Baroni

Sold Out! The BROAD cast of 2005 (Sarah Storer, me, Clare Bowditch, Katie Noonan and Ruby Hunter) with band members Dave Williams, Andy Papadopoulos and Stephen Teakle.

Performing *String of Pearls* for its 25th anniversary in 2016 at Memo Music Hall with (left to right): Clio Renner, Willy, Louis Gill, me, Niko Schauble. **David Harris**

Zygier Family singing The Go-Betweens' 'anthem' 'Streets of Your Town' at the Reclink Community Cup annual fundraiser event, 2017.

Between takes on Peter Greenaway's film *Prospero's Books* with composer Michael Nyman, 1990.

Alma Zygier's Very Jewish Christmas (left to right): Alma, Hettie, Syd and me, 2020. Alma's annual concert of Xmas songs written by Jewish composers and performed by some of Melbourne's musical finest.

Backstage after our last show of the Epic tour; the 25th anniversary of *Bitch Epic* and the launch of *Words of Men*. From left to right: Daniel Farrugia, Willy, Hue Blanes, me and Simon Starr, 2019.

In 2022 after a long period of sitting on the couch through endless months of lockdown, the flood gates opened. We flew from Sydney, where we were performing, to the Peninsula Festival on Victoria's Mornington Peninsula, before heading back to the airport to catch a flight for our evening show in Newcastle, which we almost didn't make because of traffic jams, closed roads, detours and a very confused GPS. The other side of the rockstar lifestyle. Mark Moray, Wicked Rock Photography got a good pic. **Mark Moray**

Mr and Mrs Zygier, 2023. Hector Clark

By the time Virgin had dumped me and consigned the dance album to the landfill of pop pulp, I had realised the rewrite was a mistake and embraced the sunny optimism of the original. We recorded the track at Metropolis Studios, and Peter Jones's pick-up fill into Richard Pleasance's gorgeous and immediately recognisable descending guitar line was irresistible ear candy.

The song came out in June 1991 and was picked up by every commercial and community radio broadcaster. One afternoon, driving, I heard it on three different stations at the same time! I turned up the volume and with the windows down and the breeze in my hair, like a Roger Voudouris film clip, flicked between stations on my push-button car stereo.

A hit is fun. I've been lucky, I've had a few: 'Standing on Wires' and the first version of 'Man Overboard' were both community radio chart-toppers, and 'Sweet and Sour' went Top 10 on the Australian charts in 1984 (though only a handful of people knew it was me singing it).

The re-recording of 'Man Overboard', the first single off Do-Ré-Mi's first album *Domestic Harmony*, had reached Top 5 on the mainstream charts in 1985, and invaded the public consciousness. Nothing too intrusive, but suddenly I was recognised pretty much everywhere I went. People were nice about it: comments like, 'Love your work!' shouted by a boofy bloke in Yakka work shorts from the building site across the street, or, 'Oh man, that's a great song' from hipsters out and about. Comments you might get on social media now were delivered in the flesh. My childhood fantasy of being famous had come true and I was enjoying it. 'Man Overboard' has had a long life lived in the brilliant sunshine of popular song.

But 'It's Only the Beginning' is a signature song in a different way. Maybe it has something to do with the plus-fours I'm wearing on that autumnal golf course in the video clip, a controversial decision, according to my record company boss. Gudinski didn't appreciate my homage to *Bringing Up Baby*, a favourite film of mine starring Cary Grant and Katharine Hepburn. He didn't think I had done myself justice in the costume department, but we agreed to disagree, something I always appreciated about Michael.

Despite the plus-fours, the song, hit number 19 on the charts and remains my most recognisable song, my most played song and the song most identified with me even if, curiously, it is more outlier than representative.

For a start, as I mentioned, the song is particularly cheerful, at least on the surface. Lurking beneath is a bit more cynicism about the fleeting nature and interchangeable properties of love and lust, but to be fair, not many people really listen more than superficially to the words. As long as you can sing along to the chorus, which is dewy with rosy, glowing glee, that's the takeaway.

And, well, I am grateful, really, incredibly grateful that I have contributed a song to that rarefied number of pop songs that endure past their year of release to remain among a few beloved classics, that three decades later people haven't yet appeared to tire of.

My chosen career is pretty strange, really. Historically, musicians signed to a record deal were subtly encouraged to remain ignorant of the machinations of the business and focus on the artistry, with getting a song onto high radio rotation, the ultimate short-term goal. But statistically the chances of a working musician having a recognisable hit song are rare.

Think of the legions of working musicians out in the world; the jazz sidemen (and women); the members of our many orchestras; the musicians who are playing most nights in cover bands at little corner bars, at weddings, bar mitzvahs, New Year's Eve and fiftieth anniversary parties; the pit musicians at the theatre, in church, playing community events; the myriad working stiffs eking out a living as jobbing musicians who get picked up by solo artists or as extra players for pop bands. The horn or string sections for a touring rock act; the big and small ensembles, musicians who have never been inside a recording studio, or have managed to make a record but received zero attention, or have played on a successful recording but remain uncredited and anonymous—they all vastly outnumber the tiny few who do make it, even ever so fleetingly. And success is not always predicated on talent.

All this is by way of saying that I am aware of the absurdly remote chances of that song becoming so successful, let alone enduring all these years. But its success has bred a peculiar love/hate relationship towards the song. I am frustrated when it's always 'the hit', my musical calling card, that is acknowledged, while the iceberg of all my other material is left unseen below the surface. I also know it's my job to find a way of getting inside 'the hit' again and again to bring a fully technicolour, meaningful new relevance each time I sing it.

Sometimes the relevance leans more to the ridiculous than the sublime.

One morning in September 2006, I got a call from an excited ABC journalist, who said, 'Deborah, were you aware that the champion mare Makybe Diva has used 'It's Only the Beginning' to get in the mood for her first covering with the stallion Galliano?'

'What? Really . . .?'

It turned out my song was beloved not just of *Homo sapiens*, but of equines too. I had had a good betting record with Makybe Diva's three successive Melbourne Cup wins, and now she had 'chosen' my song to conceive a future track champion—an outstanding contribution to horse racing/rock trivia. I used it with audiences in the form of a guessing game: 'Which famous Australian female athlete used "It's Only the Beginning" as the backing track to conceive her firstborn?' I also wondered aloud if any human babies were conceived to that song . . .

There are times when the hit comes to own the artist. Mostly I think the song no longer belongs to me; it belongs to the women singing along in a crowded venue, to the people who write and tell me how much it got them through a difficult time, to the dancers who fill the dance floor and abandon all decorum with their depth of feeling. To play the song on request at a house party and find that the entire room from eight to eighty is singing the chorus with me elevates all of us, it is meaning enough and ownership I am bound to.

17

Under My Skin

I'd written down the phone number on a scrap of paper with the name 'Willy Zygier'. I called it now.

'Hello, is that Willy?'

'Hi, yes, who's this?'

'Hi Willy, my name's Deborah Conway . . . I'm looking for a guitarist. Peter Farnan and Richard Pleasance thought I should talk to you.'

I told him my touring dates and he checked his diary while I was on the phone.

'Oh, I'm sorry, I can't do it, I have a show with my band.'

Huh? One show? I'm offering him the best part of a year's worth of touring and he's a holdout for one show? Crazy.

'Okay, that's a shame. Well, thanks anyway.'

We said goodbye and hung up. And I sat there thinking, *I really want to hire this guy.*

Richard had mentioned Willy first. I needed a guitar player and Richard's dance card was full with his own new album and tour. 'You'll like Willy, he's very musical, inventive and unpredictable'—all the right adjectives. A few days later I was speaking to Richard's former bandmate in Boom Crash Opera, my old pal Pete Farnan, and he echoed Richard's sentiments.

And then he said something weird: 'But he's got a girlfriend.'

'So . . .? I need a guitar player, not a boyfriend!'

I had a boyfriend, and I had a career. I just didn't have a guitar player.

I called Willy Zygier again a few days after our initial conversation.

'Hi, it's Deborah again. If I put my start date back to accommodate your show, would that work?'

We arranged a meeting to discuss details and listen to the songs.

A week later Willy Zygier knocked on the door of my East St Kilda flat. I opened it.

It was a strange heart-stopping moment of recognition. A jolt. A tiny current of electricity passed between us. We both took an imperceptible step backwards. All in a split second. All unacknowledged.

I made us cups of tea and we talked about our musical histories (I'd heard of his former band, Government Drums, and he'd heard of mine), our mutual friends, touring expectations, music in general, what you'd expect from a first encounter . . . and then . . . he left.

We saw each other again a week after that. Willy's current band, Tootieville, were making a video clip. The idea was to ask every 'celebrity' known to the band to mime a few lines of the song to camera. I was happy to be part of it. Willy's keyboard player and friend Amanda came with him to help film. Apparently, I was wearing a see-through shirt when they arrived. I hadn't thought of it as flirting, I was just trying on something that might have worked for the clip, but, hey . . . actions speak louder.

I ended up changing into a Memphis Minnie t-shirt. The song is called 'Basic', and the clip is called 'Tootieville Rides the Coat-tails of Success', a brilliant little marketing initiative showcasing Tootieville members alongside some of Melbourne's finest: Paul Grabowsky, Red Symons, Magda Szubanski, Rod Quantock, Lou Richards, Wilbur Wilde, Frankie J. Holden, Senator John Button, comedians, actors, bands. Tootieville knew a lot of people.

I watch the clip now and think, *I look awkward*. I'm not my usual goofing-off self, not until the final seconds when you see a shot of Willy and me sitting together in my office broadly grinning at the camera, completely comfortable. Did we know then . . . ? Maybe . . . ? Somewhere? . . .

I arrived at our South Melbourne rehearsal room, where our new band had already set up. Willy had invited Bill McDonald (bass), while Al Harding (keys) came via Richard. I'd invited Peter Jones (drums), but they all knew each other from the Melbourne music scene.

We launched into 'Release Me', the opening song on *String of Pearls*.

I slid right into your hands
And you grabbed me and told me how you'd understand
Whatever I wanted to be
And I believed for a while you believing in me

I'm turning circles again
Caught in a spin
I'm a high fly trapeze
To you little worm
Earthbound and dirty and still on your knees

Release me
You know I want to come down
The air is too thin off the ground
And my head's not clear
Way up here

It was one of those magical sessions: this incredible energy and precision, the notes tipping into the room and then building on themselves. We all felt it; everyone was grinning. Before we got to the end of the song it felt like we'd been a band for years. I called us The Mothers of Pearl.

Pete Farnan told me recently that even before we'd started playing on that first day of rehearsal, Al Harding was already looking at Willy and me and saying, 'Oh no, it's going to be one of those tours.'

We had spent the rehearsal period harmlessly flirting. I hadn't realised it was that obvious, but the attraction was intense and mutual.

One lunchtime we'd all gone to one of the local cafes. While we waited for our order we talked about stupid combinations of food when one of our number, it may have been Willy, said, 'watermelon and feta'. That did it: Willy broke into incomprehensible, hysterical, uncontrolled laughter, which despite defying sense was so contagious we were all weeping with him. Every time he does that he adds years onto my life. (Not long after this, watermelon and feta salads somehow became a thing—the craze was short lived.)

Anyway, maybe I wasn't falling in love yet but I was definitely falling in lust. Willy was tall, slender, angular, refined and strikingly handsome—to me anyway. Not the Soap Star version of good looking, he was slightly androgynous and at that time—which was probably 99 per cent projection—he felt risky, unsafe.

He had beautiful hands that cradled his guitar, a way of curling into his instrument that made it an extension of himself. His playing was as advertised: exceptional, unexpected, highly musical. He played like Ziggy played guitar (people of a certain age often unconsciously referenced David Bowie and called Willy 'Ziggy').

And he was Jewish. Maybe I already knew it before we met; seeds were planted.

We played our first show in Fitzroy at the Royal Derby before we hit the road to play our second show way out of town in Traralgon. Bill had a holiday house nearby in Cape Paterson where we all stayed that night. I paid Willy a late-night visit, because it had to be done. We were like magnets, irresistibly pulling together. It was 23 October, 1991.

As the tour progressed we thought we were being so clever, sneaking into each other's rooms, trying not to make it obvious; but everyone knew. (It might have been that one early morning when Al Harding encountered Willy walking down the hotel corridor, shoes in hand, and Al said, in his Curly-from-the-Three-Stooges way, 'Hey, what are you doing?' And because Willy has an abiding love for the Three Stooges, he revealed all; if Willy has one flaw it's not keeping secrets.)

The tour came to an end. Not knowing what was going to happen next, we danced cheek to cheek to music coming out of a transistor radio at Coolangatta Airport, coming home from the last gig of the tour; not yet fully committed to upending our lives.

We faced stomach-churning weeks as we confronted life-changing decisions; to ditch our respective five-year relationships and the futures they implied, for something gossamer, only partly known. It was a dismal time, contemplating the awful, wrenching sorrow we would inflict on people we loved.

Not doing it would have been worse.

18

Now That We're Apart

I went back to my flat on the railway line and tried to process what had happened. Alex had just arrived in Melbourne and was staying with friends. We'd spoken before he got on the plane in LA and he knew something of the turmoil he was about to walk into—I'd given him veiled warnings that we had probably reached our end point.

He was justifiably furious, hurt and bewildered. Our long-distance phone communication was entirely lacking in bluntness on my part. Bluntness was exactly what was required, but we had been conducting our relationship over two continents for the best part of a year and some part of me needed to see him to feel sure.

I was radiating equivocation. My absurdly complicated love life had me recovering from the doomed affair with the English sculptor by secretly getting into bed with a local piano player, all while I was officially in a long-distance relationship with Alex, who until yesterday had been residing in Los Angeles . . . and now I'd met Willy. I really needed to streamline!

I sat in the kitchen of the mutual friend's house Alex was staying in and I told him I'd fallen in love with Willy. I don't know if I was completely convinced of that reality at the moment of confessing it, but I'd gone far enough down the path to make an ongoing relationship with Alex, no matter how relaxed about infidelity we both were, untenable. I had to be a bastard.

Willy came home from the tour to the house he and his girlfriend had bought together, knowing he had to be a bastard too. He moved out with his cat, Tootieville, who wasn't happy about any of it.

Willy and I were now free to continue our affair openly; would it still be as intoxicating when it was no longer covert?

'Now That We're Apart', *Bitch Epic*, 1993

What's the point you're trying to make here
I'm so tired I'm losing heart
Talking round and round
Your mouth is forming sounds
Nonsensical, now that we're apart

Here we go, the words spill over
We say the same thing it's a start
Little fingers locked, little prayers fly up
Wishful thinking, now that we're apart

Look outside the sky won't fall
We're little things trying to muddle through
It all could be so smooth, we could be so good
But darling you're so cruel

It's getting dark and you can't stay here
My sweet thou doth protest too much
Kiss me on the cheek, tell me that we'll speak
So very soon, now that we're apart

Look outside the sky won't fall
We're little things trying to muddle through
It all

I'm so mad, my hand is aching
To plunge a knife into your heart
I want to see you bleed
I need to see you need
Me
Now that we're apart

'Now That We're Apart' came into being in those tumultuous weeks, written among the packing crates in a haze of uncertainty. Willy had moved into a dingy basement flat off Eildon Road, St Kilda. In my memory the flat verges on subterranean, the windows covered in a green hedge that rendered it dark on the brightest day, like a monastic cell for someone seeking self-flagellation.

I was there for dinner when Willy asked me if I would listen to something he'd just written. He played me a song, wordlessly vocalising a tune. I told him I'd like to try writing a lyric, and it became our first collaboration. Done with sincerity, I believe, songwriting is one of the most intimate activities you can engage in with someone. I crafted a lyric around the misery of relationship breakdown, the morass of mistrust, betrayal, momentary hopeful delusion and finally murderous fantasy. My *mea culpa*. Beyond conscious reason, I had summed up the treachery we had visited on two people who didn't deserve it.

19

She Prefers Fire

Willy and I were in our different dwellings, trying to figure out our messy lives. The ancient gas oven in my flat had four burners and three of them weren't working. I summoned assistance. The Gas and Fuel man came and spent some time pulling apart and putting back together the upright freestanding cooker. Eventually he stuck his head around the corner of my office and told me he'd fixed the problem.

I continued writing for another hour until, as I wandered towards the kitchen for a tea break, the smell of gas hit me hard. *Uh-oh, he's left the stove on.* But all the knobs were pointing up. I opened the oven door and found the culprit, gas hissing out of the pipe.

And this is where it got weird. My first thought was not, *At least I noticed the smell and I didn't light the stove*; no, my first thought was, *I'm going to be gassed; I need to light the oven to stop the gas leak.*

I reached for the matches, opened the oven and put the lit match inside.

Predictably (though apparently not before I did it), there was an explosion that lit the stove and engulfed me and my little kitchen in a ball of flame. I was flung across the room. The gas burned itself out almost instantly, leaving only a small amount of damage—to me. Nose and cheeks blackened, eyelashes and eyebrows singed . . . Fortunately I was wearing a hat so, other than my fringe, my hair was still intact.

I slammed the oven door shut, and grabbed some ice cubes from the freezer, filling the bathroom sink with water and ice. Plunging my face in, I wondered why I had thought it would be better to light the flame than leave the damn thing alone and get out of the flat. When I emerged from my ice bath, I looked like a panda bear. I rang the Gas and Fuel office and told them what had happened. They sent someone over to fix the gas leak, and paid me $1200 for my trouble.

I made a note:

> Sometimes I dream my house would burn down and I would be left as I stand, fully in the present, owning nothing, owing nothing, my fantasy to be free of all my accumulated past. Homeless, possession-less, past-less, memoryless.

It described the shape of things at that time; there was something appealing in being exonerated from the past, physically escaping the myriad threads of connection that tie you down. The piles, boxes, trunks, cupboards of photo albums, old letters, parking fines, mementos, clothes you don't like but can't yet give up, outgrown relationships, unwanted family ties, old ideas, outdated versions of yourself—STUFF—that felt more dead than alive, more constricting than comforting.

'She Prefers Fire', *Bitch Epic,* 1993

She stood on the steps behind a man
He lit a cigarette and leaned on the rail
The smell of burning made her head clear
Thinking all the thoughts she hadn't thought for years

Everything that we have
Reminds us what we have lost
Old friends go to war
Love comes love goes
Everything that we have
Echoes what we desire
She prefers fire

Tomorrow no plan will carry her away
This evening the man well he wonders what to say
The sparks are lighting up the night sky
Possessions, letters, now just fuel for history

Everything that we have
Reminds us what we have lost
Old friends go to war
Love comes love goes

Everything that we have
Echoes what we desire
She prefers fire

And from the bridge she's seen
Water pale and green
She still prefers fire

Sometimes I dream that everything I own
Could burn up and leave me no sadness no home
A flame collapsing from the inside
Antiseptic, hottest blue and purest white

And everything that we have
Reminds us what we have lost
Old friends go to war
Love comes love goes
And everything that we have
Echoes what we desire
She prefers fire

The great purge remained a fantasy, until suddenly it became real.

Diary entry 10 January, 2015

My mother is moving house, downsizing after forty years in the same family home we moved into when I turned fourteen. My steamer trunk has been sitting on bricks in the basement for a good ten years, full to the brim with letters, postcards, diaries, old lyric books, photos—loose and in albums—slides, newspaper clippings, drawings, the collected detritus of the previous two decades waiting for that rainy day to arrive and me to claim, sort and file the memories into a more dignified resting place. Well the rainy day came alright, about four years ago, with a deluge that flooded the basement, crept over the top of the bricks and invaded the trunk. I had been cavalier and then forgot about it. But yesterday I opened the trunk for the first time and all that was left was a soupy sludge of blur and crumble and hard lumps where the water had glued entire packets of photos together and turned the images into watercolour abstracts. It was like the titles to *Treme*, beautiful and ghastly, depressing but with an element of liberation. 2015, *tabula rasa*.

20

Alive and Brilliant

'Alive and Brilliant', *Bitch Epic*, 1993

Way above
The clouds are black
They say it's gonna pour but I haven't been keeping track
So now we're here
In this cage
The Ferris wheel of love, my love what a charade
It's been a long time since anyone meant what they said

One step forward
Two steps backward
I won't wrestle, you won't talk back
Three deep breaths I'm still alive and brilliant

Turn around
And be polite
I'm so sick of listening to your crap about the breasts you like
Look at me
I am restrained
I'm not screaming like some jealous adolescent here in vain
It's been a long time since anyone meant what they said

One step forward
Two steps backward
I won't wrestle, you won't talk back
Three deep breaths I'm still alive and brilliant

So you got me
On this ride
What was it darling, what exactly did you have in mind?
Ferris wheel
Up and down
Is this some dumb metaphor to tell me you're not hanging 'round?
It's been a long time since anyone said what they meant

One step forward
Two steps backward
I won't wrestle, you won't talk back
Three deep breaths I'm still alive and brilliant

Spring 1992 was busy. Willy and I were unequivocally together, cautiously positive we'd done the right thing. By night

I was frocking up in white body paint and donning a toga to tread the boards at Belvoir St Theatre in Aristophanes' *Frogs*, directed by Geoffrey Rush. It was a stellar cast of the veteran and newly minted. Robyn Nevin, Bill Zappa, Paul Blackwell, Toni Collette and Paul Capsis all happily descended to the underworld together.

Geoffrey had commissioned me to write a song for the production, called 'The Parabasis'. The term refers to the ancient Greek comedy tradition where the stage clears, leaving the Chorus to break the fourth wall and address the audience directly. My guitar and I played the Chorus, the little rip in the theatrical universe.

By day, the Coogee flat overlooking the glassy sea where Willy and I were staying became a fertile songwriting sweatshop. It was where 'Alive & Brilliant' found its way onto the carpet; the inspiration came via Brian Eno and David Bowie who documented how, when faced with writer's block, they'd jot random words on slips of paper and pull them out of a hat. The exercise could produce marvellously curious combinations, 'Bitch Epic' being another. By the following year, Mr Zygier and I had written enough songs to record my second solo album. I wanted him to produce this record; I knew that we shared a vision and I trusted him to get the job done. I also knew that it would be far less expensive than hiring a hotshot record producer from somewhere exotic. But the thing about hits is that no one can predict them and the thing about record companies is that they delude themselves into thinking they can. If you believe that a hit has a price, then the more money you spend the more likely you are to buy one. I'm not sure why this weird equation has held sway for so long because it doesn't reflect reality.

A heated discussion with Michael Gudinski ended with him saying, 'If Willy is your producer, Mushroom will pull support from your project.' Perhaps it was a bluff, but I blinked and we went with the expensive overseas producer. Jim Rondinelli was not a producer with a track record, but he had engineered Matthew Sweet's album *Girlfriend*, which was doing well and which I liked the sound of. Also, Jim was from New York, which for the record company was a credential in and of itself. After Jim signed on, I fought for and won the right for Willy to take the co-producer credit.

It wasn't the greatest beginning to a working relationship. There was a lot of jockeying to be top dog in the stuffy little space we called home for the next six weeks.

Jim had a tendency towards perfectionism and petulance; he had been a drumming wunderkind and he took a dislike to the way Peter Jones played 'Holes in the Road'. Jim would have Peter snapping that snare for hours trying to hone his sound; the difference between the start and finish of the exercise was something only a dog could hear.

One morning, Jim came in early to try and play drums on the song himself. We walked in on him, at which point he threw his drumsticks aside, either because he hadn't wanted us to know or in a fit of temper at not being able to do it. The resulting tension set the mood for most of the recording. The credits on *Bitch Epic* read like a who's who of Melbourne's music scene but Jim liked only some, not all of the musicians, and who knew what he thought of Mr Zygier and me.

Jim also had allergies, or he claimed he did. A sniffle would occasion him cracking the shits and demanding the entire studio be steam-cleaned before he would set foot in it again. It happened more than once. (I should have bought him a box of Telfast.) As the days and weeks ground on, he became increasingly cantankerous, sometimes storming out in the middle of a session.

Fortunately the co-producer was more than capable of continuing in Jim's absence, but unfortunately there was the risk that Jim would fly into a rage because we had somehow strayed from his vision. *His Fucking Vision! Whose record was this?!* There were wild fights between Jim and his assistants, between Jim and my manager Amanda, between Jim and the studio staff, between Jim and just about everyone.

And there were monumental fights between Amanda and me, most often over the phone because she was travelling, though we never let the cost of a long-distance call curtail our free-for-alls. It was Godzilla vs King Kong. I'm not sure who was who, but neither of us was afraid of a confrontation and they could escalate rapidly. I remember, after one particularly savage slugfest, I looked up to see an empty room. My band had slunk out in horror.

The fights were mainly about Jim and his growing demands for more authority and more perks, which would be added to *my* expense account and which incensed me no end. I didn't think Amanda was defending Jim, but she was between the proverbial rock and a hard place and I wasn't letting her off.

Back at Metropolis Studio, the moment had arrived to record the 'Consider This' guitar solo. Jim mentioned that the legendary guitarist Richard Lloyd, from seminal New York punk band Television, was in town, moonlighting with another touring act, and had the day off. Mr Zygier and I both thought it was a tremendous idea. Richard turned up to the studio the very next day. Hours flew by overdubbing solo after solo after solo, all at glass-shattering volume. No complete performance was making Jim or Richard happy.

But this is the wonder of recording; the 'extremely loud lead guitar break', as credited on the album, is an amalgam of highlights of all the takes, stitched painstakingly, lovingly together by Jim after Richard departed. It was a testament to Jim's perfectionism that it really was a stunning guitar solo, and probably Jim should have got a co-credit for it—but that would have been telling.

The recording was close to the end when our relationship reached its absurdist Samuel Beckett-style denouement. Jim walked into the studio one morning more ruffled than usual and slightly hysterically announced that he was devastated because he'd just had word that '70 of my closest label friends have been let go'. We didn't quite understand how to respond. How do you begin to unravel that statement? 'Seventy closest label friends'? We were confused, trying not to giggle at the absurd image and trying not to panic that the power dynamic between us had finally become unhinged. Clearly Jim was a long way from those who best understood him.

We had concerns that he was past his breaking point and we still had an album to finish. We held ourselves together until knock-off time. Fortunately the bulk of the work was behind us, because after this glimpse into Jim's strange universe our working partnership became yet more vexed when Jim micromanaged and curtailed our attendance at Studio 301 where the album was being mixed.

Bitch Epic was mastered by the renowned Bob Ludwig and released in November 1993 with a huge push from Mushroom. It remains my highest-charting solo album, peaking at number 18 on the Australian ARIA charts.

Jim now makes occasional reappearances in our life via social media, commenting warmly on things we have done; he has clearly softened and looks back in nostalgia at working with us, though curiously, when I looked at his discography, *Bitch Epic* does not appear on the list.

21

Today I Am a Daisy

Nineteen ninety-two. Forgotten town, forgotten gig. Hotel room; beige. The television was on the ABC, an arts program that followed Jackson Pollock around for a few days. He was in an aged care home, where he had brought many 4 litre pots of paint in multiple colours and had arranged an extensive length of canvas or paper from one end to the other, in what looked like the central activities room. Pollock was encouraging the residents to pick a colour and splash some on the blank canvas.

They were mostly a little hesitant, but one gentleman, well into his eighties, was enthusiastically dipping a brush and flicking yellow paint over the surface. He was asked, 'What are you painting?' He replied in a quavering Polish accent, 'Today I am a daisy'. I reached for my pen and notebook.

Top floor, Mushroom Records, Dundas Place, Albert Park. We played the track to Michael Gudinski as our pick for first single from the album. He struggled to punch the air in time with the polyrhythm (a 12/8 time signature; a quirky re-interpretation of a Soweto beat, utterly dissimilar to any rock or pop music on Top 40 radio at the time), and demanded to hear something else. The first single ended up being 'Alive and Brilliant', another awkward time signature in 5/4, so not exactly a dance-floor-filler either, but somehow to Michael it had the imprimatur of rock. 'Today I Am a Daisy' became the second single.

Flinders, where we shot the clip for 'Today I Am a Daisy' on a late summer day in 1994, became the backdrop for a circus troupe running, cartwheeling and cavorting around the hills, chased by a film crew and a props person wrangling carts full of sunflowers. I guess they last longer than daisies? Everyone except Willy got hay fever. 'Today I Am a Daisy' became my parents' favourite song.

'Today I Am a Daisy', *Bitch Epic*, 1993

Today I am a daisy
Tomorrow I will be the chain holding up your heart
Today I am a waitress but tomorrow I could be an astronaut
Flying to the moon, playing amongst the stars
Seeing the galaxy from inside a jar
Today I am a seashell
Tomorrow I will be the ocean roaring in your ear
Today I am your daughter
Tomorrow I will make your disappointments disappear
And you will come fly with me
We will play leapfrog through the years

And life will be elegant
We can chase away the tears

Goodbye goodbye
Today will be tomorrow
Goodbye goodbye
Tomorrow's almost here
Goodbye goodbye
Today will be tomorrow
Goodbye goodbye
Something might be clear

Today I am a daisy
Tomorrow I will be Vincent's sunflowers,
Claude's lilies anything I want
Today I am a waitress but tomorrow well I might be an
astronaut
I will be bathed in love
I will be soaking in tenderness
And you will be standing there
The one who loves me best

Goodbye goodbye
Today will be tomorrow
Goodbye goodbye
Tomorrow's almost here
Goodbye goodbye
Today will be tomorrow
Goodbye goodbye
And everything will be clear

The Sports' 'Who Listens to The Radio?' had come out in 1978 and I knew the answer: it was me, everybody I knew and a whole lot more. I'd had my ear glued to a transistor radio tuned to 3AK 'Where No Wrinklys Fly' since before I turned eleven. A few years later, 3AK had switched to broadcasting 'Beautiful Music' and I switched to 3XY, which had picked up the rock music baton where 3AK dropped it. I remember it being a slightly bumpy transition getting my head around who was now 'groovy', but I coped.

Before FM took over the driver's seat for rock radio, playlists were looser, DJs played stuff they liked, and you generally didn't hear the same song more than twice a day. It was personal, in the way that community radio is now. There was energy, there were surprises. A few years later when FM radio kicked AM radio to the kerb on ratings and competition for advertisers became fierce, programming became something head office took over. It was too perilous to allow a DJ to decide what they would play; someone might flip the station.

Programming became unbearably risk-averse. All music was assessed by focus groups with market researchers in charge. It got scientific. It was Big Business. Breaking through those barriers to get your song played on commercial radio was immensely difficult—but it was powerful. Radio DJs were cajoled, massaged and often bribed with concert tickets, aged bottles of single malt, leather jackets, drugs, cash, whatever a record company mogul could arrange (and a DJ might accept) to get a single added to high rotation on a station's playlist.

This simple act of being added to the playlist could make or break an artist; it was the difference between recouping the money you spent to the power of ten or more, or having your investment sink without a trace. And breakfast radio was the king of the heap.

To participate in breakfast radio, you must be up earlier than early to ensure you are fresh, alert and not prone to letting down your guard and saying something you may regret. Wendy Harmer was enjoying massive ratings hosting breakfast on 2DayFM. Wendy was an old friend and we were comfortable bantering on and off the air.

After the interview in which I was asked about the imminent release of *Bitch Epic* and the new single 'Alive and Brilliant', Wendy invited me to stay in the studio and participate in the 'Battle of the Sexes' contest they had going. I would be representing women, and asked questions on topics that traditionally men were considered to know about; a random male caller would be representing men, answering female-centric questions.

'On your marks, get set, go!'

The atmosphere had suddenly intensified. There was the smell of competition in the air and a great deal of barracking for each representative. I was on the spot first. 'Name five Arnold Schwarzenegger movies.'

I rattled off, '*Terminator*, *Terminator 2*, *Conan the Barbarian*, *Twins* and, and, and . . .' Oh no, I'd blanked. Wendy chimed in, '*Total Recall*' and I, unable to control my newly-acquired Tourette syndrome, under the pressure of competition and completely LIVE radio, burst out, 'Of course—*Total* FUCKING *Recall*!' before clamping my hand over my mouth and watching the panel operators, producers and other dogsbodies circulating in that small studio go into overdrive meltdown. Think Chernobyl, button punching, hand wringing, complexions turning shades of green through white. To give credit where it's due, Wendy remained cool and we carried on to the end of the contest. We laughed about it off-air and I left.

That afternoon I received a call from Gudinski. He was the crossest I've ever heard him, absolutely enraged with me. It was like I'd gone and sworn on live radio deliberately to be a trouble-maker. I assured him that was not the case, but apparently that's what station boss, Brad March had accused me of when he called Michael in a white-hot rage. No one had complained; the segment had received enthusiastic positive feedback, and it was probably the panel operator's fault for not having the seven-second delay switched on. But the fix was in.

I was given Brad March's phone number. He sounded like he accepted my grovelling apology. But Brad being Brad, he hung on to the grudge. He refused to play 'Today I Am a Daisy' when it came out and for as long as he remained at the helm no Deborah Conway record was ever heard on 2DayFM.

Maybe that was the moment I could call the beginning of the end of my formal relationship with Mushroom Records, though it would be many years before we officially separated. Amanda and I concluded our relationship just after *Bitch Epic* was released.

What has never reached its use-by date is my relationship with Frank Stivala.

When I signed with Mushroom in 1990, a relationship with booking agency Premier Artists was part of the deal. Frank Stivala was the boss, Premier *numero uno*, the co-owner with Gudinski. In those early days, as with Amanda's management, I didn't question what was going on. Amanda was liaising with Premier to book the gigs, I was having a ball, I wasn't asking questions.

But when *Bitch Epic* came out in 1994 I did start interrogating Frank's choices. This was a different kind of record and we weren't interested in playing the standard pub rock venues on the circuit. We didn't want to pit ourselves against noisy audiences who were there more for the drinking and mating than the music. We wanted rooms where music lovers could treat the performance as a listening experience, as opposed to something they had to talk loudly above to be heard. I started booking tours myself.

When I was a kid, I'd spend Sunday afternoons at Nanna's watching Epic Theatre, a double matinée of sword-and-sandal blockbusters, all of which featured a cast of thousands. When we mounted our national theatre tour of *Bitch Epic*, the name 'Epic Theatre' immediately sprang to mind and deservedly so: the tour comprised a string quartet, backing singers, percussionists, a five-piece band, all wearing identically cut suits made in a palette of bold colours, an elaborate set, lighting rig and sound system; we needed a semi-articulated truck to move us around. 'The Epic Theatre Tour'. It virtually named itself.

I had a number of costumes, including a stunning gold lamé frock with enormous breasts built in—thank you, Sally Mill—which I called my Jessica Rabbit frock. I wore it with a platinum blonde wig and adopted a Marilyn Monroe husky whisper to thank our sponsor, Poppy Industries of the famous matte lipstick, before peeling the concealed zip down and revealing a slender white sheath dress beneath. It always got a good response.

Frank came to the show; he appreciated what we were doing.

And many decades later we still work together; despite our occasional combative discussions, Frank is an enduring ally.

He is not a classically handsome man; short, tubby and balding, he has the pallor of someone who rarely sees the sun and eats too much takeaway. Whenever I walk into his office, Frank has a cigarette on the go, wafting blue smoke from the overfilled ashtray on his desk. He's like the classic Hollywood agent, phone in one fist, fag in the other.

Frank is gruff, abrupt, shy, but his sense of humour is never far from the surface; he can be cute and cuddly, though I don't recall ever cuddling him; he wouldn't be out of place in the Bada Bing nightspot in *The Sopranos*; he bears a passing resemblance to that unlikely sex symbol Lior Raz (who plays the character Doron in Israeli TV series *Fauda*). I have told him this often, but I still don't think he's watched an episode.

On 17 June, 2004, Frank walked up to the Committee Room at the Moonee Valley racecourse for a fun day of racing and punting, only to discover a room full of well-wishers in attendance for his fiftieth birthday party. Frank was truly surprised—I'd say moved. He would never have organised himself a party, not being someone who seeks the limelight, but he loved it. The top weight, Deprave, got up for the 'Frank Stivala 50th Birthday Cup' (all races were especially named for the day), and Frank was a winner on and off the track. The giant birthday bash was attended by people who think of Frank with great affection, and all of them had kept the surprise a secret.

What was particularly interesting was how many people I spoke to expressed a version of, 'What, get outta here! Frank's only fifty?' It was like Frank had always been older than fifty.

Funnily enough, it worked in his favour. All of us have got visibly older more than a decade and a half since then, but Frank hasn't. He just looks like Frank.

And after all the lives cut short in our line of work, it's Frank who is the survivor.

On 2 March, 2021, Michael Gudinski defied expectations that he would always and forever be the indefatigable hub and cannonball boss of Australian music, and went and died. I still can't quite believe it. It was way before time. Michael's sudden exit was felt acutely around the world. We all poured out our reminiscences, painting vivid word portraits that overlapped and deepened the colours of this man we each knew in our own way.

There were his phone calls at all hours, the half-baked rambling conversations delivered as a monologue in his increasingly gruff voice that would abruptly terminate only to be picked up ten minutes or two days later in another series of calls that were hard to decipher in the Queen's English but the spirit would be clear; the mad schemes he made happen that no one else could; the unending passion for music, for the deal, for the new young thing; his boundless good-humoured enthusiasm, his restless energy, his very long memory, his ability to seduce people into thinking he wasn't concentrating and to believe they might get the better of him in a deal only to pull out the trump card at game's end; the naughty stories.

He was a loveable rogue. I knew that, and I also knew I could ask him for a big favour and he'd deliver. He was a conundrum. He would call to ask me what I thought of someone he was thinking of touring, or to share a few cryptic sentences before his attention was pulled in another three directions and he had to go. He was a man of vast capacity, in his ability to work, to multi-task, to be a wheeler dealer. I railed against some of his practices, I would remain wary of him in a business venture, but I was, despite it all, always enormously fond of Michael 'Godinski'.

Michael was Atlas hefting the music world on his shoulders. He called me after Chris Murphy, famously the manager of INXS and another titan of Australia's music scene, died, sounding like he was grappling with the weight of it. We spoke briefly—I don't know why I bother to add briefly, it was always briefly—about shows he was organising that he wanted me to be part of. He rang again a week or so later, this time more reflective.

'We get on so much better now we're older. You and Willy have to come over for dinner.'

He hung up before we could make a date, and then suddenly he was gone. Hell of a way to get out of a dinner invitation, Michael.

22

Born Once

After the Epic Theatre tour wound up in 1994, we flew to Thailand for a bit of R&R. The first two weeks were brilliant, but when we headed north and started the recommended course of anti-malaria tablets, I immediately felt wretched. The sight and smell of Thai food churned my stomach, and the pungent aroma of the fish markets was making me heave. I couldn't believe the tablets had this effect. I loved Thai food, but now everything made me want to throw up.

I wobbled through the last week desperate to get home so I could eat something, anything, made without the ubiquitous bottle of Squid-brand sauce. I spent our last night in Bangkok trying to find a toasted cheese sandwich or spaghetti bolognese that didn't taste fishy. It was a fool's errand.

Back in Melbourne I was done with the anti-malaria tablets but the nausea was sticking around. My doctor gave me a pregnancy stick test to wee on. *Positive.* I was suffering from morning sickness. The nausea lasted longer than the first three months and then came back for the last three. It was nightmarish and years passed before I could eat Thai food again—even a news story on Thailand made me feel queasy.

We fronted up for the first ultrasound to make sure everything was as it should be. Mr Zygier quipped, 'Ultrasound would be a splendid name for a band.' I enthusiastically agreed. And since we were between projects it came to pass. We reached out to Bill McDonald to play bass and Paul Hester to complete the quartet on drums.

By the time we'd amassed enough material for an album and everyone's diaries had lined up, the summer of '94–'95 was in full swing and we were holed up in Tim Finn's house in South Caulfield, which he'd converted into a studio. I had spent a lot of time there in the early 1980s when Paul and I were still a couple. It hadn't changed at all really; even the plate featuring Moshe Dayan wearing his eyepatch was still hanging on the kitchen wall.

The heat added to the languid feeling in the room. I was close to term by then, and sang my vocals from the studio couch. Experimentation was in the air and we gave all ideas free rein until they either worked or didn't. Mostly they did. We were crawling all over the piano, jamming Blu-tack into strings, and finding toys to bang and crash on, like some kind of adult crèche. The ten days we spent recording were more like a holiday than work.

Paul had recently quit Crowded House, claiming he'd had enough of hotel rooms and was yearning for a different lifestyle. His public persona was sunny and laidback, a lover of life and the life of the party, and he tried to be that most of the time, but Paul had another side that manifested in depressive episodes and an anger he found hard to curb. He was in a good place at the end of 1994 in Tim's South Caulfield studio, making pots of tea and playing like a demon.

My pregnancy was a curious time. At thirty-two, I hadn't been entirely sure I would have a baby; at thirty-three, I was eschewing contraception; by thirty-four, I was pregnant. I was perfectly aware of my little alien tumour, especially after six months when I started to pop, but it was a curious detached awareness, like it was happening to someone else. I could feel the restless life inside me but not a scrap of maternal instinct. Of course it may have had something to do with the constant heaving.

My mother was keen to take us shopping for accoutrements to fit out a nursery, but I was so reluctant (and nauseous) she gave up. Friends gave us their old, soft carrycot to put a newborn inside. I looked down to where the head would be and felt not brimming, rapturous anticipation but horror (and nausea). A baby shower was completely beyond the pale. When would the maternal instinct kick in and when the *hell* would the nausea stop?

At my thirty-four-week check-up, the midwife told us the baby had flipped and was now in breech position, not ideal for a first-time mother of thirty-five. I wasn't hugely concerned; I had a month before my squatter had to vacate the premises. We tried a Chinese herbal remedy, moxibustion, to see if it might hasten the little tacker to flip back. I lay on my stomach and Mr Zygier lit a cigar-type concoction of evil-smelling ingredients and held it against my toes daily for twenty minutes, ten minutes per foot.

Strangely, it didn't work. Nor did the uncontrollable laughing as we were doing it. The creature wasn't budging.

We performed at the Comedy Theatre on 10 February. I was due on 26 February, so we had plenty of time to squeeze in a show. The collective gasps from the audience as I danced and jumped around, belly akimbo, were worth the price of admission. There was never a health and safety issue, but there was a metaphorical fireworks element. And still my occupant remained firmly upright.

Two days later, we were wandering around Fitzroy Street on a steamy night taking in the St Kilda Festival after seeing Ute Lemper prowl the catwalk, naked and close to full term in Robert Altman's *Prêt-à-Porter*. We passed the George hotel and sitting outside was jazz singer Shelley Scown holding her brand-new baby. We stopped and chatted. She was serene, and I was detached, as though this impending baby thing was happening way off in the future.

Back at our temporary house-sitting residence, I pottered around cleaning until after 2 am. (Afterwards I remembered someone saying that manic cleaning could signal a baby was imminent.) Finally, tired enough to lie down, I felt the odd sensation of liquid dribbling out without my having any control over it. My waters had broken.

We were in the car and at the hospital within fifteen minutes. Poking, prodding midwives confirmed that the future Zygier was still lying upside down—actually, right side up in any other scenario, but in this instance feet-first wasn't cutting it. My gynaecologist issued the ultimatum: 'Caesarean section or find another gynaecologist.' At 4 am neither of us thought that option two was such a good idea, but my problem of not feeling a maternal instinct remained.

I had thought that struggling through a lengthy labour would prepare me. I likened it to the difference between the World War II troops being dispatched from the theatre of combat on ships, and the Vietnam troops returning on helicopters; the former given a way to adjust to civilian life over a leisurely couple of weeks, the latter having to deal with the jarring leap from battlefront to non-combatant in head-spinning time.

I was shot with numbing anaesthetic, painted in amber antiseptic and everything below my waist was shielded from my eyes by a green hospital sheet. The surgeon took his scalpel and sliced through the seven layers dividing me from our first daughter; she was plopped onto my chest at 4.20 am on 13 February, 1995. Had she been a boy, we were going to call her Kodak Youngblood Zygier(!) but she was Syd Dolores Zygier, and from that moment I was launched into the affair of a lifetime, mowed down by a freight train of love that remains for me unequalled in its speed, ferocity and unexpectedness. Maternal instinct? I had my first hit. I wanted six.

Ultrasound still stands as a favourite album for me, inventive, relaxed, sonically and compositionally adventurous with equal weight given to instrumental and vocal tracks, a pointer for things to come. The album was released shortly after Syd was. I have fond memories of the four of us signing the covers that Paul Hester had designed while Syd breastfed. We rehearsed upstairs at Woodstock Studios while Syd slept peacefully in her father's soft-foam-lined electric guitar case.

The tour was brief, and we approached it like a busman's holiday. With Paul at his relaxed and comedic best, the shows went off on creatively charged tangents every night. We performed the entire album with one exception; 'Born Once', Mr Zygier's musically rollicking praise for the universe, which he'd written for his band Tootieville, who never recorded it. Our recording sounded alive, shifting and restless like someone who has to shake out pins-and-needles from too long sitting. But it was a difficult key for me, and my vocals had sounded either too edgy or too laidback within the song's urgency. And then came one of those studio ideas that makes things fall into place. We sped the tape up (we were still recording onto tape in those days), which put the song into a key I could sing, then slowed the tape down again. I no longer sounded like me. The shift was so remarkable that this new singer needed their own identity. We came up with the name Bodean Rochway, a jumbling of letters that yielded deBoRah conway to the keen puzzle solver. But because Bodean Rochway didn't exist except in a box, we honoured the mystery and never played the song live. Like the rest of us, the track was born once only, in a South Caulfield home studio in the summer of 1995.

I can't listen to this song or the album without thinking of Paul. My dear friend, who became my lover and then became my friend again, was an integral part of my most formative years. Through that summer of content Paul had tamed his demons to fuel his creative output but ten years later those demons got the better of him; he took his own life over Easter 2005. Syd Dolores, who had shared those sessions with him in utero, was only ten years old.

'Born Once', *Ultrasound*, 1995

Blown to smithereens
Compelled to Kingdom Come
Swing low sweet chariot
Over the mountains under the sky
The seasons are changing
I feel it inside
Over the airwaves under the sky
It is home, it is home

A clangour from the horizon
A warning a signal
The shifting of the sands towards the East
Phew, a smell I don't recognise

Over the mountains under the sky
The seasons are changing
I feel it inside
Over the airwaves under the sky
It is home, it is home

A drop in pressure
Rain in the air
The sound of a trumpet
Wheels in the sky
The beating of wings
I've nothing to hide

I hold you upright yet you still fall
With every step closer
Another step from grace
It is home, it is home

23

String of Pearls

Becoming a mother blew my mind, bringing a newly acquired empathy and perspective into everything—especially my relationship with my own mother.

Some words about my mother:

1. loving
2. impressive
3. affectionate
4. exasperating
5. infuriating
6. admirable
7. maddening

My mother (1. loving) was the most important person in my world until I was twelve years old. I adored her, hung off her every pronouncement and believed her every utterance. There was literally nothing that could shake my conviction that my mother was always right and that if I only listened closely, I would learn everything I needed to know. I told her everything too: she was my confidante.

I didn't have any close friends in primary school, I was too shy to ask any of the girls home, maybe because my father was so extreme. My mother was my best friend. She was my cheer squad, my biggest supporter, who always told me I could do whatever I wanted, I just needed to want it badly enough. Her advice held true when I was growing up (it still does). Her hands are imprinted in my most primal memories, holding me, holding out possibility, directing my focus. She had small hands but they were strong, unlined, honest, capable.

My mother was the shield between me and my irrational, unpredictable, alternately terrifying and uninterested father. He was my rival for my mother's attention; there was no competition as to who my favourite parent was, that was a lay-down misère. By comparison she was reasonable, nuanced and thoughtful, able to lead the way through the rocky paths of tricky psychological terrain and seemed to always know the right things to say and do. Her predictions and prescriptions were unerringly accurate. Maybe all mothers are like this when you're very little.

When my nanna walked into her back TV room one day and discovered me (aged nine) sitting naked on my cousin's (aged twelve) lap, playing with his penis—this was my idea—while my younger sister and his younger brother were obliviously watching TV, she called me a harlot. My mother (2. impressive) was extremely calm in the face of Nanna's fury and defended me as curious and innocent; she never wavered in her full-throated defence of me.

My mother (3. affectionate) was exceptionally good at cleaning ('shit off shag' as the saying goes), but she couldn't sew and wasn't much of a cook. Once she made ice cream that was frozen so solid that after three hours left out of the freezer was still too rock-hard to serve; we pondered the possibility of selling it to NASA as a new kind of heat shield. My childhood meals were on a limited rotation between macaroni cheese and fish fingers, both out of the packet, steak diane or, as a special treat, a burger and chips from Red Barn, the forerunner to McDonald's.

More than once, I absentmindedly threw my dental plate, worn to counteract the effects of sucking my thumb until the age of fourteen, into Red Barn's rubbish bin with the detritus of my meal. We would have to drive back to try and retrieve it. While my mother would have reason to be furious, I don't remember her being so. My other memory of her cooking is sitting in front of a side serving of brussels sprouts, which I was gagging over, and being forbidden to leave the table until I got them down. I tried to drown the flavour in tomato sauce, which didn't help at all. My will was stronger than hers. She never made them for me again. I also remember the smell wafting through the house when she cooked mushrooms which also make me gag; she never tried to make me eat those.

Mum never smacked us, though there was one time she apparently tried. Who knows what I'd done, but it was something significant enough for her to bend me over the back of the kitchen chair and bring her hand humming through the air to land on my backside—which it would have, if I hadn't moved mid-whack. She ended up hitting the metal bars of the chair hard enough to cause bruising and deep regret. I don't recall the occasion but she laughs at herself when she tells it, with appreciation for my lightning-fast reflexes.

I once found a report when I was searching for something in my mother's drawers, a psychological profile that contained things I shouldn't have been reading. But I still remember the phrase: 'Your accommodating traits have suppressed your essential nature'. I read this with recognition and sadness.

My mother is a people-pleaser. She likes it when people like her, she is high in agreeableness. (I am less agreeable.) Interestingly her agreeableness has diminished substantially, at least with me, since my father died. Maybe she feels she has to fill his shoes? I don't know what the reason is, but we fight a lot more these days. My mother (4. exasperating) drives me nuts with her disagreeableness—we can barely find anything we agree on. Every year on Yom Kippur, I have one sin I need to atone for: fighting with my mother (5. infuriating).

Lately I've been thinking it's actually not always my fault. Our fights don't last longer than the exchange of words in real time; the following day I'll call her and we'll both be as sweet as pie, until the conversation strays into some new minefield and we start all over again. I am attributing her inability to hear my side of the discussion to her being slightly hard-of-hearing these days.

I guess she is a good example of a cantankerous old lady living her best life; her exceptional good health, combined with the fact she takes no medication, is a wondrous thing. Who am I to complain if my mother's (6. admirable) longevity and quality of life result in her regular squabbling with her eldest daughter? She gets on swimmingly with her youngest, who also happens to be very agreeable.

My mother (7. maddening) is completely independent and hates using her mobile phone. I'm not the only one who expresses concern if they can't get on to her, but I am the one who will drive around to her house to check she's not on the floor being eaten by Lottie, her small grey-white Maltese Shih tzu.

Au contraire—she has usually been playing bridge, or taken Lottie for a walk, gone shopping, stopped in the street to talk to a neighbour or a stranger and ignored all the missed calls on her mobile phone. And then when I turn up on her doorstep she says, slightly mockingly, though with underlying affection, 'Were you really worried about little old me?'

24

2001 Ultrasound

'2001 Ultrasound', *My Third Husband*, 1997

My big head feels like lead
Weighed down with indecision
I might know where it starts
But where it ends is quite different
And it's out of my hands

All the wires are down
And cables on the ground
Ending of the century
Don't know where I'm bound
You might be the first to see the last time round
Tell me ultrasound

Something's growing in me
It feels like indigestion
I think I'm going to be
Someone's mummy don't ask questions
Do you mind if I sit here?
All the wires are down
And cables on the ground
Ending of the century
Don't know where I'm bound
You might be the first to see the last time round
Tell me ultrasound

Peering in, to the great unknown
The future's asleep

There are plans for next door
The tallest building in the world you know
Can't imagine what for
Except to cast the longest shadow
And I want to be there

All the wires are down
And cables on the ground
Ending of the century
Don't know where I'm bound
You might be the first to see the last time round
Tell me ultrasound

'2001 Ultrasound' was written between late-night breast-feeding sessions, on inadequate sleep, in a foreign country at the end of the millennium. We were dazed and confused, adjusting to our new roles and shucking off the old ones. The song is a contemplation of new life in a new century, a walk along a meandering line in search of comfort while negotiating our new emotional landscape. The recording takes a similar stroll between the machine intrusions of pops, whirrs and bangs, before slipping back into lullaby cadences.

We had arrived in London in July 1995 with Syd Dolores Zygier, who had just turned four months old. It was a brutal thing to rip my mother's first grandchild away from her loving arms. The long sad goodbyes at the airport were tearful for all of us, but we were off to seek our fortune and I wasn't going to let a little thing like 'becoming a mother' get in the way.

We'd left behind our newly renovated house in our end-of-the-line suburb, Williamstown. The house, sandwiched between the mouth of the Yarra River on Hobsons Bay, the beachfront along Port Phillip Bay, and near Point Gellibrand, was surrounded with an abundance of water. You could swim at the bay beach on hot days (or not-so-hot if you were hardy), or you could fish in the 'warmies' up near the Newport Power Station.

The first botanical gardens in Victoria enjoyed prime position on Williamstown's beachfront. The streets were wide and treelined like an old Victorian country town, with cars parked nose to kerb. Nature strips were broad enough in Williamstown to be able to cultivate a serious veggie patch if you had a mind to do so, but we lived in the more urban part of the suburb on Douglas Parade, next door to a junk shop called, appropriately, Willy's Bazaar.

We'd only recently moved back after camping at friends' places in St Kilda for months. By comparison, Williamstown was sublimely peaceful; the house, an early 1900s weatherboard double-fronted two-storey grocer's shop, with an old triple-brick building at the back originally built as a bakery, was a short stroll from the waterfront where I would walk Syd in her pram, both of us entranced by the pelicans gliding on the still water of Hobsons Bay. Pelicans always made me happy, as did hanging out with my baby girl in the room we'd added to the rear of the house. Downstairs was our small back garden with the granite slab our future daughters would stage shows on, and a graceful white cherry tree that told four majestic seasonal stories every year.

From our first-floor living room we could see the massive shipping containers chugging slowly past, like huge colourful office buildings, to load or unload their cargo in Footscray. The suburb resonated with their low sustained foghorns. On clear days we could see the Dandenong Ranges on the far horizon. It seemed like it was always sunny as we rolled around on the carpet together. But the three months we lived there together whipped past, and the moment came when our long-laid plans to head for the other side of the world were upon us.

In its essence, the plan was a good one. *String of Pearls* and *Bitch Epic* had sold Platinum and Gold quantities in Australia, and Mushroom Records was offering to release a compilation in the UK and Europe if we would relocate there and commit to promoting them. While Do-Ré-Mi had made small inroads on German and Dutch radio, after we'd toured there in 1986, and 'Man Overboard' had been picked up by John Peel's late-night BBC radio tastemaker program, we hadn't cracked anything with our second album. To be able to reach an audience beyond Australia was a long-held ambition; there were plenty of hurdles, the tyranny of distance being paramount, but Mushroom Records was handing me one more chance to climb the mountain.

A few days before we were due to depart, Gudinski called me with a veiled warning, which he didn't elaborate on. 'Don't go,' he said. The flights were booked and paid for, the bags were packed, we'd arranged for people to move into our house and had organised to house-sit a flat in Soho to give us a soft landing while we looked for somewhere to rent. It felt too late to pull the pin, so I chose to ignore his advice.

The ride from Heathrow was memorable, sitting in the back of the London black cab on a sticky July day listening to our four-month-old daughter laugh for the first time. Joyous, and, in hindsight, maybe prophetic.

We got oriented and over the jet lag and a few days later I called Mushroom's London office. Unbeknown to me, twenty-four hours earlier the head office 'shooting party' had delivered a stern ultimatum to Mushroom's London office.

'STOP SPENDING MONEY NOW!'

Mushroom UK was throwing all available resources at trying to get Peter Andre, an Australian dance act, into the British charts. I don't recall if they succeeded, but in the meantime, they had come close to bankrupting the company. Naturally that meant death by a thousand cuts: jobs, projects, departments, recording budgets. And there was no sweetness left for us. Despite the much-prized promises of a UK and European release, a tour and accompanying promotion to support it, everything was rescinded. The entire enterprise had crashed on the jagged rocks of hubris, theirs for the profligacy and mine in refusing to probe Michael's warning.

We had uprooted ourselves and moved to the other side of the world on the understanding that we were equal partners in the venture. To say the rug had been pulled from under us doesn't come close. It felt like a profound betrayal. Mushroom UK limped on for another few years, its stocks much depleted, until a merger with other smaller labels renamed it A&E Records, which was then sold in 1998 to Warners. With a whimper.

The grim reaper in July 1995 was the Mushroom Head of UK operations, Gary Ashley, who told us we were essentially on our own and that there'd be no UK release. We decided we would not turn around and head home. Instead, we would write a third solo album (unofficially our third collaboration). With credit to the prematurely deceased Ashley, I do believe he felt our disappointment keenly and was appalled at how events had transpired to undermine us; he managed to gift me a DAT (digital audio tape) recorder at some stage, though in the two years we lived in London we never once scored an invitation to the local pub for so much as a pint.

Heads hung in disbelief, we repaired to the oasis of the lovely little pied-à-terre in Soho in which Greta Scacchi—famous for her beauty, her exquisite body and much to her chagrin, her nude scenes—had most generously allowed us to pitch camp for our first few weeks. It was the height of summer, and London was experiencing a heat wave. The mercury soared to 33° Celsius, and we were in the centre of a big city with no sea breeze to cool the air.

I love the heat, and we were pretty happy to indulge in our own nude scenes in the comfort of that Soho flat while we tried to write the next opus but there were multitudes of challenges.

The new-baby exhaustion and the feeling of having my brains vitamised and leaking out with the copious amounts of breast milk I was making for our very hungry daughter were life-changing. But the biggest challenge was trying to process the loss of the opportunity that had been dangled and then swiped away. I was finding that shift enormously difficult to bounce back from.

In those first few weeks we wrote and wrote, though most of that material was rejected before we recorded two years later. They were days of intense work and heat, which I spent juggling the demands of motherhood with the headspace required to create something from nothing, and the frustration of not being able to write anything I was happy with. Writing songs was a job—not one I was getting paid to do, at least not in any direct way, but nevertheless a job—that demanded full creative commitment, whether I felt like it or not. I was a deep-sea diver trying to find the pearl before my air ran out.

Greta's flat was small, with the living space upstairs, and the bedroom the floor below. One sweltering day at the coalface, both of us wearing only underpants, there was a 'Yoo-hoo!' from downstairs. Our hostess had dropped by with a minor Saudi princeling after he had taken her to lunch to explore her knowledge of live theatre. She had brought him back to her flat to meet us, which meant Mr Zygier had to go downstairs past the prince, who made some disparaging comment about his gold earrings—though breeding probably prevented him complaining about the fact that he had to meet a sweaty peasant in his underwear—and grab clothes for both of us.

I guess Greta made an impression on him because shortly afterwards, by way of thank you, a brand-new, navy-blue Mercedes station wagon was delivered to her country house. She was horrified, but her protest to the prince's staff was met with tut-tuts and, 'Don't worry about it, dear, just think of it as a bunch of flowers'.

By mid-August we'd moved to a flat in W9, an area romantically known as Little Venice because of the canal. The owner of the flat was an adventurer; every room was packed to the rafters with abundant evidence of travel. After the tastefully sparse interior of Greta's Soho flat, the amount of stuff to wade through just to cross a room was so overwhelming I felt like we were museum staff. The layout had the front entrance upstairs on the same level as a bathroom and two bedrooms, one for the three of us and the other doing duty as a studio; downstairs was a living area, kitchen and laundry.

Syd became very adept at removing all the contents of the shelves, drawers and cupboards. It took me a surprisingly long time to figure out that I could leave her redecorating until she went to bed before undoing her good work. It was a ritual repeated many times a day; really a minor skirmish among the many battles I was fighting, but I was too tired to realise I should have just let it go.

We created many songs during our period of parenting in exile, most of them around the business of eating. 'Spin That Teddy' was the theme tune for the TV show Syd unwittingly hosted every time we sat her in her bouncy bassinet with the plastic spinning teddy bears to get her to eat some mush; 'Sydaleela, Sydaloola, Sydalumpkin' was another firm favourite to encourage another mouthful to go down, as was the classic 'Muncher, Muncher, MuncherLoo'.

The other hit tune was 'There's a Piggy in the Bath', a smash that kept all parties well entertained till bedtime. Sadly, however, despite enjoying full and busy days and a healthy appetite, Syd did not sleep through the night until she was four years old.

The Tube was a few minutes' walk away and the bus to Marble Arch took no time. Every week we would walk or trudge (depending on how much sleep we'd had and what season we were in) along the canal to buy our groceries at Sainsbury's. It was not as romantic as it sounded; the canal banks were littered with plastic debris and there was usually something like a half-submerged bicycle poking out of the water, plus for most of the year the skies were heavy and the weather bleak. But it was exercise and Syd enjoyed it from the comfort of her stroller.

We'd been in London a couple of months when Mushroom Australia and Polygram Publishing (Willy's publisher) came to our rescue and invested in an extortionately expensive digital recording set-up. We installed it in the second bedroom, then spent a lot of time reading manuals to figure out how to use it. Eventually we started recording the songs we'd written since arriving (though not the almost-album's worth of eating songs we had devised—perhaps that was our mistake!). Every now and again the line 'TRY TO SAVE YOUR SONG' would appear on the screen; it was a tease, as no matter what buttons we pressed we knew with sinking certainty that everything we'd done to that recording would vanish into the ether. I should have laughed but I wept. Willy retained his sense of humour. ('Try to Save Your Song' became track four on *Summertown*—nothing was wasted.)

Finally, months later, we managed to get four tracks to the point where we felt confident enough to send them off to our benefactor,

Roger Grierson, (you might remember him as the co-owner with Stuart Coupe of Do-Ré-Mi's first record company). Roger was now the head of Polygram Publishing. An intense, fast-talking, high-energy music fan, he bore an uncanny resemblance to Roddy Doyle's fictional manager and music fanatic, Jimmy Rabbitte, in Doyle's novel *The Commitments*.

Roger loved music. So when he responded swiftly, 'Don't play these to anyone,' it felt like a body blow. We took his advice, kept our counsel and went back to the drawing board to write and record another batch of songs.

Again, I should have laughed but tears were my go-to response for most things at this point; my sense of humour had taken a severe battering. I was acutely (and constantly) aware of all my lost opportunities, the sliding-door possibilities I'd allowed myself to miss. They were queuing in my head, taunting me, haunting my sleep (what little there was of that) and replaying themselves with every new setback. The king-of-the-mountain ascendancy I had lived through in the 1980s was a distant memory now. My constant nagging brain kept reminding me that a thirty-six-year-old's chances of making this recording thing successful were fast diminishing.

Absolutely everything, no matter how immaterial, felt hard to accomplish. I was living through a midlife crisis, or was it postnatal depression? Maybe the lack of sleep for so many months had finally done me in.

A year or more went by. We made friends; we visited my cousins in Surrey and Yorkshire; my parents came over and took care of Syd while we had a restorative seven-day break in Deià, Mallorca, where the English poet and author Robert Graves was buried. As well as not sleeping, Syd had developed a deep need to scream her lungs out whenever we went out for a meal, necessitating one of us always being outside to soothe her no matter the weather. We gave up going out. We still don't go out much; old habits die hard. Strangely, though, when her grandparents were her restaurant dinner companions, Syd behaved impeccably ... or so my father told me.

Finally, we wrote ourselves a batch of tunes we were happy with and found some great musicians to play them. We started performing shows around London and tried to recruit management. I took a lot of meetings and approached a lot of people who showed little interest in what we were doing until we met with John 'Knocker' Knowles. Knocker came via a friend who referred to him as 'a bit of a wide boy', which I gathered meant someone who was comfortable skating the thin line between legality and illegality but he bowled us over with his enthusiasm for our demo tapes at our first meeting, so wide boy or not, Knocker was in.

And in those early halcyon days, he didn't disappoint. He was booking the rehearsal studios for us, helping us lug gear, critiquing our shows and coming up with grand, if harebrained, schemes for world domination.

We played a handful of gigs, most memorably at the Borderline, a smallish venue off Charing Cross Road that attracted Australian expats. The night we played, the joint was heaving with an appreciative crowd, but before we could get back on stage to play the demanded encore, the staff had sprung into action, busily clearing out punters due to a significant health risk posed by the toilets in the basement overflowing with a fast-rising tide of excrement.

(Like Syd's first laugh in the black cab, this surge of shit was a portent of nothing good.)

Post-show, Knocker was beside himself with excitement. He told us he'd had a vision of how he could exploit our unique offerings in Europe. 'You guys are a European act all the way, we're gonna have to get you over there; you'll go gangbusters in Germany!'

It was the last conversation we ever had. The call he was going to make to us on Monday never eventuated, nor on Tuesday, nor anytime that week, the following week or in the following months. I was bewildered. I kept myself distracted inventing more and more implausible scenarios as to what could have transpired. Was it something I said or didn't say? Was Knocker in emotional turmoil due to his wife asking for a divorce? Had he been hit on the head, and was in hospital suffering memory loss? Had he been recruited by MI6 for an undercover operation?

I realised by the time I'd thought of that last one that I was losing my grip on reality. His disappearance was the nadir of this ship-of-fools' misadventure and I was unutterably abject. I tried to call him but never got anywhere until one day he finally did answer the phone and in a very friendly way said, 'Great, I've been wanting to talk to you, but I'm on the other line, I'll have to call you back.'

He never did.

Years later, after we had left the UK and returned to Australia with our new recording, I heard from the friend who originally introduced us that he'd bumped into Knocker at some industry night and asked him straight up, 'Why did you just drop them cold like you did?'

Knocker, in his own inimitable way, replied, 'Sometimes you just have to be a cunt.'

25

Everybody's Begging

In the early 1980s Do-Ré-Mi recorded our two EPs on an 8-channel desk over the course of two days, with minimal overdubs. After signing with Virgin in 1984, we recorded the next two albums over several months, on SSL (Solid State Logic) 48-channel desks, both in UK studios. The music business has always been one of rapid technological change, but the one constant I had thought was impervious to change was the expense. With the cost of recording technology above and beyond what an artist or band could pay, it felt like record companies would always retain the balance of power.

As you might imagine, the scale of spending between those four releases were chalk and cheese; when the record company is paying, no expense is spared, but ALL those expenses become the artists' responsibility. The equation is deceptive—and I would say opaque to most young musicians excited to be signed to a major record company—but key to understanding what happens next in terms of industry upheaval.

Put simply, the way major record companies did business was to ensure that all production costs were added to the artists' tab, but that the repayments for those advances were deducted not from the overall profits made from the sale of the music, but from the artists' share of the profits; there is a substantial difference. Maybe the artist is being paid $1 out of the $10 wholesale price of the album. Out of their $1 share, they have to pay back all the costs of recording, manufacturing, marketing, video making etc. to the record company.

In the meantime the record company has long since recouped its costs and is making a *motza* from the remaining $9 which the artist never sees. Even if an artist ends up selling a significant number of albums (units), it is still a very long time before they clear their debt, if they manage to at all.

On the upside, if the artist doesn't sell a lot of albums, the record company carries the debt and if your contract expires you will never have to put your hand in your pocket to pay that debt back. On the downside, even if you sell a lot of records, you still may not have earned enough to repay the costs.

However, the contract you signed gives the record company the right to exploit your work 'in the known and unknown worlds in perpetuity', which is a standard contract clause, and henceforth herewith notwithstanding (etc., etc.) you will remain in debt to that record company or in the event that the record company is sold to another record company, your debt will be transferred and you will never own your own recordings. (There's rarely any punctuation in these contracts!)

I accept there must be some imbalance in the artist/record company profit-sharing relationship if you look at the amount of risk-taking that record companies commit to in order to do business. But it's hard to understand the extreme imbalance I've described as anything other than rapacious exploitation.

From there it's a small step into the endless labyrinth of shadowy, often grubby, dealings that characterise the music business model. Few of the players are purer than any other; some just have less opportunity.

This is a sustainable business model only if everything stays the same.

But it never does.

Music and recording technologies have been in a state of constant change ever since the first player pianos appeared in the 1840s. In the following decade, de Martinville introduced his phonautograph machine; hot on his heels was Thomas Edison, cutting the first wax cylinder. In fact, there have rarely been more than a few years at a time where huge leaps forward in technology haven't imposed massive repercussions on the delivery and the consumption of music.

I grew up with vinyl. I had shelves of albums and singles; I wasn't a collector or a completist, but if you wanted to listen to music you had to purchase the physical thing. Mostly that was vinyl, though cassettes were creeping in by the time I was fourteen. I had a cassette deck and I liked playing my music loud. I remember listening to 'Love Lies Bleeding' with the volume knob turned up full (eardrums lie bleeding!) as my father barged into my bedroom, hurling my cassette deck across the room yelling at me to TURN IT DOWN. Goodbye *Goodbye Yellow Brick Road* but it and my tape deck survived; no doubt they wouldn't have if I'd been listening to vinyl.

When compact disc technology burst onto the shelves, the record companies were high-fiving each other. It was a gold rush. Not only did sales go through the roof with music fans buying new releases in the novel format, they were also re-buying heritage-act albums just to have them as CDs in their collection. On top of that, CDs were significantly cheaper to manufacture, a saving that, predictably, record companies decided not to pass on to the artist. Instead they inserted a clause into the standard record contract which termed CDs as 'new technology' and came with a 25 per cent loading to the artist. I know, I almost signed one of those contracts before I managed to negotiate it back to 17.5 per cent. (Still *chutzpah!*) In 1991, *String of Pearls* was released on CD and cassette only; vinyl was pretty much over and done with by 1992.

By the middle 1990s, there was a veritable explosion in the availability of digital equipment that enabled quality home recordings which were able to equal those made in professional studios, at a fraction of the cost.

Mr Zygier and I were busy making music on one of these set-ups in our London flat while simultaneously caring for our now one-year-old daughter. Since weaning herself off the bosom at thirteen months, she had become vulnerable to every cough, cold and virus going around—which I would also catch. Syd and I ricocheted from one illness to the next. It was a rough eighteen months on the health front, adding a layer of hardship to everything else that was going on, or more accurately, *wasn't* going on. No wonder the songs we were writing were so bleak.

'Feathers in My Mouth', *My Third Husband*, 1997

I fall softly into nothing
I die quietly in my bed
I'm on some Panadol
That's all you saw in my bathroom

But I'm surrounded
Getting crowded
Spitting out the feathers in my mouth

I see white lights in my future
Beating wings—out of time
I'm on some Panadol
That's all you saw in my bathroom

But I'm surrounded
Getting crowded
Spitting out the feathers in my mouth
(They're flying north and south)
While I'm spitting out the feathers in my mouth

Let's go walking at midnight
And rub against the moonlight coming off my skin
I'm on some Panadol
That's all you saw in my bathroom

But I'm surrounded
Getting crowded
Spitting out the feathers in my mouth

In the middle of our far-from-home sleeplessness, wrestling with digital recording manuals, we uncovered something extraordinary. Searching for some minor distraction, Mr Zygier casually typed 'deborahconway.com' into our computer, and amazingly, an entire dossier popped up on the screen, documenting my personal life, career, activities, likes, dislikes, names and dates, with photographs we couldn't recall posing for. We'd stumbled on a kind of shrine to our existence; perfectly respectful, a little breathlessly worshipful, flattering but surreal; like stumbling on your own obituary when you are in strapping good health.

The discovery of a muscular online world was both a milestone moment and a strange out-of-body experience, as we realised that an unknown benign entity was beavering away on our behalf.

Despite the arcade-game novelty of that encounter, we recognised an important opportunity where more agency than what was currently possible could be in the offing. We saw sparkling baubles. It was an adventure in the style of the grand European architectural enfilade, each space leading to the next. The sudden possibility of passing through how we were currently doing things, into how we might one day do them, instead gave us our first inkling that the methodology of secret record company business was about to be democratised.

Those London years marked the end of our relationship with the traditional music business, and set us on a course into the new world. We didn't quite know it, but recording into the computer in our Maida Vale flat broke with the past and pushed our careers into a second act.

And the changes just kept coming. Around the same time the personal computer had become a must-own item, Napster appeared. Napster was a rudimentary file-sharing application that users could access to download music from other users, albeit illegally and not instantly. It wrought transformative change on the way we consumed music. Napster was taken to court and eventually forced to cease and desist, but stable doors and bolting horses are a good analogy for what was coming.

In 2003 Apple launched a digital music service; then another company, Pandora, offered a subscriber model that could suggest playlists. In 2008 Spotify offered a new service called 'streaming'.

Suddenly new cars no longer had CD players, computers came without an inbuilt CD drive and state-of-the-art stereo systems no longer came with a CD slot. The CD honeymoon was over.

The internet revolutionised every aspect of our business. By 2003, Mr Zygier and I had taken complete control of our own music from go to whoa: writing, recording, manufacturing and promotion. As independent musicians we were finally making money from our musical endeavours. We rejoiced.

But there are no revolutions without bloodshed. The new millennium would be barely ten years old when metaphorical blood started flowing through the ether and drizzling down from the little dark iCloud.

The technological revolution that such a short time ago had been viewed as miraculous for musicians, seeking to free themselves from the tyranny of exploitation by the record companies, had become a disinterested disrupter to all artists seeking to make their living from selling their recorded output. Streaming was a whole new way of disseminating music, legal and desirable for consumers, but with a profound downside for artists, who were collecting only a fraction of a cent per stream. We went from exploitation by the record companies to exploitation by the streaming services; the more things change, the more they stay the same. How could we know, as Gillian Welch so succinctly wrote, that 'Everything Is Free Now'?

Musicians would be back at the bottom of the food chain, again.

But all this lay a few short years in the future. We saw it coming, but we didn't quite realise how comprehensive the change would be. In 1996 the workers owned the means of production and it was liberating and exciting.

Crowdfunding became an ingenious method by which musicians could do business. In 2012, Amanda Palmer, formerly of The Dresden Dolls, crowdfunded her yet-to-be-recorded new album, raising $1,192,793. With numbers like that, it wasn't surprising that overnight everybody was crowdfunding. There was a conga line of newly independent musicians trying their luck in this brave new autonomous world.

I received a dozen requests in a week to buy everything from a souvenir t-shirt to a tea towel, to paying the artist to sing 'Happy Birthday' to a loved one over the phone. You could receive a postcard sent from the tour-bus; you could pay for a horse-riding lesson (these are all real examples!). You could even buy the music—though as the crowdfunding cavalcade grew more intense, and the pleading letters were coming thicker and faster, the music appeared to be the item of least interest.

Rightly or wrongly, Mr Zygier and I resisted resorting to crowdfunding, feeling that musicians were being reduced to begging for support. One part of this so-called business had become a cap-in-hand experience.

'Everybody's Begging', *Everybody's Begging*, 2016

Beggar man keeps company
With soldiers, sailors, spies and thieves
Everybody's got a scheme
Beggar man wears his on his sleeve

The priest is begging for a soul
The rabbi's begging for the scroll
The ferryman begs for his toll
The jelly's begging for the roll

Oh oh everybody's begging

You have a lot of everything
You have someone to do your every bidding
And I see you living like a king
But you know there's still something missing

The dog is begging for a bone
The heir is begging for the throne
The poor man's begging for a loan
The unknown are begging to be known

Oh oh everybody's begging

Nothing like an earthly hell
To bring out all the self-styled angels
But the ones who spell it out can't spell
You give them something and they want something else

There's writers begging to be read
There's voices begging in your head
There's blood that's begging to be shed
There's hungry begging for some bread
There's hookers begging to be paid
You think it's fun just getting laid
There's junkies begging for a fix
That's not enough until it is

Oh oh everybody's begging

We are the miserable mammals
Every day's so hard to handle
The path to salvation's one long battle
The darkness lit by one lone candle

There's secrets begging to be hidden
The future's begging to be written
There's fuel begging for ignition
I'm a soldier begging for a mission
In the dark begging for some light
In the dark begging for a fight

You can just point me at the action
Everyone's begging for distraction

Oh oh everybody's begging

Everything you've ever owned
Every place that you've called home
Every piece you thought would fit
The physical and the spirit
What we are is less than what we're not
And what we're not is less than what we want
And what we want is where we're always heading
And all I see is everybody's begging

26

It's a Girl Thing

By the time 1997 rolled around, things were looking a lot less grim. We had new management, had moved flats and we'd found a producer we liked. Before the recording started, we took the Easter break to holiday in Tuscany with my sister, her partner and their newborn son Levi. Mr Zygier and I inadvertently worked on extending our family, and by the time the week was up the little seed of future joy, mystery and havoc that would become our second daughter was planted and dividing.

It didn't take too long to figure out. I seemed to have an almost instant response to pregnancy: morning, afternoon and evening sickness. We arrived back in London, still in holiday mode, and had a day out at the historic Kew Gardens. I encouraged everyone to go on without me, though Shellie, watching me turn a paler shade of green, volunteered to join me on the park bench while as discreetly as a crowded Sunday afternoon in spring would allow,

I threw up into the adjoining potted palm. A subsequent visit to the doctor confirmed I was indeed up the duff again, and the future progeny was due on Syd's third birthday.

But there were shows to play, songs to road test and an album to record, plus a general need to make some money, that I was determined nausea would not derail. After a particularly high-energy performance at the Garage in Highbury, Willy had to pull the car into the kerb so I could heave. A constable, stopping to see if all was okay, saw me in my frock and lipstick and snarkily recommended I think about drinking more responsibly.

Meanwhile, we were making headway with our darkly layered, machine-like electronic album. We'd taken a convoluted route to reach this musical point but having begun we were thoroughly enjoying it. Our band at the time was made up of Martyn Swain of The Waterboys on bass, Roy Dodds from Fairground Attraction on drums, Fine Young Cannibal Andy Cox, who we recruited as our drum programmer, plus our very English producer Dave Anderson and engineer Jock Loveband.

We were all finding great joy in the refuge of the work. Studios are strange places, a kind of time machine, seeming to extend or shrink the fourth dimension, so that days could disappear as you microscopically home in on parts of a track until you hear what you want to hear. Satisfying and consuming to the exclusion of everything else happening outside the studio door, it's easy to work eleven hours without pausing.

We'd been in various studios for many weeks, tracking (recording the drums, bass and rhythm guitar) and overdubbing (recording keyboard parts, percussion, lead guitars and vocals), when we realised we were probably short a solid, commercially friendly track. We decided to record a version of Talking Heads' 'Psycho Killer'.

Syd used to dance around to it singing 'syko kia', so we thought we had the youth market covered. But apart from the vocal, what we recorded was so unrecognisable that when Mushroom Australia brought down the verdict that the song wasn't a single, we rethought it, wrote a new melody and lyric and repurposed the existing backing track into a completely new composition titled 'It's A Girl Thing', over which you could sing 'Psycho Killer' perfectly if you wanted to try.

In retrospect it was a frustrated, high-energy dummy spit, full of opaque innuendo and obscure imagery—*Ah fat boy, you're all gland, all gland, all gland, all gland / Ah, it's a girl thing*—but the song's heritage was entirely concealed and we got to hang on to the publishing.

We returned to Australia from the UK in the second half of 1997, bringing home the fruits of our two-year labours with our new album *My Third Husband*, ready to release. Bitter fruits they turned out to be. Triple J, our best hope, brought down their verdict quickly—too 'mature', which was a completely meaningless critique unless they were referring to my age. 'There are lots of immature tracks on *My Third Husband*!' I wanted to scream, as if that would have made the slightest difference. As they almost say in the classics, 'The bitch barks, but the caravan moves on'.

Possibly if I'd had a heroin habit I might have stayed on their radar for a couple more years. Suffice to say, not only did I *not* have one but my pregnant belly was out there and I looked altogether just too darned wholesome.

I'd experienced failure before but this was definitely my most significant and extended encounter. It shouldn't have been surprising, after all, we had unwittingly managed to confound everyone's expectations. I had left Australia as the good-natured girl on the golf course, with songs that people could effortlessly sing along to; they weren't challenging, they weren't difficult and now I had betrayed all that good faith in making an album that provoked hostility or, worse, disinterest.

I don't know that I recognised it at the time because the entire catastrophe of the English experiment had bounced me between debacle, negligence and malfunction for the best part of two years. It seemed like we had ploughed through a lot of money for no good reason other than to prove the adage that what doesn't kill you makes you stronger. I was the engineer of my own fall from grace. We'd made a dense, dark, difficult record, a reflection of the years of frustration, in which I stubbornly juggled motherhood, the creative impulse, lack of sleep and thwarted intentions.

Maybe it was an album ahead of its time—or, most likely, it just wasn't the album anyone wanted to hear from me. But we had turned a corner and there was no going back. I had bedded down a new way of looking at the world, no longer so careless, more cautious and with a background hum of imminent disruption. Some of it came from becoming a parent, gazing upon my newborn and being overwhelmed in equal parts by love and the dizzying sensation of staring into a bottomless well of potential calamity.

When we started touring in support of *My Third Husband*, I was moving into my third trimester. I designed a dress especially for the tour—full-length, red-sequinned, mandarin collared and short-sleeved with a gold mesh heart-shaped cut-out edged with rhinestones over my protruding belly. The effect of taking my guitar off was dramatic, equal parts Las Vegas glamour and high-camp hijinks humour.

That tour was hard, hot work; making sure there was a fan on me through the Queensland leg, and timing my throwing up between the end of the set and the encore, became second nature. The venues were packed, and the responses to the new album were antithetical to radio's disinterest. And, thankfully, I never passed out.

We played twice on 26 January, at the Williamstown Festival and at an Australia Day Celebration at the Treasury Gardens with Kutcha Edwards and Paul Hester. That night I had a long luxurious bath. Strangely, I appeared to have sucked up the water, because later that evening it started pouring back out of me. My baby had decided to come three weeks early. Alma delRay Zygier, born on 28 January, 1998, already a veteran of the road.

27

Something's Right

When I first became a mother, I started to understand my mother in a new way. When our second daughter Alma was born, I gained perspective on my relationship with my sister.

I was three and a half when Shellie Miriam Conway was born. I have no recollection of how I felt about that auspicious addition to our family unit. There is a story my mother thinks sheds light on my innermost feelings, though I believe operator error is where the spotlight should be directed.

Our parents liked to go for Sunday drives in our sky-blue Ford Falcon. On this particular late spring day, the Conway family was heading to St Kilda Beach to take advantage of the nice weather. The route took us up Toorak Road before my father made a brisk left turn onto St Kilda Road, perhaps a little too brisk. We had barely gone 90 metres south when my mother, feeling an odd breeze behind her, turned around to see the car door swinging open and Shellie, approximately twelve months old, sitting on her well-padded rear around twenty metres back in the middle of the service road.

I was apparently nonplussed at the sudden absence of my backseat companion. 'Nonplussed' can either mean 'so surprised and confused that one is unsure how to react, or the reverse'—*Oxford English Dictionary*. I think that sums it up really. I mean, 'Easy come easy go', or perhaps 'Gee, that doesn't seem right, I wonder if my parents meant that to happen by not shutting the door properly?' Who knows what was going through my young mind, but clearly I was processing before reacting. These were the days before compulsory baby seats or even seatbelts, and fortunately also the days when a Sunday drive to St Kilda Beach was undertaken with few other cars on the road. And so what should have been an uneventful day turned out to be anything but for my parents. I was exonerated—there was no way a four-year-old could have opened a heavy Ford Falcon door. My sister was more or less unscathed and we all have a good story to tell.

As we've got older we've begun to look more like sisters, but it wasn't always like that. I was an angular child with knock knees and scraggly, frizzy black hair that stuck out at all angles. When I was seven, my mother took me to the hairdresser and told them to give me a crew cut (she was hoping to thicken my hair up). I wept bitter tears through the entire procedure, which was repeated often enough that my hair became as thick and lustrous as fencing wire.

Shellie, on the other hand, was sweetly plump with enormous pale-blue eyes and literally perfect hair, long, blonde and wavy. She wore it in two pigtails high on either side of her head and every morning our mother would fix them into place. I would beg to be allowed to brush that luxuriant hair but was mostly denied.

My earliest memories of Shellie are fragmented. We're sitting at the kitchen counter eating dinner together, one of us spills the milk (almost always me) and Mum yells; we're playing some game and then we're fighting. I think she told on me a lot, and no doubt I told on her too. Shellie remembers my father smacking her because I'd complained to him that she was annoying me. He was making the point that we were both annoying him by smacking Shellie hard while asking me if I thought she should be smacked harder. Shellie says I was upset about this, proving I wasn't a terrible big sister.

We were co-conspirators when we stayed the night at either of our grandmothers' houses. We would retreat to the back spare bedroom—they both had one, and they both smelled of camphor—build cubby houses and sit inside playing games for hours. We would range from having each other's backs to being at each other's throats, but ultimately we were allies in a household where there was a lot of other fighting going on.

When I was ten and we moved house, Shellie and I shared a room and ricocheted between being best friends to driving each other spare. Around four years later, I guess when Liz and Carl couldn't stand us bickering anymore, we moved house again and got our own rooms. This was the start of me discovering boys and Shellie discovering horses, which maybe just meant she was getting in some practice first.

I was considered the rebel in our family, though that's an incorrect characterisation. I was conscientious as a child, my rebellion came much later: dropping out of uni, joining a rock band, buying my impractical car, and moving out of home as soon as I could. But behind that angelic face, Shellie was an early adopter of rebellion.

On school holidays our parents regularly sent us to Grantulla Country Club near Sherbrooke Forest, where city kids could walk through blackberry brambles, fall in mud puddles, ride ponies, feed ducks, fight battles with wooden swords, and on rainy days, form teams for talent shows or make films on Super 8 cameras. We had our own age-group cohort that we sat with for meals but through that first stay, I was suffering terribly from homesickness. Meanwhile, Shellie was scarfing down the bacon. I was sure my absence from home meant my parents might die without me, and breaking *kashrut* would just ensure their fate. Shellie was oblivious to their wellbeing, either far better adjusted or . . . 'This bacon is just too good.'

Once I'd left home and left Melbourne a year later, Shellie and I occupied very different spheres. I would come down from Sydney once in a while and give a pep talk about getting out from under the parental yoke, but Shellie was being bribed with a car if she enrolled in the ceramics course at Caulfield Tech straight out of school. There was a condition: if she dropped out they'd take the car back. She dropped out, and they sold the car to me, cheap.

At nineteen, Shellie, the quiet rebel, waited until Mum and Dad were overseas and moved in with her boyfriend John Archer and his bandmate Greg Perano, both members of Hunters & Collectors. Shellie was recruited to sing backing vocals on 'Say Goodbye', and lent her skinhead dance skills to the video for 'The Slab'. She was making money as a check-out chick, modelling and singing in jazz outfits, before she decided to go back to studying and enrolled in a printmaking course at the VCA. She parlayed that into a business, making stationery, sold her company to the highest bidder and then, decades later, went back to college to study interior design before establishing her second business.

In lots of ways our lives have mirrored one another; I left Melbourne when I turned twenty-one and came back at thirty-one, while Shellie moved to Sydney within three years of my return and has been there ever since. I met Willy in 1991, she met her husband in 1994, and our children were all born in the same five-year span.

We have been in a long-distance relationship for most of our adult lives. When we see each other we are frequently wearing versions of the same thing, bought at different stores in different cities. Her response to this is always warm and amused, mine usually slightly irritated. Some years ago I bought myself a wraparound dress in Sydney. She liked it a lot, so I was deliberately cagey about where I'd bought it. I know, petty! And then I found the frock in her wardrobe the following year. She'd actually hunted it down. Siblings are allies, but the other side has been that maybe, for as long as she's been alive, we've been competing for the same scarce resources. If I'm going to be brutally honest—and why wouldn't I be at this point?—then I could say we have been engaged in a many decades-long skirmish with extended peaceful truces. How do such different people work out the delicate balance of intimacy, interference, criticism, support, space and grace?

Shellie and I have very different approaches to life, that curiously have resulted in both of us indulging in a pattern of behaviour that is hard to understand. We seem to unconsciously assess the time we spend together and make sure to leave a percentage to allocate to a fight, and then allow a little more time to make up before we go our separate ways. The kind of relationship that can engender this behaviour is so deep, so elemental, it is really only found in siblings.

I'm not saying this is our plan exactly, but I've seen the pattern often, and once seen it is hard to unsee. I love my sister fiercely and if anyone wounds her I will always spring to her defence, but it doesn't mean that I can't be the one doing the wounding. It could happen if she was visiting me, if I was visiting her, if we were on holidays together . . . the pattern repeats again and again.

She had a worse deal than I did as the younger, softer sibling. Dad picked on her more than me, since I was harder to bully. Shellie was the silent victim of his terrible excesses. As an adult, she was given the task of checking Mum and Dad's post office box when they were travelling overseas. On one occasion, Liz was hospitalised for some minor ailment. She was discharged within thirty-six hours, but not before Carl had called Shellie and given vent to a full-blown panic attack over the phone.

'YOUR MOTHER'S IN HOSPITAL AND IF SHE DIES IT WILL BE YOUR FAULT!' And then he hung up, leaving Shellie frantically trying to a) track down her dying mother in an unnamed London hospital and b) figure out what the hell she'd done to put her there. When Liz was released, she contacted Shellie to let her know it had been nothing to worry about—which was a relief, but didn't undo thirty-six hours of rising panic. Carl had convinced himself Shellie was lying about the mail so, after days of inventing an imaginary problem, when Liz was stricken with something real he was happy to blame Shellie. No apology was ever forthcoming.

Our shared family experiences have guaranteed that we can fall back on each other's reserves when the other is going through difficulties; despite the geography, we are close. I've sung *Dumbo* songs with her during the protracted labour of her first child; we've holidayed with our children for a dozen summers; I've nursed her through panic attacks after the hellish breakdown of her marriage—they turned out to be episodes of vertigo but either way they were scary; we've post-mortemed the endless fights with our crazy father; we've cheered each other on through the worst times; she has forgiven me for my appalling mistreatment of her; and I've almost forgiven her (kidding).

Shellie is soft to my tough, messy to my neat, passive to my aggressive, dreamy to my direct. She avoids confrontation where I pursue it, and she is more forgiving than I am, except perhaps of me. We speak on the phone regularly, or daily if she is struggling with something. If she were asked to name my worst traits she would say I am judgemental, insensitive, impatient, thoughtless. If I were asked to name hers, I would say she's a needy, over-sensitive drama queen.

She has a better memory than me; she can be hilarious, and when she is in the right mood she cracks me up. We recently went on a horse-riding holiday together at her instigation. I was reluctant, having not ridden a horse for decades and not a lot back then, but she talked me into it and we had a brilliant time. We shared a tiny bedroom at night and by day we careened, slightly pissed, through wineries and forests, up green hills and down stony dales. And then, after getting on swimmingly for four days, we had our 'moment' in the car on the way home. I was fed up with her backseat driving.

Ah, the lifelong patterns of rivalrous siblings. Instead of being grumpy I could have reminded her of the dangers of being in a metaphorical backseat with me.

28

Exquisite Stereo

In 1998 I was still smarting—*My Third Husband* was too mature? Try this!

Exquisite Stereo was spectacularly immature, in the noble tradition of loud-soft bands like Nirvana, The Breeders or Sonic Youth, pure beautiful noise jammed through a continuous fuzz box of feedback. And that was just the bass.

We had mostly finished touring *My Third Husband*, parted ways with Mushroom Records and had a second baby all in quick succession. The baton was officially passed from Syd, now sleeping through the night, to Alma, who took on the awesome responsibility of sounding the night-time wake-up call every few hours. She was up to the task.

We had recovered our self-esteem sufficiently after the searing experience of those two years in London and the soul-searching since we'd returned. The muted response to *My Third Husband* definitely modified our own reflections about it. We decided, rightly or wrongly, that the album was overproduced, and that we had become disconnected from the raw material we'd started out with, taking good songs and layering them too richly. We'd been too clever, too modern, and had incorporated too many bells and whistles.

What we needed instead was the gritty, dirty sound of amplifiers, distortion pedals and drums, recorded with the sound of the room front and centre. We needed to rock out with a band, to collaborate with like-minded musicians; to rehearse our songs with them—not just make demos in a box, but give other musicians autonomy over their parts—and then road-test the material by playing it live before we set foot in another studio.

Before any of that could happen, we had to write the songs. I sat upstairs in our north-east-facing living room in Williamstown overlooking Port Phillip Bay, trying to shake off the milky-breast-fog and tap into inspiration. It shouldn't have been that hard. We were back in our lovely house, which was no worse for wear from having hosted any number of homeless wayfaring strangers through our two-year absence, but, though I was comfortingly back in the bosom of family and friends, song ideas were coming glacially or not at all. It's hard to remember much about this period I was so sleep-deprived, but when Mr Zygier came up with the phrase 'exquisite stereo' I jumped on it like a lifeline.

'Exquisite Stereo', *Exquisite Stereo*, 2000

Driving solo off a mountain in a rainstorm
Got your voice on my tape deck

I don't even remember what I did yesterday
Seems I've always been
All alone with you
I'm all alone with you
In exquisite stereo
Singing in the dark and in your heart, your head
I'm glistening, listening, whispering your sorrow

The words evoked my time living in Laurel Canyon in Los Angeles in 1992.

After I'd finished touring *String of Pearls*, I joined the troupe of Australian acts, under the auspices of 'The Wizards of Oz', who Mushroom Records sent to America to wow record executives, booking agents, publishers and managers with a series of concerts. Willy came with me. We all landed in Los Angeles a few days after the acquittal of the officers accused of brutally beating Rodney King and in the middle of the six-day-long riots that followed that extraordinary court decision. As the fires burned in downtown LA, you can imagine this was not the optimum time to be trying to score a record deal. The theatre was close to empty but for a few of our countrymen abroad.

After the concerts, Willy left LA to go travelling. My manager Amanda had rented a house in the Hollywood Hills, so I could write songs and 'take meetings' with LA musicians and she could explore if a North American release could be in the offing for me. The house, owned by Queen guitarist and astrophysicist Brian May, wasn't particularly remote but, due to the topography of the Hollywood Hills, it felt isolated. The local roads were heavily wooded and it wasn't unusual to see a coyote skulking on the verges. Alex McGregor was back in LA and while our relationship was over, we were still spending time together. It was confusing.

I had my car stereo permanently tuned to NPR (National Public Radio), a more eclectic music mix than you were likely to get on the more straight-ahead pop or rock stations (in fact, they had a daily radio show called *Morning Becomes Eclectic*, whose playlist was delightfully unpredictable). That entire period was suspended between languid and urgent, before children but after substantial career success, the feeling of abundant possibility, the unoccupied space between opening and closing doors, between the high road and low road, between yesterday and tomorrow, all felt infinite, like everything was moving in slow motion.

I was heading into town one night, maybe to eat Mexican food and drink margaritas with friends, and had just rounded the corner to drive down the mountainside on Laurel Canyon Boulevard when a soft rain started falling. Over the airwaves came an extended mix of 'Lullaby'. The delicate bell of a cymbal, *ticketty-tocketty, flicketty-flocketty*; the whispering unintelligible prayer-like voices; the bass and guitar, un-rushed, chocking away on a hypnotic mouse wheel of endless circular seduction; and, finally, like a regal empress entering with long velvet train, the melody that simultaneously coalesces everything you have already heard while effortlessly elevating itself to starring role.

The refrain went around for endless slow miles of winding wet road, my headlights catching the glistening trees on every curve, the wipers swiping intermittently, before Robert Smith started singing, 'Spiderman is having me for dinner tonight . . .' There was nothing else. Just the road, the ride, the rain, The Cure.

It was a perfect moment, the sweet-centred nucleus of that time capsule of magic I was in, a sugar hit that lasted until I turned on to the well-lit main drag heading toward West Hollywood.

All through those months I spent in Laurel Canyon, I was living in the perpetual moment, writing songs, ever hopeful for the North American record deal, which sadly never materialised, while indulging my petite trauma of decision-making, toying with the beguiling option of never having to choose. Fortunately for me—and the other parties involved—I instinctively understood that choosing not to choose is still an ineluctable choice. In the end I had chosen which door to exit and which to enter. I committed, which, as my old boyfriend used to say to me, is freedom. And it was. I chose Mr Zygier, I chose Melbourne, I chose children. Seven years later and enough water to fill Port Phillip Bay had gone under the bridge, but when Willy plucked the words 'exquisite stereo' out of the ether, it was all there, an entire album's worth of inspiration sprung whole from a phrase that called into the present that frozen-in-time, evocative, dreamlike drive. With few exceptions all the songs from *Exquisite Stereo* were touched by the ripples that emanated from that short commute.

We recruited a willing cadre of kindred collaborators: Cameron Reynolds on keys and through Cameron his friends, the rhythm section of Augie March, bass player Edmond Ammendola, and drummer Dave Williams, a generous player and a delightful man who would become an integral part of our recording and touring lives for decades to come. We called ourselves The City of Women. I booked some shows; the recording would begin after these road-testing gigs.

Sometime between the shows and recording, we were invited to our friends John and Lisa's house for a themed 'wig party'. On our way there we took a phone call telling us that a friend of Willy's eighteen-year-old niece Tully had, in a desperate state of mind, swallowed formaldehyde, then had a change of heart, rung her mother and told her she was sorry, she'd made a terrible choice. An ambulance was called but the damage was done and nothing could change the tragic outcome.

I managed to get myself as drunk as I had been since I was a teenager to forget what I could never unhear. It resulted in a dreadful hangover, which lingered to the point where I went to see my doctor—himself the host of the party—to check if it wasn't something else that was up with me. He had first-hand knowledge of my party-girl peccadillos, but when I described my symptoms—nausea, over-sensitivity to smell, dizziness—he gave me a pregnancy test. I told him it would have to have been an immaculate conception; but the dipstick told a different story.

The one occasion we'd had the bed to ourselves without nocturnal visitors had slipped my mind, as had many things. And (don't laugh) the withdrawal method had let us down. I took home my pink urine-soaked positive confirmation and presented it to Mr Zygier, who promptly fell to the floor in a perfect James Brown routine.

I was disgracefully nauseous throughout the tracking. In fact I developed the same Pavlov's dog response to our engineer that I'd had to everything Thai through pregnancy one and the songs we were composing through pregnancy two. Every time the poor fellow turned up at our door for a day of recording, I had to excuse myself and run to the bathroom.

Exquisite Stereo was released in 2000; independently produced, and licensed to Shock Records. Hettie Ira Zygier was released two days before the start of the new millennium. We were the parents of three little girls. All good choices, even the one we didn't technically make.

29

Interzone

'Interzone', *Exquisite Stereo*, 2000

Interzone
On my own
See the phonies
Competing
Completely, they don't know
What I know
The last train home's
Just gone
Interzone
All alone
And the droning I'm hearing
Is the ceiling caving in
Still we cling to this skin

That's gone
Everyone's a star
We belong there
Drive me in your car
To interzone
It's pounding through silence
It frightens animals
But all the fools
Rush in
I don't scream anymore
What for, they're so sure
Interzone
Interzone
I am yours

We loved Radiohead. So much of what they did felt like an invitation into a labyrinth of human pain but distilled something useful and beautiful for the listener. They were dark but not for the sake of darkness, more in keeping with the task of exploration undertaken in less light. Radiohead created a language that lived in the resonance between melody, chords and lyrics. Radiohead were architects of mood. They erected skyscrapers, cities; they were masters of ambient construction, and there was always mystery within their creations; they didn't table-thump a message but rather devotionally designed a seductive landscape for self-discovery.

We were writing *Exquisite Stereo* while listening to Radiohead, engaging in that conversational exchange that musicians and songwriters across all genres work within to build on what has gone before—and maybe, provide something for those who come after.

Musical quotation has always been in style. Careful detective work from musicologist David Buch, using primary sources, reveals that Mozart's *The Magic Flute* owes a lot to *The Beneficent Dervish*, an opera composed by musicians in Mozart's circle and performed (very likely with Mozart in the audience) before *The Magic Flute* was written. Mozart wasn't the only one. Berlioz, Beethoven, Richard Strauss and Shostakovich all did it, the last in blatant fashion, with his use of 'We Wish You a Merry Christmas' in his 'Prelude No. 15 in D Flat Major, Op. 87'.

No one was contemplating court battles for copyright back then. Nor had they been considered in the early days of folk, blues, jazz and the beginning of rock 'n' roll; it would have instigated chaos if everyone had started taking each other to court and accusing each other of using the same melody and/or chord progression every time a familiar musical phrase came up.

But pop music is different, primarily because there is so much money involved and too many people who bring an adversarial approach to a dispute that needs more nuance and longsightedness. George Harrison wrote 'My Sweet Lord' and ended up in 'one of the longest running legal battles ever to be litigated in [the United States]'[1] when, in February 1971, Bright Tunes, the publishers of Ronnie Mack's song, 'He's So Fine', a hit for The Chiffons in 1963, sued for breach of copyright.

The court case concluded in March 1998 with the (some have said generous) verdict that Harrison had subconsciously plagiarised 'He's So Fine'. Cases like these have a chilling effect on the free exchange and influence of musical inspiration. Harrison declared he was too 'paranoid' to write anything new for a while afterwards, and no doubt he wasn't the only musician/songwriter looking over their back catalogue or nervously checking that their current project was free from references.

In Australia, we had our own contentious ruling: the litigation brought against EMI and Men At Work for retaining 100 per cent of royalties in the case of the song 'Down Under' after Greg Ham 'stole' his flute riff from the melody of Marion Sinclair's 1932 song, 'Kookaburra Sits in the Old Gum Tree'. The financial gain from a successfully litigated case would be very lucrative for Larrikin Records, who had purchased the copyright from the deceased composer's estate in 1990 for $6100 and were now claiming 60 per cent of the songwriting royalties from 'Down Under', a song that had been a hit around the world and had sold copies in the tens of millions, for a musical quote lasting just a few seconds.

It's not hard to understand why Larrikin sued—nothing personal, just good business—but I, along with many of my musical contemporaries, thought it was an appalling and extraordinary court judgement in favour of Larrikin, twice, the second time on appeal. The payout was substantially less than Larrikin's original (I would say ambit) claim but they got 5 per cent of the royalties generated since 2002. Small comfort might be taken in Larrikin probably having spent most of it on lawyers' fees and court costs.

A much higher price was exacted from every improviser/musician/arranger/composer/songwriter who quotes an existing work in their recording. In the case of 'Kookaburra' and 'Down Under', the entire episode would have likely been avoided if a television music trivia show hadn't asked its competing players to figure out which song 'Down Under' quoted. There were still *oohs* and *aahs* from the panellists, who like nearly everyone had missed the reference over years of listening to the song.

Clearly this was also a lightbulb moment for the new owners of the 'Kookaburra' copyright. Ham's playful quote was so integrated as to be seamless, and was harmonically recast within the context of his performance. But his flourish was not part of Down Under's composition, rather a comment on it, full of creative wit. Since that landmark case the publishing wolves have been listening more carefully and thinking about the treasure that might be generated from what was once considered a respectfully beautiful, ironic or humorous quote but is now a potentially expensive misstep.

It was another depressing decision in this delicate ecosystem; it suggested that what constitutes creativity in a fluid moment might be deemed by bad actors as theft, and an attempt to line their pockets at another creator's expense. But to me, it doesn't work that way. Music isn't a zero-sum game, but an expanding space of limitless invention that benefits all.

Because music happens in time rather than space, songwriters do engage in an intimate musical dialogue with composers dead or alive. Fleeting alchemy happens all the time. Think of Dylan paying homage to the catalogue of field holler recordings in his early songs; Paul Kelly and Kev Carmody's 'From Little Things Big Things Grow' and its similarity to Dylan's own 'The Lonesome Death of Hattie Carrol'; The Beach Boys' 'Surfin' USA', a rewrite of Chuck Berry's 'Sweet Little Sixteen' and, staying with Berry, his 1959 rocker 'Little Queenie' was a straight rip of his own 1958 classic 'Johnny B Goode'.

While Woody Guthrie's estate gave permission for his unreleased lyrics to have new life breathed into them by Billy Bragg and Wilco on their collaboration, *Mermaid Avenue*, and Natalie Cole's duets with her father Nat King Cole recorded across time are considered kosher, there is a world of territorial dispute lurking with ever greater frequency.

The Verve's 'Bittersweet Symphony' was written over Andrew Oldham's instrumental arrangement of The Rolling Stones classic 'The Last Time'. In 1997, The Stones successfully sued to the point where 100 per cent of royalties were handed over to Jagger/Richards and Oldham. The issue was recently resolved after a change of heart, with Jagger and Richards handing The Verve back the copyright.

But record labels aren't always so easy to forgive. Scratch the surface of the relaxed world of musicians on their creative pathways and you'll find a veritable game of snakes and ladders where the snakes are poisonous and the ladders precarious. Publishers, record companies, managers and not infrequently the composers are busy queuing up to take someone to court or fending off their own legal stoush. The list is horrifying, and as I started exploring I felt like a proverbial abyss had opened. Labels can be especially unforgiving when musical quotation tips into plagiarism; a distinction without a clear fine line. I vividly remember Huey Lewis and The News challenging Ray Parker Junior on what was clearly a rip-off of their song 'I Wanna New Drug' for *Ghostbusters* because I was singing along to both songs at the time.

Perhaps most blatant of all, Led Zeppelin, who had been accused (though later exonerated) of ripping the riff of 'Stairway To Heaven' from a song one of their support acts performed, were clearly executing a wholesale appropriation of Willie Dixon's 'You Need Love' for their massive hit 'Whole Lotta Love'. It is virtually the same song, borrowing heavily from the lyric as well as the melody, chords and mood, though Jimmy Page's uber-recognisable guitar riff, which forms the rock-hard backbone of the song, is entirely his own—unless you're inclined to believe his claims that the devil had a co-write. The rip is so blatant that regardless of the fact it didn't end up in court, Willie Dixon got a co-writing credit on later pressings of the song.

I could go on for chapters; there are innumerable examples of inadvertent or deliberate collaboration, borrowing or plagiarism, and whether the outcomes are to your personal taste or not, a broader view suggests there are no losers in any of these musical transactions, though the legal system will tell a different story. Music is the richer for this exchange of influences, even if the poor fucker being sued or ripped off is not.

How often does a song remind you of something else? Some of the best ones do, but you can't necessarily put a name to the original song. In the world of pop music, notes, chords and melodies are relatively limited and unwitting plagiarism is bound to occur. Plagiarism can be a compliment, a hat tip to the originator, as long as they see it that way too. Most often, there's not enough money in it to bother with.

So there we were at the bottom of the world, writing our end-of-a-millennium opus and 'Interzone' plops into being. The title came from a William Burroughs collection of short stories, the language from a science fiction gaming parlour, the intensity of lying underneath a flight path too long, the sentiment somewhere between sneering and terror. Our musical inspiration was Radiohead's 'Exit Music (For a Film)' from their album *OK Computer* but the inspiration is evocative rather than tangible.

Sometime after that, we were listening to a recording called *Great Jewish Music: Serge Gainsbourg*, executive-produced by John

Zorn and released on his label Tzadik. The last track is a contribution from New York guitarist Marc Ribot called 'Black Trombone'. It is weird. It is 'Interzone'. Neither of us recall (consciously) hearing this album (or the Gainsbourg original) until after *Exquisite Stereo* was in the public domain—the resemblance is just beautiful random serendipity.

And there you are: it happens. Luckily, we never made any money out of 'Interzone', otherwise Serge Gainsbourg's publishers might be coming for us.

30

Radio Loves This

'Radio Loves This', the first and only single we released from *Exquisite Stereo*, was our cynical dig at radio's recent clear lack of interest in our recorded output. I thought if they were receptive to a little psychology they may respond to the title. Perhaps I should have tried the reverse psychology option and gone with 'Radio Hates This', though doubtless it would have ended the same way: *bupkis*. It wasn't subtle but at least we tried.

I am dreadfully ashamed to admit—and discourage anyone else trying the same insanity—that we even tried to buy ourselves into the charts. We gave members of our family strict instructions to purchase the single in the chart stores in multiples, though not in the same purchase, which would boost us onto the ARIA charts. My father took his task very seriously, managing to clear the shelves of all copies. The stores kept ordering it, Dad kept buying them up, and no one significant seemed to suspect our terrible underhand scheme (though I can imagine a few sales assistants' eyebrows may have been raised; my dad was a lot of things but clandestine wasn't one of them).

But we didn't make a dint. The song peaked briefly in the seventies and immediately plummeted. Somewhere in storage, we still have a box or two (or three) of those damn CD singles, probably with the price sticker still affixed. I hang my head more from stupidity than shame.

'Radio Loves This', *Exquisite Stereo*, 2000

Radio likes this
Radio, oh
Radio loves this
Radio
I cry myself to sleep
Listening to you
You tell me what to dream
And I keep tuned
Radio likes this
Radio, oh
Radio loves this
Radio
It's nothing I could see
Reaching for my soul
A universe of sound
Ten billion stereos
Radio likes this

Radio, oh
Radio loves this
Radio
A quiet little life
Babbling, sighing
Static like a knife
But nothing's as loud as your crying
Radio likes this
Radio, oh
Radio loves this
Radio
Turn me on you turn me on you turn me on

Despite *Exquisite Stereo* being released through a distribution deal with Shock Records, the king of Mushroom's art department and our long-term collaborator, Pierre Baroni, shot the cover for the album. I was pregnant, suffering from morning sickness and a cold, and probably whingeing; he was unsympathetic, which was fair enough; one of us needed to be on the job. His use of his dry self-deprecating humour was a pretty good tactic for getting his subjects into line; he made me—forty-year-old mother of two-and-a-half babies—look like a movie star, with the cover a stark, glamorous sales pitch.

My collaboration with Pierre lasted longer than my relationship with Mushroom. He was an interesting mixture, wavering from enthusiastic and chatty to grumpy and curt, and what set him off on the grumpiness trajectory was unpredictable. It wasn't that Pierre was scary—it was more that you wanted him to be happy because he was delightful when he was. I worked very hard to make him happy, though there were occasions when I would just give up and work with whatever he was putting out.

A small and perfectly-formed man with an enviable aesthetic both in his work and his personal style, Pierre was reminiscent of an English mod. With heavy black-rimmed glasses and severe haircut, he was a self-contained fellow who lived with his devoted white English bulldog Toby and giant carp that swam laps in a fishpond that stretched the length of his Richmond terrace. I was over there for a photoshoot the day Pierre returned from an overseas job.

Whoever had been looking after the fish in his absence had erred: too cold, too hot, overfed, underfed, the consequence was a lot of dead carp. Pierre was inconsolable, yet he still wanted to work. Appropriately we took press shots for 'Only the Bones' that day, me wearing his long-sleeved black T-shirt printed with an X-ray skeleton.

When I signed with Mushroom in 1991, Pierre put together the multi-foldout package that housed *String of Pearls*. Polly Borland took the cover shot but Pierre photographed the pearls lying against various backgrounds that circled the centrefold. It was a sumptuous cover, both understated and eye-catching, his signature look.

The front cover of *Bitch Epic* started life in a Sydney studio as a promotional shoot for an ABC series called *The Seven Deadly Sins*. I'd sung on the soundtrack and appeared in one of the seven elliptical interpretations of the sins. On that hot December morning, which also happened to be Willy's birthday, I was asked to strip to the waist, get covered in Nutella, heft a large salver of cream cakes to my mouth and try and shovel a few in while looking at the camera. Call me Gluttony. I got one of the assistants to take a few happy snaps for me and sent them around as Xmas cards. One went to Pierre.

A few months later, when he heard what we were going to call the record, he pulled out my homemade postcard and 'snap'. He requested—and was given—the photos from that shoot which had served their purpose for the *Marie Claire* article they were illustrating and got to work. The result won the 1994 ARIA Award for Best Cover Art and I got the pleasure of seeing this extremely confronting image on massive billboards all over town.

The cover of the live recording of Epic Theatre featured me dressed in a gladiator's costume, smeared in fake blood and holding aloft a latex severed head that bore a vague resemblance to Gudinski. Pierre managed to shoot a roll of film just before we were chased off the grounds of Melbourne's Shrine of Remembrance, our stand-in for Ancient Rome. We later felt bad about the irreverence of using the Shrine and digitally erased it.

Polly Borland took the photo for *My Third Husband* in London. Pierre put the artwork together during a grumpy phase. Maybe he didn't like Polly's picture, or he hated the songs, or maybe he was fed up working for a record label. He never said what was bugging him but when the artwork came back he'd put the lyrics in a tiny red font on a black background, close to unreadable. I'm sure I asked why and he snorted and I didn't ask again.

I only just recently noticed—I don't know why it took me so long—but Pierre's credit reads 'sleeve labour'. I really laughed but sadly I couldn't call him to share my mirth because he passed away on 9 March, 2021, at the age of sixty-six.

More than twenty years earlier, Pierre had shot the film clip for 'Radio Loves This' in the old RRR building in Fitzroy and in the parking lot behind Coles in Chapel Street, Prahran. I play a bored DJ behind the studio microphone in my faux fur, performing for a cast of our band, friends and family who were sitting behind the wheels of various cars singing along with their car stereos.

I've no idea how many times the film clip was broadcast—not much at a guess—but it is unbearably adorable to see Willy's parent's and my father, who, like the locations, are no longer with us, getting into the spirit of their performances, dancing in their seats and playing drums on the steering wheel. As lovely as it was, the clip for 'Radio Loves This' made not a jot of difference to the song's impact on radio play. Clearly, I was going to have to think of a plan B.

My career was changing, in some subtle way, from successful to unsuccessful; from being part of the machine to becoming independent; and most confronting for me, from being loved to becoming unloved. That last one was about to inflict a profound and wounding scar on my psyche.

31

White Roses

The voice on the radio was so familiar. I was listening to 3RRR spruik their wares to get people signed up as subscribers when I heard it. It took me a second to place because of the context, then the switch flicked. *Dorland!*

It was a Saturday afternoon in the winter of 2003. I phoned the radio station to see if I could speak to him.

For eight years Dorland and I shared. We shared stages, dressing rooms, backstage catering (the rider), hotel rooms, living quarters, rehearsal rooms, recording studios, television studios, cars, planes, cigarettes, food, booze, ideas, songs, notebooks, gossip, running jokes, laughs, our bodily functions, memes (before we knew what memes were), friends, enemies, managers, record companies, credits, accolades and anguish.

From Hamburg to Hobart, Amsterdam to Adelaide, Putnam to Perth, we spent most of our time hanging out, like an old married couple without the sex. He'd hide my phone from me when I got pissed and try to rack up expensive long-distance calls; he knew how I liked my bacon and eggs; I could sleep though his early-morning bouts of songwriting inspiration into a Walkman; and his snoring; it didn't even bother me when during one particularly hellish tour in WA, staying at the infamous Charles Hotel in North Perth, Dorland would lie on his bed nursing his second bottle of port and fall asleep with his eyes open.

The Charles was hideous. Its communal bathrooms had mouldy tiles falling off the walls, and the only phone in the hotel was located in the bar under a poster of an ample-breasted nymph who'd forgotten to put all her clothes on. I could track the half-closed eyes of the barflies drifting between the poster and me whenever I had to make a call. It was 1984 and somewhere in the world the Olympics were on. We would go to sleep every night watching the swimmers, gymnasts, runners or cyclists. Actually, it was hard to tell if Dorland was asleep since his eyes remained open, unnerving but bonding.

After my Virgin UK deal imploded in 1990, and I came back to Australia with a swag of songs, it had been Dorland I'd gone to first. Despite all we'd been through, we sat round the dining table with my guitar in the Gotham City flat I'd once shared with Jackie and where he now lived. His response was thrilling for me, an endorsement from my mentor that I had come of age.

I toured *String of Pearls* for close to a year. Dorland was supportive, and excited for the success of the album he'd had a big hand in forming. And at the end of 1992, while I was living in Sydney, performing in Aristophanes' *Frogs* and writing during the day, Dorland came over and we wrote a song, though it didn't make the album.

He and Jackie were now married and living in the northern suburbs of Sydney, but something was eating him. When *Bitch Epic* came out in 1993, Dorland told me the cover looked like dog shit. Okay, I thought, that's a strong reaction. Once I was living in London with a new baby, it was even harder to read the signals. I just didn't get it until the poison had festered too long.

Dorland was furious with me. I don't really know why. He told a journalist later that it was because I took every opportunity I could to badmouth Do-Ré-Mi publicly, but that wasn't true and he had no evidence for the claim. Any concerns I had about the band I kept between me and my diary. I think he felt like I'd discarded him. Maybe there was an element of the student wishing to separate from the teacher, and our geographic distance made it easy for me not to confront the shift.

We exchanged letters until the end of 1996 when Dorland had an affair with a woman from his past, who he met again when he was accompanying Jackie on a work trip to Auckland. He made the momentous decision to leave Jackie and pursue his unfinished affair of the heart. I wrote to them both expressing my love and support. It was a tough time.

A few years later, Dorland called me from New Zealand. He told me a sorry tale, that the woman he'd left his wife for, a woman he'd been in love with as a younger man, who had three children by three different fathers, had recently called an end to their relationship. Perhaps it had run out of steam, perhaps Dorland had not met her expectations, but he told me the souring had coincidentally happened around the same time his mother's inheritance had run out. Not content with evicting him from the house they shared, he told me she'd also told him he could no longer have a relationship with any of the children including the boy he had raised from infancy.

It was a very distressing conversation and I had nothing but sympathy for him, which perhaps he found emasculating. We talked for a long time but I don't believe he got off the phone any happier than he had been before he unburdened himself.

Back to 2003. After several hours of hearing nothing, I called the radio station again and managed to get on to Dorland. I tried to arrange to see him but he said, 'I'm not here for long and I've only got time to see my real friends.' The words cut sharp and hard and I understood for the first time the depth of his resentment. Dorland and I haven't spoken to each other since. There was a reformation of Do-Ré-Mi in 2019, but neither Dorland nor Stephen would participate, despite Helen's and my sincerest hopes that they would.

'White Roses', *String of Pearls*, 1991

You weren't the first to send me red roses
And you weren't the first to give me away
I'm not the only one to have my fingers burned
But that was a one-way conversation and you got the final
word

Forget-me-nots forgotten
White roses
Regrets and promises collide
I'm still flying the flag for you
A blue heart, red eyes and white roses

It's true
Lovers swap red roses but white ones from you
Spell the end of everything fine
Yellow roses are for jealousy but you
Don't send me them
You send the ones that say we're through

Forget-me-nots forgotten
White roses
Regrets and promises collide
I'm still flying the flag for you
A blue heart, red eyes and white roses

You weren't to know that something was making me blue
Keeping all the sunshine away
You said forever and I took you at your word
White roses make a lie of everything I've heard

Forget-me-nots forgotten
White roses
Regrets and promises collide
I'm still flying the flag for you
A blue heart, red eyes and white roses

32

Here and Now

In 2003 we were writing a new album and moving house from Williamstown to Melbourne's inner city.

It was a big year. We had gradually been moving away from record companies and getting accustomed to the parallel universe of independence. We weren't the only ones. The previous year independent Jarrah Records was established in Perth representing a gang of musicians who were fed up with being exploited by record companies and their profit gouging. Despite my trepidation, it was time to take the plunge.

Our new album, *Summertown*, would be entirely funded by us—recording, manufacture and promotion. We would seek a 'distribution only' deal with MGM Records to get the album into shops.

I knew a reasonable amount about making records, though I felt a precipitous drop into an alternate reality when I discovered how little it cost to manufacture a CD. Depending on how many you made, it was somewhere between $1.14 and $2.70 per unit, including the booklet. This was one of those well-guarded secrets that record companies hate to divulge, no doubt because we had paid the record company between $15 and $17 each to buy our CDs wholesale to sell at shows.

Beyond manufacturing costs, I was well versed in all facets of making and releasing an album, bar one: I didn't have a good grasp of marketing, or how it was different from publicity. I had a nebulous idea that marketing was the promotion you paid for and publicity was the promotion you paid your publicist to arrange, but when I started really thinking about it, it seemed to me that marketing was the least-examined area in the operational chain and could do with some serious thought. Aside from spending money on poster runs and advertising, taking a song to radio and mounting a tour, there didn't seem to be a lot else going on.

Stylistically, *Summertown* was a very different-sounding album to all our previous collaborations. *Bitch Epic* was musically complex with its odd time signatures and layered sounds; *Ultrasound* was experimental; *My Third Husband* was electronic and depressing; and *Exquisite Stereo* was punk, loud and pissed off. I made an off-hand comment one day to Willy: 'Why don't we write more cheerful songs?' His response shocked me: 'I never realised you wanted to'.

The players on *Summertown* were Dave Williams on drums, Shannon Birchall on double bass, James Black on keys, Michael Barker on percussion, and Gerry Hale who is credited with no less than eight different stringed instruments, the force of which became the primary sound of the recording. Barker quipped at one point that the album would be right at home on the sound track of *A Mighty Wind*, a biting Christopher Guest satire on the folk scene. Only half of me laughed.

Regardless, we were committed; and despite our previous restless sonic explorations, we have remained true to the acoustic aesthetic ever since.

We were grateful for the scattered plays we got on community broadcasters, but the record wasn't going to reach enough ears based on that alone. Triple J was a youth station, so with us having hit our forties Triple J was out of the question. Commercial radio stations like Fox FM, MMM and Nova were not playing anything that sounded even vaguely like the record we'd made.

I was thinking about it obsessively, like a puzzle I had to solve—how to get the attention of the media and an audience for an album that radio wouldn't play.

I turned it over and over in my brain as the hot water streamed over me—I do some of my best thinking in the shower—convinced I could find a solution, when suddenly a different question presented itself. How do you get into people's living rooms other than via radio? Answer: walk in.

It was a lightning-strike epiphany. The Tupperware model! In the internet, we had the organisational means to take this idea to the people; we had the product, a new album which we owned outright; we had the skills to perform entirely acoustically in someone's lounge room as two singers and guitarists; and we had material perfectly suited to the mode. The promise of the power of the internet to change everything had come to pass.

I rinsed off the soap and leapt out of the cubicle like I'd been sharing it with a hairy huntsman, grabbed a towel and ran into the bedroom to tell Mr Zygier my idea. Neither of us could figure out what was wrong with it—like, why hadn't anyone else thought of this?

I knew of no one else doing anything like it. We would marry new connectivity technologies to traditional round-the-campfire minstrelsy, and conjure a completely fresh marketing strategy. We kicked it around for a while and decided that we would promote the Summerware Party (made up of the album name *Summertown* and the much-loved plastic food storage containers Tupperware) via our web page deborahconway.com. Anyone in Melbourne could book a Summerware Party by pre-purchasing twenty-five copies of our album (if you lived further afield, we would be able to do it for you when we were next in the area).

Using email we would work out a location, date and time when Mr Zygier and I would roll up to these perfect strangers' homes, offices, sheds or houseboats, pull out our guitars, sit in a corner and perform four songs for them and their gathered guests. We had some rules: we had to be paid before the party was officially booked; we never played encores (twenty minutes felt like enough time to ask people to be quiet); we wouldn't overstay our welcome or drink our host's booze. We used a publicist to promote the concept through regular media channels and it became a barnstorming hit with every major media outlet.

After the album came out, we booked multiple back-to-back Summerware Parties around the tours we were already doing in Melbourne, Sydney, Adelaide, Perth and Brisbane and regionally in Victoria, New South Wales, Western Australia, Queensland and Tasmania. The first time we organised the parties through towns in regional New South Wales we had Channels 7, 9, 10 and the ABC plus the Fairfax and News Ltd papers following our Summerware Party caravan.

It was the novelty of having a well-known musician in your personal space that made the idea an unqualified success. As a marketing tool and a way of attracting media attention it was a hit, but more than that, it was an incredible way to connect with people, to play music without the barrier of microphones and amplifiers.

What we came to realise is that you only needed one motivated can-do character to get excited about the opportunity, and they would bring the rest.

'Deborah who?' 'Is she still a musician?' 'I used to like "Man Overboard" but that was decades ago ...' Regardless of their enthusiasm for yours truly, they would all come along because their dear friend had asked them to celebrate whatever event it might be, with us as the special treat. It transformed the CDs we would sign for people at the end of the performance from a bit of coded plastic to a memento of the time they had spent in good company listening to music being played live. The intimacy of those gigs was very powerful.

We won a swag of new fans, and suddenly the Summerware Party was so much more than a novel way of getting some publicity. It was how we were selling our album. We still weren't being played on radio, but we were walking into hundreds of living rooms and playing to thousands of music lovers.

The set list exclusively featured the songs from *Summertown*. They all lent themselves beautifully to the acoustic duet format. We'd written them that way.

All, that is, except 'Here and Now', the last song on the album. I wrote the words after the photographer Rennie Ellis died.

At eighteen, just starting out as a model, I posed for Rennie, the brilliant, anarchic '70s and '80s documenter of Australia's countercultural life for whom I was happy to take my top off. He was a generous artistic soul with an adventurer's taste for danger, happy to venture into those off-off-off-Broadway places where beauty and ugliness live harmoniously together. He brought back the striking eyewitness photographic evidence.

It was an awful blow to hear of his early passing in 2003 at the age of sixty-two. I went to his funeral at the Prahran Town Hall, a hop, skip and half a jump from his studio where we'd worked together all those decades before. When I got back home I wrote the lyric to a piece of music Willy had been playing around with, a paean to living fully in the moment of which Rennie was such a consummate exemplar.

On the album, the recording of 'Here and Now' finishes with a string extravaganza of cittern, mandolin and charango, all played by Gerry Hale. Underneath the sound wall of stringed instruments is a barely audible four-part vocal chant.

The stringed instrument blockbuster finale wasn't something we could easily recreate live, particularly with only the two of us, so the vocal chant replaced it, an emotionally rousing way to not just finish the song but also the set. After we had figured out the surprise a cappella exit, often accompanied by foot stomping, 'Here and Now' became the song we almost always concluded our Summerware Parties with.

'Here and Now', *Summertown*, 2004

I don't have a single question
I met a man who opened up his arms
And everything's been heading skywards

Every switch switched on in every home
In every home

Here we are and now's the time
I am yours and you are mine
Forever here and now
Climb aboard, we'll sail away
And every moment of every day
Is always here and now

Every outline every detail
Gold and diamonds are shining in their eyes
Like every flower in every garden
Has opened up and pointed at the sky
Makes me feel so high

Here we are and now's the time
I am yours and you are mine
Forever here and now
Climb aboard, we'll sail away
And every moment of every day
Is always here and now
And now . . .
They say that today is still the first day of the rest of your life

Fifteen billion years of stardust
Or Genesis
Whatever turns you on
Maybe Baby Jesus saves us

Or nothingness is
Holding out its arms
Its open arms

Here we are and now's the time
I am yours and you are mine
Forever here and now
Climb aboard, we'll sail away
And every moment of every day
Is always here and now
It's always here and now

The project did have a slightly rocky start. The first Summerware Party we played, in winter 2004, was organised through our daughter's school as a parent get-together. I remember a lot of raucous thirtysomethings crammed into the open-plan living area with a lot of alcohol, and three or four Year 12 girls neatly attired in school uniform, all of whom were clocking in around six foot tall, handing around the hors d'oeuvres. I was amazed. (Now, I too, am the mother of giants.) I can't remember anything of the performance except a lot of very, very happy people, though that probably had nothing to do with us.

The next Summerware Party listed in my diary is a month later, on 15 July, at a St Kilda bar decorated in grey tones and lots of chrome, glass and tile—modern design that provides appalling acoustics when the place is full, and echoing coldness when it's not. There were very few people in attendance. We were told to set up on a round banquette that acted as a kind of stage and to begin as soon as we were ready.

The staff walked around the small cluster of attendees with hot and cold canapés and small serviettes; we were there to be ignored, background music only, no one could hear us sing, chat, howl, scream, or any other peep we made.

Nor did they care. Perched above the room, I felt like a twerp. I attempted to divert some focus towards us, to hush the uninterested groups with their backs turned and their eyes darting around to spot the next tidbit on a silver salver, but it was wasted breath. We finished up, announced that anyone interested could have their CD signed by us and, when no one approached or even noticed we'd finished (or perhaps started), we packed our guitars, left the CDs in a pile on the banquette and slunk out like a bad smell, disappearing out to Inkerman Road to mingle with the early evening traffic. It was a thoroughly humiliating encounter, a shit sandwich with a steaming side of indifference.

I learnt a lot from that second party. When and how to take command; how to circumvent the apathy and flip it; how to grab the party guests by the metaphorical throat and ensure they would pay attention. That was the first and last corporate booking I took for a Summerware Party; the two concepts are a match made in hell. It is remarkable that of all the hundreds of parties we played, the worst was the second one; I was lucky I'd been given a valuable lesson at a time when I could make the most use of it.

The third Summerware party, a birthday celebration in Melbourne, was booked for two days later. All correspondence had been conducted via email, the payment had been deposited and we were standing outside the apartment about to knock when we realised that we had no idea whether we were playing at a twenty-first, thirtieth, fiftieth or eightieth birthday party. It was a little bit of modern magic that we could conjure an intimate event with an unknown host, an unknown amount of people, in an unknown location, having spoken to no one until this moment.

What on earth would be behind the door? We were in the dimly lit hallway of a 1930s building and were exactly on time. I knocked. The heavy wooden door swung open and a beaming young woman stood there welcoming us into her crowded candlelit lounge room where twenty friends had gathered to help her celebrate her twenty-eighth birthday.

Lounging in beanbags and a comfy worn sofa surrounding a coffee table laden with party snacks and drinks, they gave us a stupendous round of applause just for turning up. Of course, this was an investment of trust from both sides; we were all proceeding into unknown lands and every component that worked was worth celebrating.

This was the blueprint I had imagined: no barriers between audience, performers and music. We took it, we ran with it and not only made a lot of music-lovers happy but spawned a new fashion in home concerts. The Brisbane festival scheduled home concerts; companies like Parlour promoted themselves as 'a web platform devoted to house concerts' and acted as a conduit between artists and hosts. They all owed a little something of their existence to the pioneering Summerware Party home concert.

Summerware Party bookings were trickling, and then flowing in. We played at a roundtable for the big swinging end of town at the behest of a friend who owned a marketing firm that boasted groundbreaking innovation as its core principle. The ten heavy hitters in attendance listened to us with rapt attention, no doubt grateful for a break from the endless talkfest. We played for gatherings of teachers in the classroom at the end of their busy week; we played for office workers in their canteens; we played political fundraisers; we played back-to-back shows in regional New South Wales over a weekend, mostly outdoors on verandahs or under shade trees with the smell of a barbecue redolent in the air.

We played in a Victorian town called Yaapeet, population sixty-four, on their tennis court, and pretty much every person in the town was there. We left them with thirty-two CDs and joked that their dinner parties would all have the same soundtrack.

We played for religious congregants, for members of our fan club 'The Bitch Listers', for weddings and renewals of wedding vows, for anniversaries, for disputations of lawyers, for youth groups, for end-of-year neighbourhood get-togethers. We were Christmas presents, birthday presents and New Year presents; we played in the suburbs, in the city, under flight paths, in the outback. In short we played everywhere and we were at every imaginable excuse for people to congregate and share music. How spectacular!

We flew to Adelaide for a weekend and managed to fit eleven Summerware Parties into a three-day blur. I remember big backyards, lots of friendly people enjoying an Adelaide spring day, glasses of bubbles or Barossa shiraz and plenty to eat. But the last one that weekend was a standout.

We had found our way into the Adelaide Hills with the help of our trusty *Gregory's Street Directory*. The sun had finally set in a blaze of orange and scarlet and the twinkling lights of Adelaide far below were starting to flicker on, making very pretty pictures as we wound our way up the narrowing roads to our destination.

The house was a low-slung California bungalow perched high on the side of a hill, approached by a gangway between the pavement and the house. We had been booked to play a fortieth birthday party and, at the appointed hour of 9.30 pm, we rang the bell. The door was opened by a forty-something woman wearing a very tight, very short school uniform with fishnet stockings and pigtails. Not what I was expecting.

We were led into a living room with floor-to-ceiling windows overlooking the city lit up like a Christmas tree, but our eyes were not drawn to the windows, the lights, the expansive indigo sky with the stars starting to appear; nope, we couldn't tear our eyes away from our host and his party guests, all in school uniforms like those worn at St Trinian's by the extra-naughty children with their torn skirts, ripped stockings, ball-hugging shorts, buttons straining over stomachs and breasts, blazers bulging with their expansive occupants, ties askew, straw hats and berets at rakish angles, painted-on freckles, lavish amounts of lipstick and come-hither mascara, all of them clutching a glass while already being as high as the hills we were standing on. It was a surreal vision of Adelaide letting her hair down, like we'd been welcomed into a cult for the evening.

The parties when we arrived at later hours were usually extra fruity, but this one excelled itself; it wasn't difficult to entertain the overgrown class of 1982, but frankly I think we got the better show.

The smallest party we played was just outside Daylesford for six women, one heavily pregnant and celebrating a birthday for which her partner had booked us to play. The eight of us sat around the coffee table in the Airbnb they had rented. Large sliding-glass doors overlooked a velvety day, soft rain gently weeping on the eucalypts outside, and by the end all our party girls were also weeping and I had a lump in my throat too.

Was it the music, the moment, the new life expected so soon, or just the impact of sharing so much intimacy with strangers that had undermined all our composure? Whatever the reason, it was cathartic.

The *largest* party we ever played was the Kongwak Market in Gippsland, about two hours from Melbourne. It was one of those drizzling damp days of heavy grey skies that keep threatening to open and dump torrents but instead just maintain a constant, cold drip like sodden wool hung out to dry. We finally arrived when the clouds stopped toying with us and broke out the big guns.

We were expecting an open-air market but there was no one around. It was deserted and pouring and we thought, Well sure, why would anyone turn up to market day in this kind of weather? We had been paid. Rain, hail or shine, we would play for whoever was here; we just had to find them.

After five minutes of searching for evidence of life at Kongwak, we noticed someone scurrying towards a big barn. *Okay, I guess that's where whoever's turned up has taken shelter.* We hauled ourselves through the mud to the wooden building and couldn't believe what we saw as we rounded the corner of the building: the joint was packed to the large wooden rafters with 450 or 500 people. And us with two guitars, two voices and twenty-five CDs; it was gonna be like the loaves and fishes. How on earth would people hear us?

But they did. They stayed pin-drop quiet as we played our full-throated hearts out for them. The end of each song was met by thunderous applause. It gives me goosebumps writing about it now.

A few weeks before Kongwak we had played another Gippsland Summerware Party. It remains my favourite.

We had communicated a lot with the person booking us, to work out all the details, but I knew nothing about them, including whether this Gabriel was a man or woman. We had a date, a time, an address and a street directory, and after a two and a half-hour drive, the last part through rolling green fields dotted with dairy cows, we entered the gates and drove onwards to a low-slung modern house.

A pre-teen boy and girl were playing in the garden and as we knocked they ran to the front door, opened it for us and immediately sang out to alert the adults. A beautiful dark-haired woman in her late thirties came to greet us with the warmest smile. I reached out my hand and said, 'Lovely to meet you, Gabrielle.' She said, 'I'm Gabriel's wife. Please come in and I'll introduce you.'

The room was full of light and people smiling, chatting and drinking against the backdrop of great expanses of glass overlooking lush cow-studded meadows.

'Please meet Gabriel.'

I was taken aback to see Gabriel in a wheelchair, clearly living with cerebral palsy. He had organised this party, where he was surrounded by about forty loving friends, his family and wife and children, and it was clear that his condition was no impediment whatsoever to a fulfilled life. He never stopped smiling. He looked beatific. I found his speech difficult to understand, but his party guests didn't.

We were signing the CDs at the end of the performance and I asked everyone how they knew Gabriel. There were as many diverse responses as there were guests: they worked together, lunched together, were in a book club together. His physiotherapist, his library friends, the woman he bought his coffee from, they'd met at the local pool. Gabriel was a connector. I felt overwhelmed by the strength of character of this man who apparently had overcome a condition that would have been for someone else (I was thinking of me) an obstacle that would have crushed my spirit. He was indomitable, an inspiration, an example of the best kind of courage. A man who wore the love of the whole room on his sleeve. We broke our cardinal rule that day: we played an encore, 'It's Only the Beginning', at Gabriel's request. He was a hard man to say no to.

In 2010 the Summerware Party became the Half Man Half Woman Party. In 2013 we offered Stories of Ghosts Parties. In 2016 we promoted Everybody's Begging for A Party. And in 2019 we got back to basics with The House Party. But the format stuck, as did the exhilaration of coming up with a new way to perform. A seed was planted: being a musician was an elastic calling.

33

Into the Blue

All through my meandering patchwork quilt career, I had three little girls busy growing up. Family life imposes the unavoidable routine of school holidays, and the lure of escaping Melbourne over January for the seaside is irresistible for me. I was always a bit envious of my friends' long summer holidays at their family beach houses. My childhood holidays were nothing like that.

For a couple of years Mum took Shellie and me to Surfers Paradise while my father did other things. I have good memories of digging up sand on the beach and finding crabs, eating big sloppy hamburgers with the lot, washed down with chocolate milkshakes. Basically those holidays were relaxed because my father wasn't with us. The other kind of family holidays we were taken on were cruises.

Carl loved cruising. My initiation came at eleven years old. I spent the first three days of our 'surprise' holiday on an enormous

Chinese cruise ship, throwing up violently, unable to keep even a sugar cube down. Bass Strait is notoriously rough and the weather was dreadful. All along the galleys there were small piles of vomit from suffering passengers not yet accustomed to this uncertain, unstable world. My mother yelled at me one morning on our way to breakfast as I once again started heaving, but then she too succumbed to the all-pervasive sour smell of sick and made her own contribution.

We ended up in Fiji on that trip. I remember a ceremony that culminated in the tourists drinking kava, supposedly a stimulant but I couldn't detect anything; maybe it was watered down for children. The next cruise we took was on a Russian boat. I was thirteen. I met a girl onboard, maybe a year older than me, her sexuality in early bloom. She was flirting with one of the handsome Russian seamen and encouraged me to do the same. I was equal parts enchanted and terrified of the world she was beckoning me into but I spent the afternoon in her cabin, where she used her rouge, mascara and lipstick to paint our faces.

I turned up for dinner that evening, made-up and wearing a nice frock. I thought I looked glamorous. My father took one look at me and dragged me away; in my memory it was by the ear, but perhaps not. He took me to the ship's library and told me I looked like a slut, and how disappointed he was that I'd let myself down in so many ways, bringing up all sorts of unrelated things. He commanded me to return to the cabin and go to bed without dinner.

We were all jammed into a tiny space, a single-size bunk bed on either side of the cabin with one porthole at water level. Our parents took the bottom bunks, while Shellie was above Mum and I was above Dad. In the middle of the night I woke up feeling hungry and thirsty and eyed the orange my father habitually left on his bedside table, already cut into quarters. I ate it. I was awakened by a slap on the head—hard enough to shock me out of sleep—from my father at 6 am demanding that I search the ship and find him another orange. Scared and bewildered, I stumbled to the galley. I can't remember what happened next; it doesn't matter. I have never gone on another cruise. The very idea fills me with horror.

Once I was in charge of the family holiday, I was looking for something more in line with my unfulfilled childhood wishes.

Holidays in my own family would start as soon as we left home, our people-mover full to bursting with the accoutrements we needed for two weeks at the seaside. We had everything from a good pepper grinder to a full selection of oils, vinegars, spices, sharp knives, cutting boards, wok, aprons, alcohol. The obligatory selection of board games; a Casio keyboard, cassette deck, guitars, notebooks, linen for the bedroom, towels for the bathroom and the beach. We never packed light. Good grief, we were a mobile Bed, Bath N' Table.

When the girls were little, the drives had to be tailored to make sure the restless energy in the back seat didn't go rogue. We had frequent stops for toilet breaks, snack breaks, lunch, photo opportunities, sometimes 'just because' . . . and because that wasn't so much fun on the main highways, we'd always open the map and navigate through the back roads. I loved rolling into tiny towns, where the main streets were a throwback to more architecturally elegant times. The trick was to sense an imminent insurrection before it could break out, declare amnesty and find the nearest motel, no matter what or where.

That inaugural summer holiday we piled into our basic chocolate-brick room and the girls immediately pulled off their shoes and started jumping from bed to bed around and around like a bouncy castle. Somebody (either Syd or Willy) plugged in the Casio and hit the first button, which played the schlockiest instrumental version, of the Bee Gees' 'How Deep Is Your Love?' (or as our family liked to call it 'How Deep Is Your Glove?' the proctology anthem.)

It was the first time we all shared a single motel room; what ensued was the purest form of joy, the three little girls going mental, dancing and shaking off the six hours they'd spent cooped up in the MPV. We joined them because they were an unstoppable force and we were all in this together. Syd, who had the most trouble sitting still for any length of time, kept pressing the repeat button, until she discovered the second Casio programmed tune, 'Superstition', also the first verse only, also unbearably schlocky. By the time the button had been pushed thirty or so times there was no linen left on the beds.

Our destination for nine summers was Parma Farm, on the south coast of New South Wales. Sometimes there were three families on holiday together, Sydney friends or Shellie and her family, always with a gang of kids roaming around, doing all the things that kids do on farms. Also there was the beach (or choice of beaches depending on wind direction) where we would go with a picnic lunch, an esky of cold drinks, boogie boards, snorkel gear, buckets, books, tents, towels, hats, a litre of sun cream plus a selection of bright fluorescent zinc sticks for sun-safe face painting.

On grey days we might head into Nowra to take in the sights, buy some oysters or shop at the best supermarket on Australia's east coast: Nowra Coles. It sounds like cheap thrills and it was, but there was always some treasure you hadn't seen at any other Coles; cool sandals or a sunhat, or some cheesy trinket that would give you a minor endorphin bump because you'd discovered a diamond in the rough. It became a tradition, and you know what happens when something becomes a tradition: the cheesy becomes sacred and eclipses the mundane.

When the sun set, there was the Huskisson Carnival to which we would make our yearly pilgrimage, buying the girls hot dogs and fairy floss and then a ticket to ride one of those sickening mechanical monsters that whizz you mercilessly at Formula One speeds, impervious to gravity, until those children were begging to stop even as they were begging for more. Getting home after dark entailed disrupting the myriad cobwebs woven across the lane with their makers glimpsed scuttling away as the car destroyed all that painstaking work.

As you can imagine, after 200 yards or so of collecting spider-webs and some of their inhabitants, none of us was happy about getting out of the car. We had to run the gauntlet, car door open, a mad traumatising dash for the farm house, screaming and laughing or laughing and screaming; bloody nature!

Mr Zygier cooked big dinners for many people every night and I began my romance with bread baking, which continues to this day. The other thing we did on our summer holidays was write songs.

On 19 January, 2008, we were booked to play Tamworth Entertainment Centre, supporting Melinda Schneider. It was our first time being welcomed into the sanctified country music cabal that was Tamworth, but since we were coming in with Melinda, a queen in that world, we were rendered kosher (so to speak).

The only drawback was the long drive. Even though the girls were a bit older now—thirteen, ten and eight—a nine-hour drive is a weighty ask for anyone and my memory is that we drove from Parma Farm to Tamworth in one leg. The question was going to be how to keep the girls from killing us or each other. A bit of lateral thinking resulted in us writing a song they could perform with us at Tamworth; they'd learn the words and the melody in three-part harmony on the way there and that would hopefully keep them occupied.

'Into the Blue' is a coming-of-age piece full of yearning, ambition, impatience and a sprinkling of nostalgia. The girls sang separately and in harmony, I took the last verse and Willy played ukulele. As they learnt it on the car trip, they fought most of the way, accusing each other of getting the tune, the harmony or the lyrics wrong. There were tears (Syd), yelling (Alma) and unadulterated fury (Hettie). We tried to defuse the endless flare-ups but those gorgeous girls were demonic, they drove us crazy.

Then we got on stage in front of Melinda Schneider's 800-strong audience and the little darlings sang like angels and had the crowd going wild. We recorded it the year after and made it the second-last song on *Half Man Half Woman*. It is an idyllic memento of the time, sans the warring. Beyond anything else we gave our girls, growing up with a summer holiday they could depend on was one of the best.

'Into the Blue', *Half Man Half Woman*, 2010

Rock me in the cradle
Sing a lullaby
The moon is big and round and high
Wish me tall and graceful
Wish for me to fly
And when I'm able please don't cry

Don't come find me I've gone wandering
Don't know where I'm wandering to
Daddy's working Mama's busy
I'm falling into the blue

Into the blue, into the blue, into the blue
Daddy's working Mama's busy
I'm falling into the blue

I'm gonna be a ballerina
Well I'm gonna be a big star too
I'm gonna climb the highest mountain
And wave a flag into the blue

Into the blue, into the blue, into the blue
I'm gonna climb the highest mountain
And wave a flag into the blue

Out there mothers wait for children
To sleep soundly all night through

Soon those children will be mothers
And wonder what their children do

Into the blue, into the blue, into the blue
Soon those children will be mothers
Singing out into the blue

34

Serpent's Tooth

British writer Cyril Connolly famously wrote, 'There is no more sombre enemy of good art than the pram in the hall.' And fair enough, Cyril, I get it; as I might have mentioned a few thousand times in earlier chapters, being chronically sleep deprived and transformed into an open all-hours milk bar are not ideal conditions for the muse. But once the tide of chaos retreats, there's a lot of treasure to explore.

When Syd was ten, she was already as tall as me. She was home from school for a few days, feverish with a temperature. She had walked into our room a couple of times the previous few nights, unaware of what she was doing, and I'd put her back to bed. We were reading *Artemis Fowl* at the time; well, I was reading it to her, an aid to her recovery I thought. *Artemis* is a modern fairy-tale heist incorporating sci-fi, high tech and a bad-ass faery.

On night three, her sleep talking woke me up and I went to

her room to check on her. Syd wasn't there. She was standing naked in the bathroom, clearly asleep, brandishing a comb as a weapon. She was cautioning me not to come any closer. 'Don't you know what happens when a human sees a faery?' she hissed.

Several thoughts came to mind:

1. Are there any sharp objects in the bathroom that I need to get to before she does? (Yes. I cautiously took the scissors from next to the bathroom sink and shoved them into a back corner of the cupboard.)
2. Have I got time to grab my video camera so I can show her this when she wakes up in the morning? (I reluctantly decided no.)
3. How can I talk her into going calmly back to bed? (I'd need a good cover story.)
4. That line from *Eraserhead*: 'You really are sick, aren't you.'

I managed to talk her down, telling her that I was the faery queen—I had to make it convincing—and could take care of her. Fortunately, she was compliant and I tucked her safely into bed and sat with her, watching her breathe. The following day we made a doctor's appointment and she was prescribed a mild sedative to help her sleep for the next few nights.

The vulnerability of your child is so apparent when they are asleep, under the sway of unconscious impulses, all the bravado of daytime assuredness set adrift, subsumed by darker forces. Peaceful until a terrifying nightmare wakes them with a jolt. You can't protect them. A tiny almost unnoticeable alarm reminds you of all the terrors and the disappointments and the pain you can't shield them from. All you can do is fortify your offspring and teach them how to protect themselves.

Syd moved out of home at age eighteen to study in regional Victoria, at which point her sleepwalking became her own domain. As did many other things. She still sleepwalks and sleep talks but now it is someone else who brings her back to the light.

'Sleepwalker', *Summertown*, 2004

There she goes soft as a snowfall
No one would know she was there
She's a child, I want to hold her
But I can't protect her from fear

Sleepwalker, she was a sleepwalker
Dancing in moonlight with music playing
Sleepwalker, she was a sleepwalker
And all of us sinners are straining to hear the refrain

Here you are lying beside me
Dreaming whatever you dream
Breathing slow, I slip into darkness and lose you across the ravine

Sleepwalker, she was a sleepwalker
Dancing in moonlight with music playing
Sleepwalker, she was a sleepwalker
And all of us sinners are straining to hear . . .

Everything stopped
By the beat of your heart
The band waits to strike up a waltz

Just for you
In the dark

Where oh where, where are you sleeping?
Where are you sleeping tonight?
Who will wake and follow your footsteps?
Who'll bring you back to the light?

Sleepwalker, she was a sleepwalker
Dancing in bare feet with music playing
Sleepwalker, she was a sleepwalker
And all of us sinners are straining to hear the refrain
Sleepwalker, she was a sleepwalker
And all of us sinners are straining to hear

Before I had a child the only thing other parents told me was how hard it was. No one ever mentioned the love. Isn't that curious? Without the love the whole exercise would be a disastrous experiment and the human race would become extinct because IT IS SO HARD; you'd probably just murder them or at least run away. But there is one single factor that offsets all the grief that no one thought to mention, maybe because I was just expected to know it: unconditional love.

And then they become teenagers. And everything changes again.

And it's not that you love them less, you certainly don't, but if you have a difficult teenager then you and your love are being challenged like nothing has ever challenged it before. The sleepless nights, the terrible twos, the fussy eating, naughtiness, emergency hospital visits, not doing their chores, the screaming . . . all the childhood difficulties pale beside the onset of puberty.

We were incredibly lucky. Two out of three girls sailed through the hormonal years without becoming unbearable, though the scars of some of their worst excesses are still in evidence if not bubbling just beneath the surface. Our third daughter became my very own karmic payback.

'I Can't Photograph Your Smell'

I can't photograph your smell so I thought I'd write it down
But now I'm in front of white paper
with my black Super Grip Pilot pen
I don't know how to start . . . maybe . . .
the smell of you is like nectar from
a small sweet cherry—there's never enough.
A smell like baked bread, warm, fresh, rising or
like new cut grass, essentially vegetative.
It's layered—the smell of your night's sleep, damp
head on a feather pillow mingled with the milk that
has seeped from your bottle; the breakfast
you've just alternately eaten and smeared across yourself,
cheese, hot buttered toast, banana; last night's bath with
strawberry bubbles;
the pungent but as yet underwhelming bouquet of a recently
filled nappy.

The smell I can't photograph belongs to Hettie, who was barely a year old when I wrote this. In 2001, I was on a six-month tour with *Always, Patsy Cline*, staying in five-star accommodation around the country. Every night I was lauded for singing country classics and managing to stay upright on teeteringly high heels. After the shows I came back to my hotel and enjoyed a full uninterrupted night's sleep. That is the pinnacle of luxury for a sleep-deprived mother of three under age five. During the day I put photo albums together and wrote.

Well-wishers, interviewers keep insisting it must be exhausting with a schedule of eight two-hour shows a week, but compared to home life it was a cakewalk. I was a FIFO mother; home on Sunday night with a little something pink for each of my babies—lots of hugs and kisses to remind them I was their mummy, and leave again on Tuesday. Mr Zygier was 'handling' the nightly hijinks, vomiting sessions, nappy leakage with attendant linen changes, nightmares, sore tummies and runny noses, and three little girls in his bed on rotation or sometimes all at once; he took it in stride and recounted the war stories in the morning like a comedy routine.

Hettie as a baby was smiley, easy going, loving her *cumma* (cucumbers) and *manu* (tomatoes) and the best sleeper, possibly because by number three we weren't so easy to manipulate. Even the fact that her slightly older sister could be prone to some overly aggressive play—Alma wasn't completely sure about getting a little sister at the time and is still working through it—didn't bother Hettie. She was so physically coordinated that she could hold a pen perfectly before she turned two.

She loved to dance; her hips wiggled as she launched into accompanying hand movements, arms held close to her side, hands rotating around her wrists. We dubbed it the Bubba-liggle and she danced it often, usually to express joy. The Bubba-liggle largely disappeared after we moved house.

Between moving out of the house we sold and into the house we bought, we were invited to become guests in a friend's four-storey St Kilda mansion. It was so substantial that when our host declared he was off to Europe, the five of us were a little disconcerted at being left alone.

Four of us got used to it but Hettie was traumatised by the scale of everything. The artwork was nightmarish for her, the staircases too wide; behind every wall who knew what lurked and everyone was potentially so far away. It is hard to imagine that moving house at the wrong time could have such a profound impact, but it's also hard to view Hettie's personality change without taking the house into account.

By three years old Hettie was ferociously independent, unable to tolerate being read to and very bad-tempered; there was a lot of screaming. She screamed every time she put her socks on, if food took too long to arrive, or a drive was too long; she screamed with annoyance if someone was tapping on a surface; she screamed when she wanted something and the something didn't materialise immediately. Hettie's impatience bred frustration, her frustration bred fury and everything annoyed her.

Around four, after Willy had told her firmly that she was not allowed to do something (I can't remember what, maybe play on the road), Hettie responded, 'I've never loved you and I'll never love you.' Funny, devastating and memorable.

Unsurprisingly, Hettie's puberty exacerbated everything we had been through to this point. Hettie would scream that she needed help with her homework, and then scream if you didn't understand exactly and instantly what she needed. She would scream if you helped too much. If I swallowed within her earshot I was disgusting; if I was not available to take her somewhere exactly when she required it, she was furious; when we were in the car, she was uncommunicative, all my attempts to draw her into conversation resulting in single-syllable answers until we were locked in silence. I caught her once at age thirteen about to leave the house dressed (barely) in a boob tube and mini skirt, to catch public transport. I told her she had to put some more clothes on and she said, 'No, I'm a feminist, I can wear what I like.' I won that skirmish.

All of this was exacerbated because alongside Hettie's puberty, I was also wrestling with menopause. The two of us were constantly locked in battle, like a domestic-scale version of the twentieth century: World War I, followed by the Great Depression, followed by World War II, the Battle of Stalingrad, the Cold War, the Suez Crisis, the Tet Offensive, and the Six Day War—sometimes all in one afternoon. We took no prisoners. It was completely exhausting and totally unproductive. I was left devastated, and she was too.

There are plenty of books for parents to read before they become parents, though I didn't read any of them, nor did I read anything about the effective parenting of a teenager, and I'm not sure if it would have made any difference. I wrote a song instead and then I took my own advice, as much as I could. I surrendered.

'Serpent's Tooth', *Everybody's Begging*, 2016

Leave your armies at the border
I surrender
You won't need your slings and arrows
I surrender

Take down your hair my lovely
All the pins that hurt my hands
The sharpness of your judgements wound
You leave me dumb
Please still your tongue

Leave your weapons at the entrance
I surrender
You won't need your guns or bullets
I surrender

All my heart is yours to keep
The tenderest of all my parts
Be careful of your brutal feet
Don't trample me
Beneath this love

Leave your armour on the doorstep
I surrender
You won't need your wall of silence
I surrender

All the sleepless nights we spent
In the comfort of my arms
Your tangled legs your warm sweet scent
My pillows dent
In remembrance

Leave your tempest in the hallway
I surrender

You won't need thunder
You won't need lightning
I surrender
And you won't need that moat around you
I surrender

We had decided that with two musicians as parents we should be prepared for our offspring to be musical, and arranged for piano lessons for each of the girls from age four. Sometimes there would be arguments about practice but, strangely, all we'd have to say was, 'Alright, you don't have to have piano lessons anymore,' and they were back thumping the ivories. It sort of defies explanation, but certainly had the desired outcome. All three girls play piano and write songs and have all followed very divergent musical paths.

Syd has a soft spot for pop and musical comedy; Hettie is the singer and guitarist for a three-piece-girl punk rock band; and Alma fell in love with early jazz. When Alma sings she eschews the technical pyrotechnics to honour the song from deep inside it. She gives herself totally, without a shred of artifice, to the essence of a lyric. I have seen her reduce grown men to tears.

Alma was eight or nine years old when we were writing the songs for *Half Man Half Woman* but she discovered the last track, 'Say Goodnight', recently and put it in her set. The song is a paean to the grief and acceptance that go hand-in-hand with our instinctive understanding of the sorrow of endings, even if they're happy. She sings it with such a profound understanding of finality it confounds the listener when they realise she has chalked up just twenty-three tender years on the planet.

The girls are all unique and splendid singers in their own right but when they sing together, it is like angels have materialised in physical form.

In 2014, we were contacted by film producer Julie Byrne, who asked permission to use 'Into the Blue' as the closing song over the credits for her film *Touch*, a road trip story of a mother and her disturbed young daughter. Willy and I saw a screening of it in a Melbourne cinema. It is a haunting and profoundly sad picture; by the time 'Into the Blue' was playing both of us were weeping.

'Say Goodnight', *Half Man Half Woman*, 2010

Say goodnight, don't say goodnight
Have one more drink to be polite
We'll watch the moon sink to the floor

We're feeling fine, we're feeling fine
The music and too much red wine
So don't go rushing out the door

Hold me 'til there's no more shadows
I'm still pretty when it's light
Don't say goodnight

It's time to sleep, it's time to sleep
But all those pleasant dreams will keep
I'd rather hang around with you all

The late show's done, the late show's done
We've screwed around we've had some fun
But curtains always have to fall

Hold me 'til there's no more shadows
I'm still pretty when it's light
So stay with me tonight
It's definitely quite . . . wrong
To say goodnight
The late show's done, the late show's done
We've fooled around we've had some fun
Now the curtain must come down

35

City of Women

City Of Women is a Federico Fellini film from 1980. It inspired Willy to write a song of the same name for Tootieville, who never ended up recording or performing it. That was to come a few years later when 'City of Women' made the cut for the *Ultrasound* album released in 1995. The song, a darkly humorous, moody reverie like the film, is a fantasy of a secret world populated predominantly by women. I love singing 'In the city of women all the bitches are good friends'—it never fails to make me smile.

Around 2004, a producer approached me to devise an all-female festival in the style of Lilith Fair, an American all-female festival that was enjoying success. Could I go away and think about it? Mr Zygier and I left our daughters with their grandparents and went to Daylesford to lie around for a couple of days, eat, drink and think up ideas: potential venues, artists, program concepts, names. We came up with a blueprint for the producer who, shortly afterwards, lost interest, citing the potential expense.

We forgot about it until I was approached by a new management team at the Malthouse Theatre, Melbourne, who commissioned me to curate an event for their venue. The Daylesford ideas, modified, came into their own. We called it BROAD, a take on the old American slang term for women and a nod to what would be the artists' contrasting musical approaches. I would be ring-master, and we would cast four other female singer-songwriters from wildly different spheres to boldly expose our audience to the absurdity of 'Female Singer-Songwriter' as a category.

We'd break down traditional barriers between performers and genres and play on each others' songs. Discussions on stage would then reveal each artist's songwriting secrets. Sounded great on paper. We got the green light.

We had to figure out who to pull from each genre, to emphasise not just musical difference but also to highlight artists in varying stages of their careers. The next stumbling block was explaining the concept to agents and managers, and of course they wanted to know who else was in it. 'Well, me', I'd say. Yep, who else? Hmmm, this was tricky, because each person would determine who the next choice would be and if everyone was hanging back for someone else to make up their mind, we could bloody well be here forever.

The business folk were remarkably reluctant to cross the line. Maybe more money would have motivated them, but I wanted to pay everyone the same amount, and I had a budget. I'm sure if I'd been dealing primarily with the artists it would have been easier, but I understood the natural hesitations of people protecting their clients' reputations from this yet-to-be-proven, could-go-disastrously-awry concept. (Hat tip to Katie Noonan who just said yes, simple as that; she trusted me and she came on board. Her participation got me over the line in 2005.)

Next phase was picking the songs. Everyone chose three songs of their own, on top of which Willy and I picked another three songs to arrange for the ensemble. We were trying to keep rehearsals to a three-day maximum so all the parts could be distributed in the months leading up to the show for everyone to learn. I'd even joined a gym to get in shape so I could feel good hauling my forty-six-year-old arse on stage alongside all my gorgeous and mostly younger colleagues.

Things were trucking along nicely until the unthinkable happened. Out of the blue I got a call from Malthouse Theatre. They'd gone back over the budget and come to the conclusion that BROAD was 'too expensive' . . . it was *deja vu*.

Crestfallen doesn't really cover it. It was months of work I was watching implode, not to mention my reputation. Having persuaded the cast to come on board, I would now have to admit that I was a loser, out of my depth. FUCK THAT, I thought quietly to myself.

Mr Zygier and I were both fans of Mel Brooks's *The Producers*. The line, 'Never, never, never put your own money in the show' should have been ringing loud alarm bells. I'm not saying we didn't think of it but we definitely didn't dwell on it. Instead, as we walked our large, stinky American bulldog around Caulfield Park, I said to Mr Zygier, 'Hey, let's do it ourselves.' We went full Judy Garland/Mickey Rooney: 'We'll book the theatre, we'll write the blurbs, we'll hire the publicist—hell, why limit ourselves to Melbourne? Let's take the show on the road!'

We booked venues in Melbourne, Canberra, Sydney, Brisbane and Adelaide. No turning back now. We were producers and were definitely putting our own money in the show. We hired the theatres, the publicist, the photographer; we wrote the blurbs; we booked the advertising, the poster runs, the flights, the hire cars, the hotels; we chose the songs and arranged them; we distributed the parts among our artists.

I wrote the scripts and dragged myself to the gym, which I hated. We parented our three daughters, we moved house(!), we lost sleep. Every morning at the producers' witching hour of 4 am, I'd be lying in bed, staring at the ceiling, going over and over all my potential screw-ups. Describing it now, it's like one of those montages in movies when you go from the kernel of the idea, fast forwarding through all the blood, sweat and tears until you're almost at the glorious denouement months later.

Then, the squeal of brakes . . .

I have a few moderate talents but budgeting is not among them. I finally got around to working out what producing this beast would entail; if we sold every single ticket in Melbourne's 900-seat Athenaeum Theatre, we would break even. The other towns were much the same. It was pre-Facebook marketing days and each city was costing around $20,000 just to promote! By November, with only a few weeks to go before the first show and despite the crippling marketing tab, ticket sales could be generously described as slow.

Sleep was harder and harder to come by but we were committed (or should have been!).

I was racking my brain to come up with ways to promote that first Melbourne show. I ended up handing out flyers to audiences queuing outside The Famous Spiegeltent during the Melbourne

Festival; they seemed to be our crowd. A few weeks out, I was spruiking like the loudest barrow boy at market just before closing, bellowing 'BROAD—All Singing, All Sitting!'

We sold that show out—on the day! I have a photo of the five of us standing in front of our poster outside the Athenaeum, looking ecstatic, relieved, almost feeling vindicated but not exactly; we were only just beginning. We had broken even in Melbourne, but in other towns that first year, we didn't. Nor did we over the four years we mounted the concerts. Our financial headwinds were due to my inexperience and stubborn optimism: forgetting theatre staff wages were double on Sundays; over-estimating ticket sales and/or merchandise demand, and the fact that each BROAD concert took eight months of preparations. Our wages were definitely not in the budget.

The other all-consuming elephant in the theatre: I am not a natural harmony singer. Aside from the squillions spent on marketing, this was my most significant obstacle. I had spent the best part of thirty years being the lead singer. Now I was thrown in the deep end of vocal harmony and I had to sing or sink. The combination of getting older and my discomfort with harmony unleashed a demented vibrato; so as well as building up my triceps to counter my nanna arms, I was also sweating balls to banish my crazy inner-opera lady.

'Confidence is key,' says Willy Wonka to Violet Beauregarde in Roald Dahl's *Charlie and The Chocolate Factory*. He's right. It's a precious commodity. You can have it spades and it will let you fly: then someone shakes it and suddenly you are curled on the floor in a foetal position, moaning that you're shit. I needed confidence to sing harmony, as opposed to being the rabbit in the headlights mesmerised by a choir of otherwise-perfect voices.

Conquer the absence of confidence, and half the battle is won. The nerves will fry you on a theatre stage looking into the warm breathing quiet of a room full of expectation. But if you can find the belief in your own ability, and spend enough time practising, you give yourself a chance to meet the challenge.

Since Do-Ré-Mi, working with other women (with a few notable exceptions) had become a rarity for me, so BROAD was a long, cool drink for a thirsty soul. The five of us would begin by singing a group song in harmony, followed by each of us playing our own tunes with contributions from the other women. The country artist might get the blues guitarist supplying licks and the indie pop singer providing backing vocals. There was any number of variations. A comfortable synthesis of rehearsed and informal engagement set this thing apart. And the feeling that you could break out of your genre to perform in someone else's sphere was kind of magical.

Audiences found it moving, an unintended but wonderful consequence. These are the best kinds of discoveries, those serendipitous moments when you are so caught up in what's happening you lose the boundaries between yourself and your co-players; you're all together inside the tube of music rising like a wave that you are suddenly cruising effortlessly down the face of. We glimpsed that mighty musical force during those concerts.

The legitimate question you might ask is what makes playing music with women different from playing with men? Surely a musician is a musician is a musician? That is true, but it's more nuanced to me. Maybe it's the increased need to impress my female colleagues that I don't feel quite as much when my colleagues are men. I naturally feel more competitive with women, not in a way that eliminates the camaraderie but certainly in a way that lifts my game. I want to be the best I can be, because I know that they will bring their best to impress me.

That doesn't happen between me and a male musician. I heard a podcast the other day with Joe Rogan holding forth on why competitive sports are essential for men, who naturally thrive on competition. And I thought, *So do I, and so do most of the women I know*. It makes us all better at everything we do if we have that fire in the belly. I can't hold with the notion that women are less competitive. Women dress for other women, because they're the ones that notice; we have a deep need to impress our female friends and there is absolutely nothing wrong with that. A little competitive frisson serves to heighten the adventure.

BROAD had a phenomenal roll call of talent over its duration. In 2005 Clare Bowditch, Ruby Hunter, Katie Noonan and Sara Storer signed on; in 2006 it was Mia Dyson, Ella Hooper, Kate Miller-Heidke and Melinda Schneider. In 2007 the line-up comprised Abbe May, Anne McCue, Jade MacRae and Sally Seltmann. And in 2008 BROAD featured Dianna Corcoran, Laura Jean Englert, Elana Stone and Liz Stringer.

Our inaugural BROAD Concert opened with the iconic, uplifting and very Australian 'A World of Our Own', by The Seekers, heralding our fresh and singular concept. For the encore in that first year, we gave the audience 'City of Women' arranged for five voices. It brought the house down and the audience to their feet, applauding all of us bitches and good friends.

'City of Women', *Ultrasound*, 1995

I dreamed I was a girl
Saw through all men
And went to live
In the city of women

I dreamed I had a dress
As pale as mother's milk
I bared my breast
In the city of women

In the city of women
All the bitches are good friends
In the city of women
All the bitches are good friends

No men to watch me walk
Down the scented streets
There is no baby talk
In the city of women
It smelled just like an ocean
As warm as little children
I would never tell
About the city of women

In the city of women
All the bitches are good friends

In the city of women
All the bitches are good friends

I dreamed I was a man
Just like any man
So what is there
Beyond the city of women?
(She said) When the erection finally falls
There is the softness of the tongue
In the end
There is the city of women
In the end
There is the city of women

36

Third Time Down

Erica Hart was a deliciously plump 5 foot 4 with flyaway curly hair often dyed hot pink or deep purple, though between hairdresser appointments it faded to a dusky rose or gentle mauve. Erica had fabulous posture, a fluty voice with a laugh within easy reach and an astounding recall of names, places, dates: spending time with her was like being with a living, breathing Google. Scouting the pick-up point outside Brisbane airport on a bright, sunny May morning in 2008 I spotted Erica in her zippy little Japanese hatchback. The car trip into town whipped past. We had a lot to talk about.

By early 2008 I had three versions of BROAD under my belt with one more scheduled later in the year and, possibly because of them, I'd been offered the role of artistic director for the Queensland Music Festival. This was a big deal, my first proper job in any real sense. (There was a strong argument that artistic director of the Queensland Music Festival (QMF) wasn't a 'real job' either, but it was the closest I was ever going to get.) My elastic singer/songwriter/producer gig had just stretched a bit more.

The QMF was biennial with festivals in the odd years. The next one was scheduled for July 2009. I'd arrived in the middle of QMF's scheduled period of semi-hibernation; in fact Erica, the program director and I were at the time the entirety of the working staff. On day one, we wandered through acreage of empty office space, desks in open-plan formations, private offices, all at the ready with their computers. They foretold arts factotums bent over their looms, weaving my dreams. But for now we had it to ourselves.

'So what do you do, Erica?'

'Anything you want me to,' she said, and went to make us cups of tea.

It was such a complete answer and not one I was used to hearing. I was unaccustomed to working with anyone else apart from Mr Zygier, and *we* took it in turns to make the tea.

I was replacing Paul Grabowsky, who was offered the same role at the Adelaide Festival. The new Executive Director, an Englishman called, in particularly English fashion, Nigel Lavender, had only just been appointed, and his arrival from the UK was imminent. Also coming in was the new Finance Officer, Christopher Smeed. They were names that sounded like we should have been playing Cluedo—Mr Smeed in the library with a sharpened spreadsheet, Mr Lavender in the lobby in high dudgeon, Miss Hart in the boardroom with a blunt program report.

My mission was to come up with enough musical events for a seventeen-day, slightly schizophrenic festival to take place across an area roughly seven times the size of Victoria. To add spice, 2009 would mark Queensland's sesquicentenary (a word I loved saying, which was lucky because I said it often).

I say 'schizophrenic' because in the regions the festival was all about community involvement, with a focus on telling relevant stories and utilising local resources like the brass band, choir and dance school. Small towns turned out in droves to support family, friends and colleagues, while in Queensland's ultra-modern two-million-strong capital, Brisbane, the QMF became a sophisticated arts festival, presenting new commissions and ticketed concerts that hadn't yet been mounted in the city.

It was an incredible opportunity to play ringmaster and connector, bringing together arts practitioners in collaborations that I thought would yield interesting results. I was bound only by my imagination. On paper I was having a ball. I had pages filled with uncosted potential. This was day two.

This job would involve lots of travelling. I wasn't prepared to desert my still-young family in Melbourne, so I would fly to Brisbane for three days every week. Once in Queensland, trips down to Logan and Coolangatta, to the Sunshine Coast or Toowoomba were made by car, but getting almost anywhere else involved flying. Heading to Moa in the Torres Strait, for example, required a flight to Cairns, another to Cooktown, another to Thursday Island and one more to Moa itself, from where, if the tide was low, you could apparently stroll over to Papua New Guinea.

Every plane going north got smaller and exponentially louder, until we landed on the outer island in a tiny prop plane with four seats including the pilot's, all of us wearing headsets to counter the decibels, though even yelling it was impossible to hear each other.

We had landed early on our first trip to Moa and our pre-arranged contact was not at the airport to meet us. We hopped into the lone taxi, which delivered us to a tin structure before driving off with a warning that our host might be a while; apparently this was not unusual. As advertised, it was quiet. We rang the bell, we knocked, we called out, 'Heya, we're here . . .' Nothing. We sat down to wait. My phone was signal-free but Erica had coverage.

Half an hour later she roused our sleepy innkeeper, who arrived with half-unbuttoned shirt hanging out, a messy mop of wiry black hair and full plush beard covering his handsome black face. He showed us to our rooms, apologising profusely as we bumped down the corridor. Not that we were agitated—island time was already seeping into our city bones.

Our morning meeting took place under the palm trees near the beach with choir members and interested parties bringing their own folding plastic chairs. There was a lot of enthusiasm for the project. Afterwards, back at our tin shed, our host brought reparations for his tardiness in the form of lobsters freshly plucked from the Strait and still warm from the cooking pot; sweet, pearly flesh peeling in soft mouthfuls, the best apology I've ever eaten.

Queensland is a state of contrasts. The great western hinterland recce trips were entirely different from our forays into the Far North. For our first sojourn west, Erica and I flew into Townsville, and then drove and drove and drove, stopping at Charters Towers, Hughenden, Richmond, Julia Creek, Cloncurry and lastly Mount Isa to chat with mayors and council CEOs in their cowboy boots and broad-brim hats, taking meetings with local choirs and band leaders or everyone together in a great brainstorming roundtable. Ideas flew, contributions were thrown into the mix and as sandwiches and cake were handed around and the builders' tea flowed, a plan would coalesce into something ambitious and thrilling.

Not everyone was as enthusiastic. Premier Anna Bligh had recently whipped through the state amalgamating some of the smaller shires for cost-cutting purposes, which left a lot of disgruntled councillors bending our ears with their grievances (like we could do something about it!).

That first drive was formative: the feeling of space, changing topography, the scene outside the car window transforming from tropical lushness to grasslands, to rocky outcrops, to red-earth desert. Between Cloncurry and Mount Isa we stopped at the memorial for Burke and Wills. They had famously set out from Victoria in the winter of 1860 to explore the interior of the country and determine whether the continent had an inland sea, but died a year later after a series of misadventures on the return trip.

The monument was a single unprepossessing plinth, but the silence was really something. Car engine off, we didn't speak, and the birds were silent in the heat with few trees around, not another car for miles. I had never heard the world that quiet; it was eerie, and beautiful. We should have prayed. We silently got back in the car and roared off.

Erica and I were Thelma and Louise without the cliff. Road trips took us to altitude in Toowoomba, north-west to Dalby, due west to Chinchilla, Miles, Roma, Mitchell, the enormous starry skies over Charleville; then north again to Tambo, Blackall, Barcaldine, west to Longreach, once more north, and finally to the spectacular Winton landscape of the towering red rock mesas jutting out of the flatness. And still, we had nowhere near exhausted Queensland. the great state just went on and on.

I wanted no corner of the state to miss out. My debut festival opened with Hidden Republic and the star-studded Black Arm Band on Thursday Island, until then virgin territory for QMF. We had barges transporting the PA, stage and lighting rigs across from Cairns and nothing went wrong or missing or broke down. Thursday Islanders and residents of the outer islands turned out in droves, and the performance was beamed live to Brisbane.

Post-show, the community dining tables heaved under a banquet to equal the occasion: platters of fresh seafood, curries, salads, roasted meats, plantains, starchy root vegetables cooked in thick nutty sauces and then desserts as if from a children's story, all brought along by a cavalcade of home chefs. We feasted through the tropical night and washed it all down with cold beer.

I grabbed every opportunity to commission grand schemes. The triumph of staging Hidden Republic on Thursday Island opened up the possibility of what I could do next time round. One Sunday, I visited all the churches that were holding a prayer meeting. The islanders are a God-fearing community, and almost every variant of Christianity is represented: Catholics, Protestants, Anglicans, Pentecostals, Seventh Day Adventists, Sacred Heart Mission and the Uniting Church. And every service I went to pulled a crowd.

I visited the library and found a copy of the Gospel According to Saint Luke, which contains the story of the Temptation of Christ in the local language, Yumplatok. It was a lightbulb moment. I commissioned a piece based on that text; we called it 'Ailan Kores'. The Devil was played by an irresistible counter tenor, Jesus sung by a baritone and the Desert rendered by a hundred-voice choir pulled together from across the Torres Strait, backed by The Queensland Youth Orchestra. It was spine-tingling. I felt my body absorbing and transmitting the music as a physical sensation.

Bowen, home to the Big Mango, is the gateway to the Whitsundays. Baz Luhrmann shot his sweeping epic *Australia* there and the council erected a sign on the water-storage tank on a hill that you can't miss when you first drive into town: BOWENWOOD. In a darker past Bowen was a centre for 'blackbirding', the trafficking and exploitation of South Sea Islanders who were lured onto ships in the late 1800s and brought to Queensland's sugarcane plantations to work for minimal or no wages.

We spent a lot of time in Bowen in preparation to present this harrowing story and with a lot of consultation among the Bowen South Sea Island community discovered an unexpected twist: there were people who had no idea that they could trace their heritage to the South Sea Islands. They assumed they'd originated from the Torres Strait Islands or were of Aboriginal heritage.

It was a world of revelation for all of us. 'Behind The Cane' was the result, a performance that explored the heartbreak and resilience in these riveting stories delivered by a local cast of 120 musicians, singers and dancers to the community of Bowen in their sound shell on the foreshore.

Erica and I drove out to Kev Carmody's place near Warwick to visit him and his wife Beryl and discuss the upcoming presentation in Brisbane of his compilation album *Cannot Buy My Soul*.

There were challenges around travel for Kev; his back pain was exacerbated by long periods of sitting and, among other things, we wanted to make sure he was happy with the arrangements for the upcoming concert.

We sat drinking tea from a china tea set on the front verandah when Beryl announced, 'Brown snake, Kev'. Kev, now moving like an intrepid hunter, got to his feet, picked up a shotgun and silently floated down the stairs, at which point an almighty crack rent the tranquillity as the brown snake met his maker.

'Gotta do it for the grandkids,' said Kev, half-apologetic, as Erica and I reached for our imaginary Victorian petticoats and let out tiny giveaway squeals of city-slickerdom. A few months later, QMF staged 'Cannot Buy My Soul, The Songs of Kev Carmody' and packed out the Riverstage in front of thousands of fans welcoming home their local hero.

One of the first projects I'd envisaged was inspired by a favourite book from my childhood. It required more preparation time than I had for my first festival, but I didn't give up on it. I asked Elena Kats-Chernin to compose the music and Rosetta Cook to choreograph 'The Little Green Road to Fairyland', which became one of the highlights of QMF 2011.

Some years before, my friend James Black had recommended I read Anna Goldsworthy's memoir, *Piano Lessons*; and now I commissioned a stage adaptation. I was able to bring to Australia all my musical favourites, legends like Dan Hicks, Randy Newman, Michael Nyman and the incomparable Dr L. Subramaniam. I commissioned 'Presidentsland', a futuristic look at where we may all be heading (no one predicted a pandemic) and 'Drag-QueensLand', a 'psychological burlesque' of what it's like to be a drag queen in Queensland.

Naturally it wasn't all beer and skittles. Waiting around airports was tedious and the motel I lived in for the first two years was something out of a Philip Marlowe story during a down-on-his-luck phase: after a long day at the office, I would climb the external steps to my ~~cell~~ motel room, reach blindly for the motel tissue box on the bench just inside, and then, while I balanced my foot against the weighted fire door, tear a chunk off the box, roll it into a wedge and shove it along with the plastic key into the slot to activate the electricity. Different room, same routine. Every. Single. Time.

I never complained. I wanted to spend money on festival events, not my accommodation. In 2010 QMF decided to move offices and my new accommodation enjoyed views of the giant Lego-like Story Bridge.

Then there were the internecine squabbles. The CEO had to be the caution to my throwing caution-to-the-wind, to play the part of the cruel farmer, hunting down the lame lamb in my flock to put a bullet through its brain—metaphorically speaking. I understood, but nevertheless it hurt when the bullet went in. We lost some, but I saved some as well.

In those heady early days Erica, Nigel and I were quite a team. Nigel—with his pale-blue eyes that popped slightly, and slightly more when he was about to lose his cool, which he did on a semi-regular basis—was often my adversary, but I loved having someone to do battle with. Every time we'd fight over whatever I held dear and he said we couldn't afford, the overall structure of the festival became stronger for it. It is no fun wrestling a feather pillow and

Nigel was not that. Nigel was yin to my yang and he always had my back.

My co-workers were tremendous at what they did. Exactingly efficient, quietly formidable, deliberate and indefatigable, they embodied extraordinary energy and passion about each project. Whatever was needed, the army of QMF staff were unwaveringly up to the task.

The festival launches took place in a black box theatre with performances from artists for the press, our sponsors, patrons, other arts practitioners, staff and Friends of the Festival. This was my big set piece. Funding came largely via Arts Queensland with help from the Australia Council, corporate and private philanthropy, but the scale was ambitious and a $7.5 million budget doesn't go as far as you might think.

Fundraising wasn't part of my remit but I did manage to sweet-talk quite a few Friends of the Festival with expansive pockets. It was often a matchmaking exercise of working out who would be excited by what and then bingo, everybody was smiling. And thanking them was important.

For the first launch I wrote a lyric set to the tune of Geoff Mack's 'I've Been Everywhere'. Geoff wasn't a Queenslander but he'd spent a lot of time there—close enough. I had met him a few years earlier in Tamworth, sitting in a living room with Melinda Schneider and her yodelling mother Mary. Geoff (who was quite elderly by then) was nodding off in the corner, though he did raise himself to sing, at Mary's insistence, 'Hey Jack Brrrrrrabham', which he did with total commitment in his 'sound effects voice'. Then, like the Dormouse at the Mad Hatter's Tea Party, Geoff put his guitar down and nodded off again.

A few months after launching, the QMF was open for business, by which time my job was largely done. I just had to conquer my fear of public speaking. I'd made a lot of speeches in the lead-up to opening, but bowling into one off the cuff always felt like I was faking it. I needed a little preparation, notes written on scraps to make it less harrowing.

The trip to Gladstone stands out. It was just a regular function put on by council to welcome us and I had checked, as I always did, whether I would be called on to speak. I was assured that no, there would be plenty of speechifiers and my words of wisdom wouldn't be needed. *Great, I'll have a drink.*

It didn't work out that way. And there I was, Debbie-on-the-spot. 'Please,' the MC announced into his mic, 'welcome the Artistic Director of Queensland's Music Festival, Deborah Conway, to say a few words.'

Oh bugger. What the hell am I going to say? I smiled broadly, walked to the microphone and said, something I have laughed about ever since, because I really had no idea what was about to come out of my mouth, 'Gladstone, what a great community you are, I love your salt, I love your mines.' I believe my comments were received with reverence . . . 'She loves our minds!'

There is a photograph of this occasion where I am standing out in front of a line of council members and other QMF staff including Nigel, who is leaning back and looking at me disbelievingly.

Just a few weeks after the 2009 festival I turned fifty. I celebrated with friends in a local Chinese cafe I'd hired for the night. We drank champagne, ate dumplings and played rotating whist, the card game equivalent of square dancing, with lots of changing partners. I was feeling fine, revelling in the sense of achievement of having delivered my first festival successfully and, as a bonus, overcoming my phobia of public speaking.

In January 2011, five months before my second QMF, nature was on a rampage. One of the worst-hit areas was the unlikeliest. Toowoomba, 700 metres above sea level, is a pretty town with two slender creeks running through it. On 11 January, after continuous heavy rainfall for days, the creeks broke their banks and transformed into raging torrents that engulfed the town. Intense rainfall east of the Darling Downs caused massive flooding in the Lockyer Valley when a line of storms hit. The surge of water swept through, leaving houses and cars crushed as an inland tsunami caused floodwaters to rise to 8 metres by the time it reached the town of Grantham. Death and destruction stalked the valley.

The subject matter for 'Third Time Down' was not generally the kind of material I would look to for inspiration, but a year later it was something I needed to write about. It is hard to find redemption or sense amid extreme disasters. For us mortals, an indifferent universe or the unknowable acts of G-d are equally opaque.

'Third Time Down', *Stories of Ghosts*, 2013

The drought broke hard without much warning, it rained, rained, rained
Floods filled the pretty parks, houses and cars float away

First time, the water closes over I'm going down
Second time, all my sins forgiven
Redemption on the third time down

To Postman's Ridge, below the mountain, the torrent roared
Covered everything, the devil himself could have done no more

First time, the water closes over I'm going down
Second time, all my sins forgiven
Redemption on the third time down

Creeks turn to seas
People lost in disbelief
I was held by the tide but now I am released

Close the doors, lock all the windows, it's wet outside
Turn on the radio, you can pray but I'd rather dance tonight

I delivered my second and last festival for QMF in July 2011. It was wild and stimulating fun but after almost four years of commuting I needed to be at home; the girls had started calling me 'Daddy'.

37

Only Girl

A few months later my daddy died.

Episode 19, Season 2 of *The Simpsons*, 'Lisa's Substitute', was particularly poignant for me. 'Eight-year-old Lisa struggles with her identity after substitute teacher Mr Bergstrom (played by Dustin Hoffman) proves a more desirable role model than her father.' Lisa's distress when Mr Bergstrom moves on to his next job cuts to the emotional quick. Lisa does her level best to engage Homer at the same existential level as her teacher but gets nothing back. In her frustration she yells at her father, 'You wouldn't understand,' to which Homer replies, 'Hey, just because I don't care doesn't mean I don't understand!'

It summed up, in one hilarious and cruel one-liner, the way I felt about my relationship with my father. We were operating on different planes.

My father, Carl, was born between the wars in Leeds, Yorkshire, to Hettie and Solly Cohen. His grandparents on both sides had fled Russia in the late 1800s with the pogroms in full swing, sweeping through the small *shtetls* around Minsk, Vilna, Kiev and Odessa with monotonous regularity. Like so many other Jews desperate to escape persecution, they emigrated and headed for England to make a new life.

My father's family—once called Podnow and before that Podnovsky—were newly named Cohen when they arrived on the shores of Merry Old England. (Cohen is a very recognisably Jewish name but maybe to their ears it sounded more Anglicised than the name they gave up.) And without being hunted down and slaughtered every few years they did pretty well. My paternal grandfather Solomon was the youngest of six children and the only male; his sisters were Mary, Hilda, Annie, Fay and Dolly.

My paternal grandmother, née Hettie Garb, was one of nine offspring, with Julius, Sarah, Morris, Vera, Annie, Rosie, Lottie and Harry; I never knew any of her brothers, who all perished serving in the British forces in World War II. Cruel irony: if they'd stayed in Europe they could have been killed by the Germans without having to change their names or emigrate.

There were many little Garbs and Cohens running around at that time but, in the end, the grand total of the subsequent generation was a lousy six from both sides. Sarah had three children, while Hettie had Carl and a younger sister who didn't survive infancy. On the other side, Solomon's sister Fay had a son, also called Carl, and a daughter Bette, and that was the end of that.

Dad grew up as a treasured only child. Not only his parents but his battalion of maiden aunts doted on him, nursed him through a lung condition that kept him bedridden for twelve months, and comforted him through the nightly German bombing raids, all of which would have proved challenging for even the most even-keeled individual, which he certainly was not.

He was raised in an observant Jewish home, going to *cheder* (religious Jewish school), to which he wore his *kippah* and *tzitzit* every day, and being pelted on his way there and home again with some kind of makeshift missiles (sticks, stones, marbles, eggs) was a regular occurrence, though a definite step-up from the Russian bayonet, Berdon rifle or boot dealt out to previous generations.

At nineteen Carl, having emigrated with my grandparents and many of my great-aunts to Australia, repressed his true desire to become an actor and instead made his parents happy by reading law at the University of Melbourne. On opening a law office in the mid-1950s, my dad swapped the 'Cohen' for 'Conway' to avoid any possible antisemitism.

My mother had a very different start to life. Elizabeth Leah Mendes grew up in Melbourne on *Melways* Map 58. She had boyfriends, or suitors as they were called, but Elizabeth was a protected and dutiful young woman who would not have dreamed of engaging in anything more advanced than some necking until she'd stepped out from under the *chuppah*. Born in 1934 in Australia, and insulated by distance from the vicissitudes of World War II, Elizabeth's innocence was preserved in aspic for most of her young life. Her biggest bugbear was her mother, Dorothy Mendes, a formidable, overbearing woman who could be a terrible bully.

My mother tells a story that she's rather proud of. When her very unsentimental mother told her how plain she was, my mother replied, 'That's interesting, because everyone says I look just like you.' A moment of sweet vindication for young Elizabeth just before she got slapped.

In 1952 Elizabeth was a darling, diminutive bridesmaid for her friend Cherie. My mother just gave me an old black-and-white photo of the three lovely teenage bridesmaids sitting in height order on a chaise longue with the tall, elegant bride standing to one side. By virtue of her size, Elizabeth is sitting on the far end smiling broadly, her hair bobbed and perfectly posed with her identical floral arrangement. She was adorable.

This is possibly where my mother first laid eyes on my very handsome father who happened, also, to be a terrific dancer. I can't be certain it was at this party but whichever shindig it was, square dancing, that great aphrodisiac, was involved.

One of the truly tempting lures of marrying the handsome Englishman Carl Cohen was getting away from her mother, though ironically, as my mother frequently tells me, 'I married my mother', referring to the inescapable fact that both her mother and her husband were very difficult, disagreeable people.

My dad wasn't like anybody else's dad I knew. Carl Conway was larger than life, big and theatrical; he could emotionally sweep up everything in his path, he was the soul of the party, he had a magnetic pull and he loved a spotlight. He wore Liberace jewellery, a toupee on weekends, smoked cigars constantly, ate boxes of chocolates gloatingly in front of his two daughters and never shared any. He knew how to get the CEO of Sony on the phone just to interrogate him about his TV remote control. In fact, one of his favourite pastimes was tormenting unsuspecting workers, at whatever organisation he was calling, to complain about whatever he was complaining about. It was a sport for him. No wonder he could get Sony's CEO on the phone, no one else wanted to deal with him.

He was predictably unpredictable, and though he might have been difficult he was never, ever, ever boring. He was also bipolar.

Carl had a fantastic collection of musicals on 12-inch vinyl. I played them all—it was my whole musical education growing up. *Oliver*, *The Bells Are Ringing*, *Camelot*, *West Side Story*, *Oklahoma*, *Sweet Charity*, on and on. He had a fine deep voice, which worked well for all those Robert Goulet songs he loved to sing. And he loved to mime; Shellie would be ordered to man the curtain in the living room, using the pulley to reveal Dad miming to 'If Ever I Should Leave You'. I was commanded to film him.

He got himself a third name, a stage name—Carl Carmichael—and gave his first love, acting, a reboot; among other roles he was in a Playbox production, cast alongside actor Bud Tingwell, and featured in an advertisement for a product called Piles Cement, where he had to perch on a fence looking uncomfortable.

Carl was a formidable lawyer: intelligent, erudite, and with his neglected acting skills usefully employed. Notwithstanding, he took an early retirement, which left him with a lot of time. He made money, lost money and made it again in mysterious ways that he never tried to demystify for me. He was always hinting at dark forces but we never knew what. The stock market, the money market, and the real estate market were his playground but if I expressed interest he would explain things in such a way as to further muddy the waters.

He often told me I had only half a brain, referring to me being young, but I was always going to be younger than him, consequently always possessing only half a brain. He was an investor in outlandish contraptions like a bread-slicing machine that also spread butter (the butter went everywhere, the invention nowhere).

I would wake up to the terrifying sound of my parents fighting most mornings; the word d-i-v-o-r-c-e was hurled frequently until I ran in sobbing and begging them to stop. I had no idea what they were fighting about. As far as I could ascertain Liz was bending over backwards but it made no difference; Carl was either high as a kite or flat as a tack. Putting my key in the front door after school, I'd be full of anxiety. Which Carl would be waiting? Both were equally terrifying, for if he was up, down was coming.

For all of my childhood, he self-medicated. I remember one afternoon at our family friend's pool when Mum was somewhere else, leaving Dad in charge. His response was to pop one too many Valium and then struggle to stay upright or talk coherently. He was in a filthy mood that day, full of sneer and snarl. I was nine, but fuck me, I realised I was in charge. Reasons to be traumatised—or tough. I picked tough.

He was selfish and narcissistic with a cruel streak. He only hit me once but he did throw my mother's typewriter across the room; ripped up all her dresses, and put his pen through her car radio because the station she was listening to was annoying him. He loved animals but when one of our several attempts at pet cats made the felonious error of scratching him, the animal ended up in the dryer, which Dad turned on. The cat emerged dazed and confused and then went MIA.

When we were young he frequently sat with us at bedtime, but instead of reading us a story, he would talk about death. These conversations weren't abstract; there were yearly suicide attempts.

One night, after my mother had left the house after another one of their mighty rows, Shellie and I were in my bed together, commiserating, when our family doctor, Dr Levin, startled us by walking into my bedroom saying, 'Don't worry, your father will be fine.'

I didn't immediately recognise this dark, swarthy gentleman who appeared unexpectedly in my bedroom after dark, which was discombobulating right there, but the rest was like a horror movie. We had no idea what would 'be fine', having been unaware of how Carl had once again spun off the rails.

He'd constructed a tableau in the basement, surrounded himself with carefully placed props, candles and photos—of his mother, not us—popped his pills and then apparently put the call in to the doctor. All the different manifestations of his screams for help were terrifying, but that year he excelled himself. Our father was the epitome of extreme, undiagnosed mental illness, which tortured and tormented him and us by turn.

My father was intrigued by technology, all technology; in fact he was in love with it, but it was a terrible unrequited love. He was the first on the block to get the latest gadget, the last to know how to use it. Whether it was the roll-down scenery depicting a sunny day in Tuscany or a stormy night in Transylvania, complete with spot-lit moon, or the theatrical LSD-influenced, trance-inducing light show on the wall, or the TV that at the push of a button would descend into the basement and then re-emerge when required, he was the proud owner of it and he loved nothing more than an audience to show it off to.

One day I rang the bell and Mum answered, saying, 'Oh, I thought you were the TV man.' I walked into the lounge and saw Dad overseeing the descent of the TV into the basement below.

'But I thought the TV man was coming to repair it,' I said.

'He is,' Dad replied.

And eventually the repair man did arrive and got the floor show, literally, as the lounge room floor opened and the TV rose majestically from below. It was actually less than majestic and rather more moribund as it creaked upwards but my dad had a look on his face like he was cutting the ribbon on the *Queen Mary*.

The phrase 'get the man in' was bandied about often. It usually meant maintenance. When 'the man' came around, Carl recorded all conversations on one of his strategically placed hidden microphones, which would be played back if the completed job was not up to scratch. It was rarely up to scratch.

Not only the tradesmen were surveilled; Dad eavesdropped on all my phone calls, literally every one. We had many telephones in our house. For the entire duration of my teenage years, if I got a call, I would hear that spacious telltale sound of my father picking up a phone in another room and listening in. All conversations with my friends were punctuated with 'Dad, can you get off the phone, pleeease?' He was unusually patient on these calls, silently pretending he wasn't there until he deemed it the right moment to interrupt, throwing in a comment when he became sufficiently bored. It's actually remarkable that my friends talked to me on the phone at all.

His culinary skills were limited to making a cup of tea (with a teabag, as loose-leaf tea was deemed archaic at our house) and boiling an egg, but since my mother cooked all his meals for him and served them on a tray in front of the TV it wasn't a problem. As he ate, he watched the news. If we children dared to speak during this ritual, Carl would reach for the remote control and adjust the volume until it was thunderous, the equivalent of yelling at us to shut up.

One night I cooked my father a steak for dinner when Mum was out. I didn't really cook; my mother did it all and she never shared her limited culinary skills with either of her daughters. I served my father his steak on a tray and went back to the kitchen to take advantage by making a phone call he wouldn't listen to. Within moments of me sitting down and getting on the phone, a steak was hurled at my head from the corridor outside the kitchen and Carl was screaming at me, 'It's raw!!!! Put it back under the griller!'

The man was a fucking lunatic! His reaction served the dual purpose of terrorising me and ensuring I had to immediately desist from talking on the phone so he could listen to my call later.

Carl was a good-looking man, impeccably if flamboyantly dressed, but his hair was an ongoing issue for him. At around age twenty-five he had already started balding and despite having a handsome head he was always looking around for remedies. There was a lotion on the market that promised, with a few drops rubbed into the scalp each night, increased hair growth. Dad, in what I would have to say was typically enthusiastic fashion, thought that if a few drops worked, what would half the bottle do? The answer was a little hairy mound on the pillow the next morning.

He eventually progressed to wearing his famous toupee. I was acutely aware of my duty to keep my father's toupee a secret even from my closest friends, but Shellie had no such qualms; she told everyone, her small act of revenge. I have a vivid memory of my friend Caro staying over and going downstairs in the middle of the night to get a drink and seeing Dad, or the back of him, watching TV. She came upstairs freaked out about the strange bald man in the living room. I had to fess up. Secrecy was an ongoing theme.

Shellie and I never knew with certainty that our father was gay. My nanna did once say to me cryptically, probably during a period when my parents were fighting a lot, 'Well you know about your father!' which sounded like it should have explained everything, but only mystified things further. As we became more cognisant of such things as young adults his behaviours started to reveal themselves and point at something.

His love of Barbra Streisand, Judy Garland and Liza Minnelli, the theatre; his complete disinterest in competitive sport, or any sport for that matter; his meticulous approach to his wardrobe; he liked to wear a little mascara; he dyed his hair and had regular manicures; he had several facelifts; he wore fake tan; he never, and I mean never, expressed admiration for the way a woman looked, other than what she might have been wearing; he loved the *Golden Girls*, Frankie Howard, Carol Burnett, Bette Midler and Benny Hill; my parents always slept in single beds and had separate bathrooms.

Every summer Dad would fly to San Francisco, leaving Mum to oversee our holidays (always more fun without his simmering turbulence); photos of him lying grinning on a hotel bed clad only in a sailor's cap with a pink hibiscus flower between his legs turned up in his bedside drawers when I was rummaging around for something, as did suggestive appurtenances I discovered concealed in the basement cupboards.

Test results came in for Carl Conway stating a negative result for HIV/AIDS while our parents were on one of their lengthy overseas sojourns in the mid-1980s. I had moved to Sydney, so Shellie was tasked with collecting their mail, opening it, banking cheques, and reporting anything important to them when they called. It was one more piece in the jigsaw puzzle of circumstantial evidence that was my father. We never took it seriously, after all, he was also a hypochondriac. His being gay was the kind of thing we might speculate about but not in earnest. I mean, how would Mum not know?

It would be late in 1997, after yet another ghastly episode where Dad ended up in the Melbourne Clinic, a private mental health hospital, when Shellie spoke to his psychiatrist.

'Do you think my father is homosexual?'

'He is.'

Mum and I got together for lunch after that revelation, and I said cautiously something like, 'We've thought for a while that Dad might be gay.'

And she said, 'Yes, of course he's gay. I knew that when I married him.'

She had always known. She had married a gay man who was trying to lead the life that was expected of him, to become a father and enjoy his children, to have a loving, accepting, long-suffering wife at his side, someone he could trust to keep all his secrets. My mother knew everything and had never breathed a word. It was like the ground I stood on became molten quicksand. I was sinking into a completely new frame of reference.

The fact that Dad was gay is not the headline by any stretch of the imagination. I spent twenty years living with an undiagnosed psychotic. It was more that my mother couldn't trust us with this information—well, neither of them could. I kept my new knowledge a secret from my father until the day he died. I have told virtually no one in my circle of friends. Habit of a lifetime, secrecy. But I hate secrets. Especially those that make so many people wretched.

'Only Girl', *Bitch Epic*, 1993

Father I'm so disillusioned
Can you see why?
Easily let down disappointed
I know you tried to make things right
It's not possible

Light the candles fill the ashtray
Empty your heart
We can sit here talk for hours
Work out the part where we lost the plot
If it's possible it could be possible

Tell me father what's the matter?
Don't end it all
No one round here lives forever
That's not your role we rise and fall
That's possible
I'm your only one and only girl

See me father I have your blood
Your eyes and bones

Hear my voice my laugh my temper
I am your own
Don't turn to stone
Make it possible
Could be laughable
So untouchable
Irreversible
Is it possible?

My father was constantly competitive with me, making it impossible for us to have a reasonable conversation. When I played him my song 'Only Girl', he sneered, 'I don't suppose you wrote that about me.' It was hard to say I had, so I didn't.

He never got involved with my studies; wasn't there to assist me with my homework or turn up to parent-teacher meetings or, on the upside, never expressed any opinion on my scholastic results. But to celebrate me completing the HSC he took me on a father-daughter overseas trip. I wasn't all that keen on going, for obvious reasons, though we had a few good times. It's just the times I most easily recall are the nightmarish ones.

I got lost in Paris one late afternoon walking around; it was January so the days were very short. I couldn't find the hotel we were staying in, and by the time I'd figured it out it was well and truly dark and my father, despite seeing that I was freaked out, unleashed on me a tirade like I'd done it on purpose. It was on this trip that he co-opted me as his nurse and I had to apply medicated cream to his anus. Was he trying 'The Method' approach for his upcoming appearance in the Piles Cement ad? Good grief.

We went to the Paris Opera and saw a ballet, which he snored through, me poking him in the ribs when it got too loud. He took me to the Moulin Rouge nightclub and I had to endure the large-breasted semi-clad dancers flirting with him, both of us reasonably uncomfortable. We stopped in England to visit family. Lunching at Fortnum & Mason's, my father had gone to the restroom when I was approached by a young diamond dealer with an invitation to go to dinner. Strangely, my father gave permission. That's what sticks; I have no recollection of the dinner itself.

Our last stop on this commemorative trip was Boston. We had family there I didn't know existed; it's an extremely strange date with destiny when you walk into a stranger's house in a town you've never visited, in a climate you've never encountered (Boston was under several feet of snow) and a nice old lady brings out a photo album full of pictures . . . of you.

We got through the trip without killing each other, but it definitely didn't have any side benefit of bringing us closer together. I came back and spent all my time thinking about how I could move out. I needed my own income stream and I needed it fast. Carl disapproved of me living independently and told me categorically I wouldn't get a penny from him if I moved out. I wouldn't even get to take the four-poster double bed I'd been given as a birthday present.

That's when I put a photographic portfolio together and started modelling. The proceeds bought me a car, the Karmann Ghia. He disapproved of that too, of course. I can still hear him yelling at me from inside the house, after I left to pick it up from the dealer.

He disapproved of all my boyfriends. I came home one day shedding tears as I'd just broken up with the boy I'd been sharing a house with for over a year, the one who'd been cheating on me.

'What's wrong?' my father asked.

'I've split up with Peter,' I sobbed.

'Who's Peter?' he said.

That one made me laugh, though not at the time and certainly not because it was supposed to be a gag. ('Just because I don't care doesn't mean I don't understand.')

He disapproved of my career and had sent me to a shrink when I joined a band, but cried tears of joy when I gave him my first gold record. He loved to come and see me perform and was happy to offer a 'no fear, no favours', as he liked to call it, critique. 'You weren't wearing enough makeup,' or 'You didn't enunciate clearly enough,' or very rarely, 'You were wonderful'.

One night at Melbourne nightclub the Continental, my father booked a table next to the stage, directly in front of me, and was sitting with half-a-dozen friends. He spent most of the night trying to get my attention while I was trying my best to ignore him. He had shoved white cloth napkins into each ear and was doing his best impression of Peter Rabbit, writing notes in capital letters that he showed me in the middle of songs saying, 'TOO LOUD, I THINK IT'S THE SPEAKERS'.

I had always known my father was a difficult human being but walking into a psychiatrist's office in London, in my early thirties, my relationship with him was not what was uppermost in my mind. Unlike in my early twenties when it was my father insisting I should see a psychiatrist to work out why I was doing something as 'self-destructive' as joining a band, this time I had come for clarity. I was trying to solve what at the time seemed conundrums

I couldn't untangle without professional assistance. My life—love, career, future—seemed hopelessly and unbearably confused and I needed to try and work out why.

I outlined to the therapist what I'd come for and she asked me to tell her about growing up. And that was it. I was reduced to a puddle, a box of sodden tissues, barely able to catch a breath between sobs. How did that happen?

We had an intercom in the family house we lived in from when I was fourteen. I never got used to that obnoxious grating buzzer being continuously pressed by my mad father in his upstairs domain, demanding my mother's presence, a cup of tea, to issue a directive to us. It was the kind of sound that would shred nerves, and it became a warning to flee.

One time we all ran away from home, including Mum. We came back. My poor mother soldiered on and they forged a truce. But she covered for him; she thought that pretending my father wasn't as crazy as he was would convince us that his terrible behaviour was normal. It was the ultimate gaslighting, really.

It made no difference to me; I couldn't live with him; as soon as I was able, I fled. Liz and Carl stayed married, sharing their deepest secrets with strangers on passenger liners sailing for months in foreign waters, strangers they would never meet again.

I recall one conversation with my father not very long before he died, in which he sounded sane. I got off the phone, stunned. He hadn't been competitive, angry or distracted or furious about some trivial thing. He was in the moment, with me, having a reasonable conversation about nothing in particular. It was really wonderful, and it was all I'd ever wanted from him.

Carl's favourite toast was, 'Here's to an easy death!' He died suddenly, choking on his lunch in a rehab clinic, where he was recovering from a probably unnecessary knee reconstruction. It was 20 November, 2011. Theatrical to the last. Maybe not surprisingly, he is in the category of 'too big to miss'. Always with me, and in me. I am formed by him but not a victim to him.

He would have loved this.

38

Outside of Zion

In 2013, we toured a four-piece band plus sound engineer across regional Queensland to promote *Stories of Ghosts*, taking in the best of the Boy's Own attractions that are a feature of that great state's hinterland.

This tour wouldn't have happened without financial assistance; after my years with the Queensland Music Festival I knew that the magic fairy dust for any successful arts application were the catchwords 'workshop' and 'mentor'. Willy and I offered a song-writer/performer workshop in every single town on that trip, from Blackall to Winton, Longreach to Charleville and Mount Isa. The kids were completely engaged. The adults ranged from keen to passionate to mental.

The Dalby and Winton workshops stand out. Dalby was full of amateur songwriters looking for inspiration. A gentleman told us he was writing a song about his recently deceased canine friend;

he broke down as he emotionally undressed in this room full of amateur songwriters. It was brave and unexpected and made for a very authentic session around what you can write a song about.

Winton's workshop took place in the Opal Museum with a class of primary school kids and a smattering of adults. A newly widowed older woman who had been finding solace in her local church community had decided she needed to exercise her creative muscle writing lyrics. Another very odd man was initially super-enthusiastic but increasingly aggressive as he interrupted our presentation to make grand statements about Bob Dylan and The Rolling Stones being pretenders to the craft and charlatans who were only good at making money. He worked himself into a minor frenzy, throwing his arms around and swearing. I told him he should get a hold of himself in front of the young kids.

He went quiet for a while until the schoolteacher wanted to take a photo, at which he began swearing at her to stop because he thought she was taking his picture. Having freaked out all the children, he was escorted from the room, still yelling.

It was an extreme performance and we mused for a while about his circumstances; perhaps he was an outlaw on the run, pausing to take advantage of a songwriting workshop to help him hone a good song about his escapades? Hmmmm.

I'm always discomfited by requests to teach songwriting. I am neither a natural teacher nor particularly patient (Mr Zygier possesses both qualities in spades), nor do I feel cognisant enough of the process to communicate the 'how to'. When I am expected to be able to articulate the nuts and bolts, I start feeling like a fake.

How the hell do you write a song? I have a few fallback tricks that I've read in books on songwriting: have a list of titles to start from; record everything you sing and play; suspend judgement.

These are all useful instructions to impart to a student starting out, but it doesn't get to the core because by the time I'm at the core I am no longer fully conscious; it's a kind of alchemy and that is hard to teach; it eludes explanation. I can be hammering away on an idea and everything I come up with feels effortful or missing the mark in some way; and then somehow, without quite being aware how, I will have written something I like. It works and feels in some way separate to me, like I didn't really write it, but rather channelled it. Hank Williams, asked how he wrote his songs, answered, 'I don't write 'em, I just hang on to the pen and God sends them through.'

Strangely, teaching got me closer to understanding the mechanics of songwriting than actually writing songs, and for that I am grateful. Deconstructing an approach and piecing it back together while figuring out a loose set of rules to communicate to students supplied a template of how to get closer to that sensation.

How can you tell what makes a good song? I don't have a definitive answer, but there's the feeling you've heard this before though you haven't; the feeling you get when you've tried every key from the bunch in your hand and finally one smoothly turns the lock; the feeling of finding the last piece of the jigsaw you've been working on and seeing the complete picture for the first time.

It's marrying words to melody, mood and rhythm and they all want to live happily ever after. That is the ultimate beauty, the essence of what it means to communicate, the ability to generate a little mystery in the world. That's my favourite kind of music, the songs or pieces that don't lay it all out so there's nowhere to go; the best kinds of music provide a multitude of pathways to discover meaning, layer on layer.

There is craft and art to songwriting. The craft is everything you do in draft after draft to capture art, that initial inspiration, and fashion it into a song. When the door to magical mystery opens, you have to be ready to rush through with nary a backward glance.

Mr Zygier's and my last three albums, *Stories of Ghosts*, *Everybody's Begging* and *Words of Men*, stand as solid evidence in defence of the work; we never shirked the effort, never let ourselves get carried away with the art without paying due diligence to the craft. And we approached them as a trilogy, each building on the last, exploring the connections of ancient stories through a contemporary lens; our experience of Judaism; our interpretation of other artists' creative endeavours; our relationship to the swirling cultural climate. We were savage with each other's ideas, and the list of rejected songs got longer, but the quality control department working at full capacity meant we were not releasing anything we weren't totally committed to.

We dived deeply into our subject matter, teasing apart the strange times we were/are all living through, layering the personal on the universal and coming up with songs that spoke of contradictions, of hypocrisy, of rising antisemitism that was impossible to ignore; of confusion, chaos, love and hate. We tried to zoom out to place the material in the world we all live in.

In 2009 we were struggling with a song. We weren't happy enough to record it for the album we were making, *Half Man Half*

Woman. Afterwards we kept working on it. We ended up with thirteen different versions, with thirteen different titles on thirteen different subjects. Months passed; many drafts were rejected. I was the proverbial starving child staring in the window of the sweet-shop. Whether I wanted it or not, the process of writing this song was maybe what the song could be about; the travails of songwriting, the attempts, the failures, the effort and ultimately a stand-in for the struggles of being a human being falling short of the mark.

The story of Moses, who led the Jews out of slavery and through forty years in the desert but was forbidden from entering the Promised Land, felt like a good vehicle for my frustration. That ancient tale of human striving defeated by larger forces was perfectly current. With draft fourteen, 'Outside of Zion' clicked into focus.

'Outside of Zion', *Stories of Ghosts*, 2013

Falling at your feet
Coming apart slowly
I kneel before you now
Asking forgiveness for all that I've done
Standing outside of Zion

The Lord writes better tunes
I pray for some guidance
My work is rough and rude
There was a time when I heard your song
It rang out so sweetly, and I sang along

And it's still in my head, playing 1 2 3 1
Standing outside of Zion

Every mistake that I made
I'd make them all over again
'cos all of those wrong turns and stumbles I took
Let me glimpse perfection

I dreamt the Promised Land
But I've lost my way lately
And I don't know how this ends
There have been times when my faith was strong
There have been times when I got it all wrong
And there have been days when the people were crying
'Lord, were you lying?
Leaving us standing outside of Zion'

39

Take Pity on the Beast

Growing up in an observant but not religious house, my Jewish education was patchy. I went to Jewish kindergarten, but not day school, Jewish Sunday school, summer camp and dancing class, though I still ended up dating plenty of non-Jewish boys. (And every time my father would say, 'Another nail in my coffin, Deborah.' It was a well-nailed coffin.)

We had lively Shabbat family dinners at Grandma's. The two nights of Seder—the meal and service that celebrate Pesach (Passover)—were also at Grandma's, with Dad always spending the second half lying on the couch digesting. Friday nights were (and still are) full of ferocious debate, political and cultural—sometimes we even agreed!

As a tribe we tend towards the verbally argumentative. These arguments are not only found between family and friends vigorously discussing ethics, or cultivated by choosing law as a profession. This is what rabbis do: debate, wrestle and struggle in an eternal search to glean greater truth from the texts their predecessors were also debating, wrestling and struggling with. In Genesis 32:22–32, the name 'Israel' is conferred on Jacob by an angel he had wrestled with all night, and literally means 'to wrestle (or contend) with G-d'.

On Yom Kippur we fasted (or were supposed to) and over the day, visited pretty much all the synagogues in Melbourne in what I called a *shule* crawl. We started with the morning service at Kew Shule where Dad would take Shellie and me in our nice frocks and we'd play 'spot the cute boys' from up on the balcony (the more Conservative Kew synagogue had the men, sitting downstairs, women upstairs). Then we'd head home to pick up Mum before schlepping to Temple Beth Israel (where men and women sat together). Home again to drop off Dad, take a short snackless break, then on to the afternoon service at Toorak Shule with Mum to see my nanna.

By 3 pm I was starving and complaining bitterly about the entire 'atonement' thing. One year, Mum couldn't take my whining anymore and bought me a tomato sandwich from the milk bar on the corner of Toorak and St Kilda Roads, which I can still taste, it was so spectacularly delicious. Yet still we crawled, we fasted, we atoned, for what I knew not, maybe for all my future sins. Charnwood Grove was the last stop, where we went with my dad to see Grandma before piling into the car and back to her place to break the fast, which for me of course was already well and truly broken.

My living arrangements in the years after I left home were in share houses where I was the only Jew. My Jewishness assumed a marginally exotic background tint, where I would occasionally throw in some Yiddish to get a laugh. After a period of debauched, godless years of indulgence, decadence and putting many nails in my father's coffin on many continents, sometime in my mid-twenties I found myself yearning for this foundational element to be back in my life.

At the time I was living in Los Angeles. It was Pesach and everywhere there were Jews walking to synagogue and back home to share their Seders with family. I experienced a wave of sorrow for something missing, a feeling that demanded a reckoning. Thus began a journey of sorts, something I didn't recognise at the time, but in retrospect it was the moment when I began to join my different lives together.

There was some mess, some broken things—people, trust, hearts, bonds—but something was driving this beyond conscious thought. By the time I met Willy I had acknowledged that my Jewishness was an inherent part of me, not fashionable, and not even based in a fundamental belief in G-d, but bound up in an ancient and compelling story with many facets, a story I was ignoring at my peril. Slowly I was pulling out the nails from my father's coffin.

Very little of this reckoning crossed into my creative life until we wrote 'Take Pity on the Beast'.

'Take Pity on the Beast', *Half Man Half Woman*, 2010

Take pity on the beast
You gotta take pity on the beast
Man lives his life on a leash
Take pity on the beast

Take pity on the beast
You gotta take pity on the beast
'Til his burden is complete
Take pity on the beast

I was walking my dog in the gardens
The day rising up with the sun
A well-dressed man in leather told me
I am the son
I am the Son of G-d, the Messiah
And I see everything you done wrong
Before you is redemption
Then he blessed me and was gone

Take pity on the beast
You gotta take pity on the beast
It's always famine never feast
Take pity on the beast
Take pity on the beast
You gotta take pity on the beast
Until the sun sets in the east
Take pity on the beast

My good friend had a nervous breakdown
Truths were leaking out of her like shit
She said my whole life's a sickness
I am sick
I am sick and I'm a liar
And I drip sadness everywhere I go

I see no light, no joy, no beauty
Then she says but I'm going on with the show

Take pity on the beast
You gotta take pity on the beast
One day soon he'll be deceased
Take pity on the beast

Take pity on the beast
You gotta take pity on the beast
He's been robbed and he's been fleeced
Take pity on the beast

His skin is paper thin and worn out
His blue eyes are vacant lots
As a young man he was a survivor
Of the Holocaust
The Holocaust was his companion
A lifetime at his side
Now all that's gone with his memory
And all he says is alright, alright, alright

Take pity on the beast
You gotta take pity on the beast
He knows enough to know he's least
Take pity on the beast

Take pity on the beast
You gotta take pity on the beast

When he's crumpled and he's creased
Take pity on the beast

I know a man who denies his essence
He is a man who is not at one
When he swallows moods from a bottle
He is blind deaf dumb
Blind deaf dumb to reason
Crying out for more
Chemicals and crazy hormones
A one-man self-waged war

Take pity on the beast
You gotta take pity on the beast
If you're rabbi or you're priest
Take pity on the beast

Take pity on the beast
You gotta take pity on the beast
Like a lover just released
Take pity on the beast

We were slaves in the land of Egypt
We were dogs under Pharoah's whip
'Til the first born lay dying
And the mountains skipped
The mountains skipped the Jordan turned backwards
The sea saw and fled
And the children of Israel

Trembled and wept
We lurch from post to pillar
Repeating our mistakes
In every generation
We all ache
We all ache from our desires
From all our misplaced trust
In heroes, gods and science
But still we are dust to dust

Take pity on the beast
You gotta take pity on the beast
Whatever scare they preach
Take pity on the beast

Take pity on the beast
You gotta take pity on the beast
Its milk is sweeter than its meat
Take pity on the beast

Take pity on the beast
You gotta take pity on the beast
Life is brutal 'til it's ceased
Take pity on the beast

Willy had the title and the first two stanzas, which formed the first chorus. It was enough. I ran hard and fast and came up with a cast of characters, people we knew all too well, friends, our fathers, a litany of woes and for my climactic penultimate verse

I sought inspiration from the Haggadah, the prayer book read around the family table at the Seder meal on Passover:

> When Israel went forth from Egypt, Jacob's household from a people of alien tongue, Judah became his sanctuary, Israel his dominion. The Sea saw and fled; the Jordan turned backward. The mountains skipped like rams and the hills like young lambs. What ails you, O Sea, that you flee? O Jordan that you turn backward? O mountains that you skip like rams? O hills, like young lambs?

Is this the description of an earthquake? A mystical vision? The ecstatic response of the Jewish diaspora returning? A natural phenomenon only able to be understood through transcendent rhapsodising?

Questions don't always need answers to make sense of something. This was sense-making in the metaphysical realm. The lines came to me unbidden. After so many Seders, I knew them backwards (which is how they came out) and there we were, in a place I hadn't glimpsed before. I had written a song with the fullest sense of my being as a Jew.

It was kind of crazy I'd never done it before. Twenty years ago, I had used Catholic references in my song 'String of Pearls': 'patience of saints', 'dimly lit by my rosary'. My friend Jackie Dennis (raised a Catholic) took exception to my cultural appropriation (not that we used the phrase back then) of Catholic tropes. I found it surprising at the time and justified it as a sort of universally recognised shorthand, which satisfied her—I think. But I should have thought more about it.

Now, suddenly, in mid-life, I was thinking about it. I had finally placed side-by-side what I did with who I was. It is not so often you can point to something and say, 'Before this we were this and after this, we were something else'.

In 2010, Gary Holzman, a Sydney copyright lawyer and music buff with a special interest in Jewish songwriters, started up a festival called Shir Madness. 'Shir', pronounced 'sheer', is Hebrew for 'song'; cute pun. He invited us to play. It was like walking through a life-altering gateway; the opening of new avenues to marry our Judaism and our musical lives. We performed 'Take Pity on The Beast'. It felt electric to me, singing those familiar lines from the Haggadah to the little children dancing wildly in front of the stage.

40

As Sweet as Battles Won

By the time we were asked to perform in our third Sydney Shir Madness Festival in 2013, we'd released *Stories of Ghosts*. Lyrically the album revolved around an unbeliever's examination of Torah (the Five Books of Moses) stories from a Jewish perspective, of existential uncertainty in the face of ancient beliefs and coming to terms with the idea that life is full of inexpressible loss leavened with fleeting moments of happiness.

There is no denying the endurance and grip of biblical stories on the human psyche but, like Nick Cave, I never believed in an interventionist G-d. Even with exams coming or stricken with boyfriend grief, I was a prayer-free zone. At the Sunday school and summer camp I attended in my late teens, we discussed hot-button topics like abortion and feminism, but G-d rarely came into it. There was always enough structure to work with so that any doubts about the existence of an Almighty didn't need to be a stumbling block to entry.

But to sit down and write an album's worth of material based on the Torah . . . ? It was a step into a foreign country and frankly, while I had the visa, I wasn't entirely convinced I was gettin' out alive. I mean that in a creative sense. This stuff was far from sexy subject matter in the world of popular music. It felt like we would be taking our audience on a very different excursion to the one they had signed up to with Do-Ré-Mi's material, *String of Pearls* or *Bitch Epic*.

Being explicit about my Judaism was a kind of coming out, publicly piecing together my two halves, musician and Jew. I know Willy felt exactly the same. It was a strange kind of nervousness, hand-in-hand with the regular nervousness I always experience when releasing new work into the public arena.

But the criticism I imagined never arrived. *Stories of Ghosts* was embraced by reviewers, public broadcasters and audiences; now I'm surprised I ever thought otherwise.

'G-D', *Stories of Ghosts*, 2013

I am the creator, the violator
Of your natural law
I am pure vengeance, the death sentence
Happy to destroy
Send in the plagues, the flood, send fire
I never tire of misery
I'll slay your first born, I'll slay your second born
I'll make it easy to believe
I've done it before
I can do it again
Let's start with you atheists, a good way to begin

I am, I will, I do, I see

I am the code, the secret road
To your hidden soul
I am the noise and I am the poison
That will take you all down
Here is the pestilence, I don't want to talk sense
To anyone here
I'm not forgiveness, nor am I kindness
Or justice, just fear
I made the world
And I make the rules
You think there aren't any, you're fools

I am, I will, I do, I see

Light your candles, bend your knee, lift your eyes and cry again
Why me, why me?

No hiding friend, we're at the end
I've predetermined destiny
Too late for prayers, you think I care?
I'm gonna blow you to smithereens
I've done it before
I can do it again
Can you hear it coming, the day of reckoning?
I've done it before
I can do it again
I'll still be here after Armageddon

I am, I will, I do, I see
In every generation I help a nation to fall

The other reason I felt nervous I was uncomfortable to discuss.

Growing up, I had never experienced antisemitism, but ever since the attacks on the World Trade Towers, paradoxically there was an undeniable rise in the oldest hatred. Suddenly, conspiracy theories about a secret world order of 'globalists'—meaning Jews—began to come into the mainstream. The old European tropes about Jewish bankers had transformed into a handy scapegoat for market crashes and global financial crises.

There has been an increasing prevalence of swastika graffiti on Jewish sites, the vandalising of Jewish cemeteries. In the US, people have lost their lives for attending *shule*.

More insidiously, people have felt emboldened to question if the Holocaust really happened. Or if Israel, the only Jewish country in the world, established by a UN declaration in 1948, really has legitimacy.

Like the songs we were writing, our decision in 2015 to mount our own Shir Madness Jewish Music Festival in Melbourne, was intimately tied to the temper of the times.

'As Sweet as Battles Won', *Everybody's Begging*, 2016

I was there at the camps
I was there at Babylon
I saw your face at Babi Yar
I am gone baby gone

I felt your breath upon my neck
Smelt your perfume on my gun
I was with you in the olive groves
As sweet as battles won

I was there right beside you
When we sang the workers' song
I was there when the idols
Became dust that dully shone
I held you in my arms
As you dreamt of old Zion
I'll love you at the shoreline
As sweet as battles won
As sweet as battles won

I was there working for Pharaoh
I lay bruised amongst the stone
I heard of hearts that stopped beating
And I know we all die alone

Yet when you hold me down
With words of love on your tongue
The future is a dream we dream
As sweet as battles won
The future is a dream we dream
As sweet as battles won

I was there for your condescension
I was there to play the violin
I was there to be moved on

Again again again
You hate the fucking Jews
But you always liked Bob Dylan
It's me that you got now
As sweet as battles won

I was there for your equations
The Lord our G-d the Lord is one
I was there on the seventh day
When you said the world was done
You got other things on your mind now
Everyone's forgotten about the bomb
I heard your love's eternal
As sweet as battles won
I heard your love's eternal
As sweet as battles won

I saw the birth of a country
Saw the country near succumb
I watched them build the Temple
All that glory and then none
I was there to hear glass shatter
As the wedding songs were sung
And inside me a child's growing
As sweet as battles won
As sweet as battles won
As sweet as battles won

After futile months of looking for prospective candidates to run the festival on a volunteer basis, I realised that if I wanted it to happen, I would have to direct it and recruit Willy as reluctant Artistic Director.

The workload was immense, the learning curves steep, treacherous, terrifying and tedious. I learnt things I had never wanted to know. I had the Queensland Music Festival Artistic Director role under my belt, but that was a glamorous gig with a paid staff to do my bidding. Starting a festival from scratch, total *tabula rasa*, was another beast entirely.

I spent the first few months waist deep in grant-writing, something I'd had very little experience in, and following up every hint I was given that might lead me to someone, anyone, who could heft some of the jobs and tasks off my bailiwick.

Before I could lodge a grant application, we had to recruit a board. Without a board no funding body would take us seriously. The board was Willy and me (no board experience there); Stephen Wagen was the finance officer, Annette Charak the barrister and Fiona Sweet the graphic designer. We shared a vision of a Jewish music festival in Melbourne where none currently existed. First hurdle jumped.

A couple of grant results started to dribble in. While I had been moderately successful, none was gonna set the falafel van on fire. I decided, based on the outcome of my Australia Council (AusCo) grant application, the result of which wasn't due until February or March 2015, that if successful we would go full festival, and if not, we'd return the cheques and Willy and I would go back to making songs.

I had a few shoulders to cry on, and G-d knows I needed every one of them. I was getting a crash course in fundraising from Sydney: no funding, no festival; no moolah, no music. And then—blow the horn!—we got the grant. The Shir Madness Melbourne Jewish Music Festival could hang out its shingle.

I made dozens of phone calls in the days after the AusCo decision, running through my extensive list of potential donors. The singular essential quality required for a successful fundraiser is a thick skin, of which I am luckily in possession. I cajoled, I pleaded, I bargained, I begged. Occasionally I got stern. I got most of them across the line and we raised over $220,000. It was enough to put on a very respectable professional music festival run by committed volunteers.

We discussed a lot of different location options, until finally we settled on the Classic Cinemas in Elsternwick, one of Melbourne's Jewish enclaves, with its six separate screens and the Kadimah Hall next door. We would also set up an outdoor stage in a tent on Gordon Street if we could get council permission to close the street and erect a giant marquee. We had to arrange seating, heating, lighting, toilets (how many?), toilet paper (how much?), toilet lighting (oh yes, it's all in the detail), waste management, ambulance, insurance, catering for the public, catering for the VIPs, catering for the participants, sponsorships, the cinema advertisement. We had to organise the real-estate boards advertising the festival, and also erect the real-estate boards, arguing with council about whether we could do this without paying business rates . . .

Council was suspicious of the fact that we were selling tickets, and refused to distinguish between selling tickets to make a profit and selling tickets to fund the event. The arguments I had to have!

The other item on the laundry list of festival essentials was security; another defining feature of running a Jewish Music Festival is that any public Jewish event requires special security. The difficulties galvanised us.

We were in full swing now. The volunteer team had grown exponentially. We nominated Father's Day for our festival and when it came around, it came with a tidal force. Our wonderful, supportive, frustrating community had waited until the last moment to buy tickets.

I was pulling my hair out. We had put everything into creating something from nothing, we'd put our lives on hold, our new album into the fridge, any touring was postponed, we were giving it everything including, of course, a manic publicity schedule, and what were we getting—*bupkis*! A great sleepy yawn . . . 'Yes, yes, we know about it, we'll be there . . .' Have you bought a ticket yet? 'No, no, we'll get it on the day, we'll come a bit early.' *Oy vey*.

My Girl Friday, Nerida Stern, managed the frantic hordes who had all left their ticket purchases 'til the last minute, wrangling the chaos 'til we hung up the SOLD OUT sign, moments before doors.

On the day, Melbourne's spring skies opened at 8 pm and wept profusely into the canvas maw of a jam-packed marquee; our technical manager, Danny Olesh, had spent hours, from the middle of the night before and would continue into the early hours of the morning, pulling cinema seats out, putting stages in, setting up PAs and lighting rigs on six separate stages, and then doing it all in reverse; our team of volunteer coordinators were coordinating close to a hundred other volunteers, wrangling the gold patrons into or out of their seats.

These volunteers included our rock 'n' roll emissary angel, Ruth Gould, with the tobacco-stained voice and extensive experience, whose work was only done when she had ensured all our international musicians were able to enter the country with the right visas. Our friendly welcoming artistic liaison Carolyn Masel shunted everyone back and forth from pillar to post, airport to hotel, stage to bed. The event assistants were across all of the aforementioned ephemera of event assistance; the caterer Sandra Dobs wrangling the three tiers of feeding and watering. You get the picture.

We were a lot, we were loud, we were intense, we were argumentative, we were fractious and we were pushy. We were everything I love about Jews and some stuff I don't, but it's all baked in.

And the music was frigging incredible!

After a full day of the festival that we would all claim stood testament to a groundbreaking cultural moment, it was time to rest. I dismissed our incredible platoon of exhausted volunteers at around 1.30 am as the last bits of the marquee were packed up. And in the early hours of the morning after, like the perfect end to the perfect movie, Mr Zygier and I picked up the disposable plastic tent pegs and sodden programs that had melted into the road, still glistening from the earlier downpour.

41

Book of Life

I had first visited Israel when I was fifteen. It was wild. The streets were dusty and it felt like a frontier, like something out of American Western movies I'd seen; we'd been dropped into a way-out-west desert town for which gutters and pavements hadn't yet been constructed or perhaps even thought of. It felt like a different set of priorities was at play. The air was light and clear and the sky limitlessly blue. There was an energy in the place, palpable, electrified, breathless, vibrant.

On every street corner, groups of soldiers hefting artillery were cracking jokes and smiling broadly at each other or passers-by. It is an enduring image: a soldier didn't have to be a stern figure projecting the threat of imminent violence. These soldiers were just a few years older than me, women as well as men, manifesting in equal parts freedom and duty, competence and youthful athleticism. There was enormous magnetism in that. Melbourne, my point of comparison, felt so staid, so safe and, if not old, then very middle-aged.

We spent around ten days in Israel; I have a photo album, most of the snaps faded and slightly out of focus. My father, the photographer, never remembered to take the lens cap off until we had all yelled at him. I look surly in every photo, glaring into the camera, having posed for long enough to start attracting the attention of passers-by, the very definition of torture for an awkward adolescent. My posture reflects self-consciousness over my sudden growth spurt; I am knock-kneed and my t-shirts are too small. I look like Olive Oyl.

Our family joined a tourist group, around ten of us in all, being bussed around Israel. I climbed Masada with my dad; it was early in the day but very hot. The archaeological remains of Herod's palace are extraordinary, even a sullen fifteen-year-old could marvel at the physical feats it would have taken to complete a construction of this scale in a place of such inaccessibility. I remember the breakfast we ate at the hotel at the Dead Sea, the long tables heaped with every kind of breakfast food imaginable and some that defied imagination.

We explored Tel Aviv without a tour guide, walked to beaches and cafes, did a little light shopping or at least watched my dad do some; then the bus collected us and drove the winding road up the hill to Jerusalem, the golden stone shining in the sun.

We toured the Old City and had our family photos taken in front of the Kotel. I jammed a scribbled note into the cracks. We plunged into the Arab Market, the cramped, narrow shop-lined alleys full of trinkets, fabrics, spices, carvings, pots, bells, whistles and then stumbled into the darker parts where the butchery took place.

Goat and sheep heads covered in flies met us as we wandered; other bits of animals hung like meat curtains across the storefronts, while below were pallets of offal, soft, claret-coloured liver and kidney and the paler tripes and brains that would become some sumptuous dinner for someone else—definitely not me. I am a carnivore but I remained un-tempted.

The alley ended in an archway that incongruously led into The Church of The Holy Sepulchre. Everything butted up against everything else in this tiny geographical space, barely half the size of an inner-city Melbourne suburb.

The butchered, flyblown flesh of the markets cheek-by-jowl (pun intended) with the sacred sanctuary housing the site of Jesus's crucifixion and the tomb where he was supposedly buried and resurrected. The cognitive dissonance of crossing the stone threshold from one to the other was both jarring and animating. The insistence of LIFE in all its passionate, bloody, practical, irrepressible facets was right there in those few steps.

The cramming together of Jewish, Christian and Muslim holy sites—literally on top of each other in the case of Al-Aqsa Mosque built on the ruins of the Second Temple—makes for a fevered, often violent battle of ideas and the rest, all rubbing constantly against each other. Jerusalem is a holy city for all three major Abrahamic religions; it has blood scrawled into every chapter of its thousands of years of history with justifications from angels and villains in hair-splitting Socratic proximity.

There have been countless words written in the quest to promote one angel over another villain, in the hope of finding solutions or unearthing ancient motivations, but different tribes still cling to their own versions of this seemingly endless, intractable contest.

It is a contest that not only implicates the long-dead tribes of Greeks, Romans, Babylonians, Seleucids, etc., but also the Crusaders, the Ottoman Empire and the British and French wrestling over the spoils of their hard-fought World War I. The broken promises made to their Arab allies and the nascent Zionists fighting for a small chunk of land to call their own are the most recent culprits in this history, but it is infinitely more nuanced and complex as well.

The history of the Jews indicates they can't afford to lose; that in a minority without a state and without the ability to mount a defence, the Jews are subject to persecution and worse; it has happened over and over and over again and it is still happening. 'Never again' is freighted with meaning; a couple of hours spent at Yad Vashem, the Holocaust Museum in Jerusalem, will attest to how keenly that is felt.

My second trip to Israel was in September 2006, when we travelled en masse to attend Ben Zygier's wedding. Willy's nephew was marrying an Israeli woman whose parents were from Melbourne but had made *aliyah* before they started their own family. There was some anxiety that we wouldn't be able to go, as Israel was engaged in a war with Hezbollah from their base in Lebanon through July and August. We held on to our resolve and our tickets, and once the smoke cleared we boarded our flight.

The security was tight and, as you would expect, we were asked probing questions before boarding. I'd taken care not to wrap any of the presents we were bringing in case they were searched.

Arriving at Ben Gurion Airport was magical. The golden stone of Jerusalem featured heavily in the concourse, and it felt like a homecoming. Out in the streets, there were a few more gutters and pavements than last time, works in progress; the air was still light and clear, the sky still limitlessly blue, the energy still palpable, electrified and vibrant. It was wonderful to be back, introducing our daughters to this country that, even with so much animosity directed against it, can still function as a melting pot of humanity and be a wild all-night party yet serious enough to provide an intellectually, religiously and historically profound experience.

We did all the things I had done as a teenager; it was a hot September and we hung out on Tel Aviv's beaches, at cafes serving heaped falafel, hummus and salad plates. We visited museums and mixed in a little light shopping. We hired a car to visit friends and family. Then we went on to Jerusalem to explore the Old City, the Kotel and the tunnels under the Western Wall. The layer upon layer of multiple civilisations revealed in these digs are mind-blowing.

Willy and I visited Yad Vashem, the World Holocaust Remembrance Centre. It is a harrowing experience. I understood why my parents hadn't taken my sister and me in 1974, we made the same decision not to take our young daughters in 2006.

We drove up to Haifa to see the Bahai Temple and gardens and stayed with friends living on a kibbutz in the north, a little farm life mixed in with a little light Socialism. We went south to the Negev, and swam in the Dead Sea, the intensity of which drove six-year-old Hettie out of the water howling 'til she could wash off the salt. I revisited the scale and audacity of Masada, but this time I could share my awe with eight-year-old Alma.

These memories are precious. Ben's afternoon wedding was beautiful, the groom wearing thongs, as were many of the guests, while the bride looked radiant. Willy and I played 'The Blower's

Daughter' as the bride approached the *chuppah*, and there were tears of joy and huge amounts of love and great food and wheelbarrows of ice-cream for the kids to go nuts over. The dancing was ecstatic and the guests didn't tire until the sun began to set.

A few days later we flew to Italy and spent some time in Rome before driving down to the Amalfi Coast. We rented an apartment overlooking the Mediterranean just outside of Minori, bought ourselves local produce and sat on our terrace under the grape vines, eating smoky, creamy, crumbly cheeses, bread, figs and tomatoes. I called the girls out to marvel at our views and found all three huddled under the doona in one of their beds playing Nintendo; we each have our own version of happiness.

Four years later Ben was dead and a great hole was blasted through the middle of everybody's happiness.

The years leading up to the writing of *Stories of Ghosts* were heavy with loss. Too many of our friends and family were gone to G-d, many way too soon. We tried to make sense of it, to respond. The project felt relevant, weighty and absorbing and became a kind of receptacle for grief. Tragic stories became welded together, inextricably linked by their similarities, and the song 'Book of Life' became the howl of anguish in response to them.

The Book of Life is a metaphorical or literal book (depending on your belief) that G-d opens on Rosh Hashanah, the Jewish New Year, and seals ten days later on Yom Kippur. On Rosh Hashanah you pray to be inscribed in the book, and on Yom Kippur you pray to be sealed into it; the phrase, 'May your name be sealed in the Book of Life' is the common greeting during those ten days, the Days of Awe. For the devout Jew the time between the Book's opening and closing is spent in prayer, self-reflection and acts of repentance or reconciliation, to square away your relationship with G-d and with yourself.

All being well, prayers are answered and the good Jew can rely on another year on the planet. Of course, it doesn't always work out that way, by accident or design. Are there any accidents with G-d nominally in charge? For that matter, is there any design that G-d hasn't had a hand in? These are the key questions that the religious and the secularists have been battling out since Nietzsche declared, 'God is dead. God remains dead. And we have killed him.'

The prayer associated with these two holiest of days is called Unetaneh Tokef and was made well known beyond the Jewish world courtesy of Leonard Cohen's song 'Who By Fire', which quotes the prayer and then embroiders it. It is a prayer rich with yearning, heartache, a deep understanding of the human condition and ultimately forgiveness, without ever slackening the demand for personal responsibility. This beautiful poem has been a flint for many seeking to spark their creative fire, including us.

It was on 16 December, 2010, that we learned that someone very dear to us had walked too close to the abyss.

I had just hung up the phone after wishing my sister a happy birthday when my sister-in-law Louise rang. What I heard on the other end was an animal howl. She could barely get the words out; I couldn't comprehend what she was trying to communicate. And then like a projector clicking into focus she said, 'He's dead.' And I repeated it back to her. I was trying to comprehend it too.

It was way too much. Incomprehensible. Unspeakable. But she had spoken it. This was nothing I had anticipated, despite the excruciating uncertainty we had been living with for the previous year. But not this, not this.

Syd heard me on the phone and came running upstairs. Willy and I told the girls what had happened. It was about as awful a conversation as you could have. All of us were grappling on ground that was collapsing beneath us. There was no understanding; it was more about accepting.

Ben Zygier, the son of Willy's brother Geoffrey, had been incarcerated secretly in an Israeli prison for a year before dying in custody. Eventually he came to be known in the press as Prisoner X. Ben was in a maximum-security cell designed to be suicide-proof, in Ayalon Prison, Ramla, Israel, but he had hanged himself. He had just turned 34. It had only been four years since we'd all attended his wedding.

After Ben died, a *Foreign Correspondent* journalist spent ten months attempting to uncover the identity of the detained Australian-Israeli citizen. The media attention this family tragedy received was devastating to all of us but particularly to Ben's parents.

Despite Ben having been in prison for most of the year, this finale was unimaginable, ghastly and for the girls too shocking to process. They adored Ben and as the year had gone on, they had been asking more and more, *why hadn't he contacted them?* He had been a good correspondent and now, nothing. We had thought it was best to let the situation play out and tell them when we knew what the results of his court case would be; we felt sure there would be time.

The next few weeks were fragmented snapshots of collective and solitary grief. We spent hours every day at Ben's family home, sitting *shiva*, answering the door to endless streams of visitors with plates of food, making a lot of tea, whispering mourning in hushed voices. There was so much suffering, so little insight.

Ben's body was flown back to Australia, and we drove with his parents to the Chevra Kadisha where he would be constantly watched over until his burial. The sounds from within the chamber that Geoffrey and Louise entered to see their son are something I never want to hear again. Tearing, terrible gates-of-hell pain. The funeral was agonising. Ben was loved by family, friends and colleagues, many mourners united in complete desolation.

There would be a great deal written about these events in the years to come, but never with complete certainty or clarity. In the end the truth is virtually unknowable, even to those who knew the most. The only one with answers is gone now, leaving the memorial candle on his *yahrzeit*, the familiar twinkle in his little girls' eyes, the anguish on his parents' faces, the heartbreak on his sister's, his stricken wife, family and friends.

We went to Ubud a month after his death where I bought a statue as a kind of memorial. We placed the squatting stone boy under our maple tree outside my office window, eyes closed, hands wrapped around shoulders, self-sufficient, silent, still and now gently covered in a coat of lichen.

Maybe Ben had been seeking thrills, or maybe he had momentarily lost his grip on reality, or at least his understanding of how the world worked and how good and evil can play out. Or maybe it was simply that he had thought he was playing a game, and had forgotten the real-life consequences when others are not playing or maybe playing by a different rule book. The sequence of events following his dalliance at the edge of this abyss were beyond all comprehension, and they continue to ripple out in widening circles of sorrow and confusion that leave us questioning everything we ever understood about him.

I thought I knew Ben Zygier, but I didn't really know him at all.

As Unetaneh Tokef says, there are many ways to die: sickness, accident, foul play, or in peace. Death by one's own hand was Leonard Cohen's addition. Our song, 'Book of Life', is a kind of processing, a means of trying to understand why someone resorts to what is the inevitable final outcome for everyone lucky enough to be born at all.

It is hard to understand why some people decide that death cannot come soon enough. And it never fails to pull the rug out from everything you thought you knew. The grief and loss intermingle with anger directed wildly at them, at yourself for not knowing, at the world for not stepping in in some way, at G-d. But then what is left? Trying to make sense of cataclysmic events is challenging. An openness to the mysteries of life is a lens that allows some leeway when logic fails. Maybe that's a definition of G-d. Even for atheists.

'Book of Life', *Stories of Ghosts*, 2013

Blow the horn blow the horn
Give a voice to all the mournful souls who search to be reborn tonight
Forgiveness like the sharpest knife

Oh G-d inscribe me in the Book of Life
I've been hungry since before the dawn

Everybody's empty but it's not for food
Everybody's praying here to be rescued
Examining our sins it's hard not to conclude
We're screwed
The world's in flames these maddened days of black and white
No shades of grey to keep at bay the darkest night
There's never been a song that could save a life

Blow the horn blow the horn
Give a voice to all the mournful souls who search to be
reborn tonight
Forgiveness like the sharpest knife
Oh G-d inscribe me in the Book of Life
I've been hungry since before the dawn

Tired and full of uncried tears I still can't shed
Stored up with the unsaid things we never said
You wanted forgiveness I wasn't ready yet
Now you're dead
For all the souls who lost themselves I sing for you
Apart from that there's nothing more that I can do
And though I know it's useless it kind of helps me through

Blow the horn blow the horn
Give a voice to all the mournful souls who search to be
reborn tonight

Forgiveness like the sharpest knife
Oh G-d inscribe me in the Book of Life
I've been hungry since before the dawn

I want to see my children out in the world
Grown into women from little girls
Why wouldn't you want that too?
The older you get the more friends you lose
Next year I won't disappear in fire or flood
Next year I'll still be here to do some good
I won't be taken by pills or thrills or wine
I should be doing fine

Blow the horn blow the horn
Give a voice to all the mournful souls who search to be
reborn tonight
Forgiveness like the sharpest knife
Oh G-d inscribe me in the Book of Life
I've been hungry since before the dawn

I turned sixty in 2019. To celebrate we returned to Israel, the first time we'd been back since Ben's beautiful wedding thirteen years earlier. It was an important trip for us, to visit family and to repeat and build on the incredible experiences of both previous sojourns. We had two daughters with boyfriends, an Airbnb, Google Maps, a van and a plan.

We ate like kings, rode around on electric scooters down the Tel Aviv Beach boardwalk to Yafo and its crammed bakeries, and swam in the clear blue Mediterranean. We were dazzled by Batsheva Dance Company, spent time in Jerusalem, the Kinneret (Sea of Galilee), and stood in Mitzpe Ramon in the Negev on the edge of the world's largest cirque (crater) with an infinite starry sky above and ibex, the wild mountain goat, wandering fearlessly. We travelled back to Tel Aviv to attend a concert in honour of Zubin Mehta's retirement as music director of the Israel Philharmonic, a role he'd held for fifty years. There must have been 100,000 people in Yarkon Park on rugs, sharing picnics with family, friends, lovers; at eighty-three the charismatic maestro exuberantly conducted the orchestra and a superstar international cast of sopranos, tenors, mezzos, altos, to the delight of that enormous crowd, which gave him such an affectionate send-off. The finale was Tchaikovsky's '1812 Overture' accompanied by fireworks, the perfect farewell to Zubin.

Eretz Yisrael is an incredible place. It lives in the hearts and imaginations of many people: Jews and Muslims and Christians. As the years roll on it is difficult to have faith that such oppositional aspirations as those that exist between Palestinians and Israelis can find a peaceful resolution, but we can't lose faith; the land is built on it.

42

Love in the Middle Ages

As a young woman I was a reluctant writer of love songs. As an older woman, I have warmed to them. Youthful, bouncy, lusty, groping, perky love songs have their place, but even as a younger woman I never felt I could authentically own writing or singing them. I preferred the seedy, crusty, frayed, comfortable, maybe a little distracted variety. Shiny newness wears off quickly (I said as much in my one successful love song). The poignancy of finding and holding onto love as our human frailties, exposed by the passing of years, come to dominate, is where it gets interesting for me.

'Love in The Middle Ages' and 'Lying Next to You' are both in the genre of A-Little-Worse-for-Wear-Love-Songs. They are about the bend, not the snap. Compromises, work-arounds, the mundane journey of the unsung hero doing nothing more heroic than exactly the same thing they did yesterday without losing their mind. Some days are better than others, always helped by knowing you're not doing it alone.

'Lying Next to You', *Half Man Half Woman*, 2010

Woke up today the sky was all grey
I was lying next to you
So how could I mind if the sun takes her time
While I'm lying next to you

Thoughts come and go just ticking over slow
While I'm lying next to you
What was before doesn't matter anymore
Lying next to you

The dawn chorus choir
The alarm's about to fire
I'm lying next to you
Your breath soft and warm in the calm before the storm
Lying next to you

I'm spending today a million miles away
From lying next to you
Before the blinds are drawn
I need a moment more
Lying next to you

And tonight when I fall at the end of it all
I'll be lying next to you

Yes I know when we fall at the end of it all
I'll be lying next to you

I know how blessed I am to have found a lifelong companion in Willy Zygier, to have made a family that feels like an endless adventure playground even if some parts wouldn't entirely meet health and safety regulations. Our lives have been rich, serendipitous and joyous, and the sorrows more easily borne because we are in this together.

Life has taught Willy to embrace obstacles, to think independently; he's tech fluent and, more importantly, he can explain the intricacies of such to the less tech-savvy family members without losing his cool (this requires a huge amount of patience and innate kindness). I like to argue—Willy is happy to challenge me when it's meaningful, to let it slide when it's not. We never fight each other (not since Google Maps) and we never run out of things to talk about.

Willy has now been my lover, my boyfriend, my collaborator, my hands-down favourite guitar player, the father of my three daughters, my husband and my best friend for more than thirty years; we are indivisible travelling companions on the tricky journey of life. He has been my lifeline through the frustration, the slumps, the failures as much as the successes, which is saying a lot. He has never wavered in his support; and even as he challenges me to be better, while I'm yelling at him, Willy makes me laugh.

Mr Zygier and I met in 1991; we got married seven albums, three babies, two houses, two cats, a dog and nearly seventeen years later.

When I was in my twenties there was a lot of pushback about getting married. Neither I nor anyone in my peer group were interested in giving tacit support to the patriarchy, or becoming a chattel, or the expense, or the bother—who needed it? I went to hardly anyone's wedding (though to my eternal sorrow I missed my two oldest friends' weddings when I was living outside Australia). And still more than half my friendship group remain steadfastly living in sin, decades after no one gives a toss, apart from same-sex marriages which that same demographic cares about far more than they didn't care about their own, obviously for quite different reasons.

There *were* some good grounds for getting married, like smoothing bureaucratic hurdles when you're at the airport with a babe in arms with a different surname on their passport to yours, or persuading British immigration officers that your partner and father of your child shouldn't be kicked out of the country because you lack a marriage certificate. But still I was a holdout. When, back in 1998, we released an album called *My Third Husband*, and journalists asked about the name, I would tell them, 'I'm married to my work but I like to fuck around.'

I was perfectly happy with our arrangement. I had no interest in white dresses or walking down the aisle or our children not being bastards. Nor, as it happened, did our parents. No one cared. We had been married in the eyes of Willy's brother Geoffrey's rabbi from the first night we started cohabiting; modern parlance would call it a great hack!

But sometime in the middle of winter in 2005 I rose from my bed and went downstairs at the I-can't-sleep witching-hour of 2 am, with a line, 'love in the middle ages', spinning in my head. A smartypants song title, for which I wrote the most romantic ballad I'd ever composed. Unlike my usual drafts, which are edited, revised and rerevised, this song is etched in one page of my notebook, with barely a word crossed out.

'Love in the Middle Ages'

I'm not waiting for you to climb to some great height, not tonight
Relax, I'm here to rub your back and remove those gloves
Can you feel the love
Can you feel the love

C'mon I might have cold feet but baby my heart is warm
We're in the eye of the storm
We're in the eye of the storm in here

The sink's full of dishes, I'll wash and you dry
We all make our wishes and sometimes they fly
But like the loaves and the fishes there'll always be enough to get us by

Years, so many gone and so many years to go, oh oh oh oh
Like sea birds, flapping our way across an endless blue, for you I do
I do, I do for you

The song celebrates ordinary domesticity not with a golden hue but with acceptance—life might be enduringly tough but it is infinitely easier when we make it work together. I would introduce this song at shows by discussing my barren ring finger and dropping leaden hints (show biz-style) that after road-testing our relationship for fifteen years I was almost ready to tie the knot.

Away from the footlights, we had been discussing getting hitched for a while, and had decided that, having waited this long, we should hold off until our daughters stopped pulling focus. (Which gave me a good couple of years to milk the introduction of this song.)

Finally, in 2007, we set the date and started making preparations. But it quickly became a chaotic time.

Willy's eighty-six-year-old mother Lucia, fell and broke her hip, which sent his eighty-nine-year-old father Tadek, aka Ted, into a spiral of rapid-onset dementia from the shock. He had driven to our house that morning to tell us Lucia was on the floor in their flat and couldn't get up, which of course was already peculiar, because no matter how much you don't like the telephone this would have been the moment to use one.

Twenty minutes elapsed between the moment he arrived to announce the disaster, and the moment he had driven himself home again, ignoring my pleas to let me drive him. In those few minutes I phoned Willy (who was out walking the dog when Tadek had arrived), his brother Geoffrey and an ambulance. By the time Tadek got back to Caulfield, both sons were there to witness their mother being carried out of the flat on a stretcher, as Ted, watching his wife of close to seventy years, asked in Polish, 'Who is this woman?' As well as his memory and grip on reality, English had also deserted him.

It was a dreadful period. Lucia spent time in a rehab clinic while Tadek was admitted to a local aged-care residence under a watchful eye. However, the watchful eye was nowhere near all-seeing, judging from the number of times Tadek was able to elude it, hail a taxi and pay with one of the collection of electric razors he'd been hoarding, maybe for just such a moment.

Tadek had survived the Holocaust; now his lifelong companion, his existential bedrock, had disappeared and the dementia was at full-blown crisis level. He wasn't letting a little thing like no money, bars on the windows or watchful eyes stymie his bids for freedom. What did him in was the kindness of strangers, who would gratefully accept the razor and then return him (and the razor) to the closest police station. It became an almost daily occurrence. Once, when the sliding doors had been secured, he hefted a brick and escaped through the broken window glass. He was good at it—he'd survived the Nazis.

Lucia and Tadek had met in 1944, in Budapest, at the Polish Consulate where Polish refugees could obtain work permits in Hungary. Their eyes met in the waiting room and after Tadek walked out of his interview with a slight swagger, he asked Lucia if she would meet him later that day in the town square. Both were in their early twenties, both had lost their parents and siblings to the gas chambers, both had seen things no human being should have to see. They were incognito, Jews posing as gentiles, trying to survive another day.

What twist in the universe allowed him to ask her, what call was she hearing when she agreed? Intuition bolstered by courage, battling fear. A mistake was potentially lethal.

The meeting place would be under the town's famous clock tower. It was a perfect spot, Tadek prided himself on being punctual—'like Bank Polski', he'd declare when he arrived at our house exactly on the dot. And there he was, at the appointed hour, where Lucia was not. There was more riding on this than just a casual dalliance; he must have asked himself if she suspected something, or had informed the authorities. He was blond and blue-eyed, she had more to fear with her darker features.

He was growing impatient, even a little suspicious that he'd misjudged. And hanging around looking shiftless would eventually attract unwanted attention. As he was thinking of abandoning the wait, so she appeared; without an arresting officer in tow, she was just herself, alone.

They walked, they talked. Increasingly the small sense of her was growing on him. He needed to know, more than he needed to know anything he'd ever needed to know before. Risking everything, he asked her, 'Are you Jewish?'

She stopped and flushed, raising her voice slightly, and said 'How dare you ask such a thing!' He looked into her eyes and very quietly, no longer in Polish but in Hebrew, recited the first part of the Sh'ma, the prayer Jews say every morning and evening.

'*Sh'ma Yis-ra-el, A-do-nai E-lo-hei-nu,*' 'Hear O Israel the Lord our G-D', and she finished the line '*A-do-nai E-chad.*' 'The Lord is One.'

The fell into each other like tiny islands of sanity in a sea of chaos and remained together for sixty-seven years.

Tadek regained his grasp of English within a week or so, but his Houdini exploits hadn't waned. Just before our wedding, we were readying to leave the house on a family shopping trip to outfit the girls in something appropriately weddingish, when Tadek knocked on the door. He was beaming, so happy that he was once again at large and at our house. He joined the family excursion. He was like a good luck talisman: we found matching frocks (on sale) and matching shoes. Tadek flirted with every sales assistant and they flirted back. He was on fire, his old-world charm on full display. It was a perfect day.

Lucia emerged from rehab a few weeks later and Tadek began to regain some semblance of himself. He was home, not physically back in Caulfield—that would never again be home—but his home was not a place, it was Lucia.

Mr Zygier and I finally stood under the *chuppah* and broke the glass on Sunday, 9 December, 2007. It was the day before Willy's fiftieth birthday, which I knew he would never celebrate if left to his own devices, but a wedding was the perfect Trojan horse to smuggle in a milestone birthday party as well.

In the scheme of things, it's curious that Willy and I didn't meet sooner. The birth certificates we had to produce for the rabbi revealed the same midwife had signed both documents twenty months apart, in the same hospital. We had both gone to Temple Beth Israel Sunday school. We both grew up in the same small Melbourne Jewish community and both became musicians. Willy came to a Do-Ré-Mi gig, but stayed outside catching up with friends.

But here we were now. My mum and dad walked me around to the green space behind Hamer Hall where the *chuppah* was held aloft by family members under Melbourne's unpredictable skies, with the city outline alternating darkly and brilliantly behind us. The overflowing cup of wine was passed between our four parents. Tadek tried to drink it all. Our three daughters, our siblings, our parents, our friends, everybody I loved had gathered here to witness. My long-held ambivalence to getting hitched was no match for such euphoric certainty.

The reception was a few steps away at the Famous Spiegeltent set up on the Arts Centre Forecourt. The Stiletto Sisters' gypsy trio moved through and around us, herding everyone through the dark wood and mirrored portico, and we newlyweds circled the dance floor. Almost immediately Monsieur Camembert, our seven-piece house band, had the entire tent heaving and groaning in a *hora* that didn't stop as we spun faster and faster, more and more deliriously in clockwise and anticlockwise circles that continually shifted under the weight of increasing participation.

I ate and drank nothing all night. I didn't need to, I was high and full on the food of love. We asked musical couple friends to perform a song for us, which they all did with exquisite panache. In between there were speeches, and my father was hilarious. Friends extolled Willy and our long friendships. Geoffrey brought the sacred to the proceedings as is his wont, and drew parallels between the coinciding Chanukah (Festival of Light) and our metaphorically light-filled home.

Our three daughters honoured us with their very first gig together, (the aforementioned Tamworth gig was their second public performance) singing three-part harmony on 'You Are My Sunshine' with lyrics modified for the occasion.

Mr and Mrs Zygier chose 'I Wanna Be Loved By You' to perform. I played ukulele. And then we each made a speech. Mine was entertaining, but Willy's speech was one of those that lifts the room to somewhere else. I feel the need to reprint it here for the kind of posterity that it wouldn't receive if it was simply left to gather dust on the shelf, which is where I found it.

I can't tell you how many people have said to me when they heard about this event, 'Are you sure you're ready?' My parents-in-law, even the rabbi used that gag—half the people in this room said it. But you know what? I was ready 16-and-a-half years ago, it was blindingly obvious the moment Deborah and I met, it was one of those things.

There are people here tonight who recommended that Deborah hire me for that first tour, and who also said something about the potential chemistry and who went so far as to warn me that there was the possibility for something to happen and there you go, they were right and here we are.

And in that time since we have done everything together, work, play, shop, live overseas, raise a family, we're one of THOSE couples, so yes, I'm ready, but the question I haven't been asked, strangely, is 'Why?' Why get married, married now, after all this time?

There are the obvious jokes about our children being bastards, there's even the retort about wanting the white-goods . . . Half of you here tonight aren't married, it was our generation's little rebellion, so no one thinks to ask why?

I don't know if you know but the Zygiers have gone through a tough time over the last couple of months. My parents are also one of those couples that do everything together. Sadly my mother broke her hip and my father caved in under the pressure. It's been awful really as they have gone from two independent people living their own lives to something completely other. And yet while this was happening my brother Geoffrey and his wife Louise became grandparents and their daughter Tully, an aunt. And my amazing girls have had piano exams and homework to get in, and there have been meals to cook and floors to vacuum and music to be written, even dogs to be patted and tomorrow, well, tomorrow I become old and I turn fifty.

And it's just the stuff of life that we all experience in our own ways and for me, a lot of it is a blur, just rushing by in a beautiful mad uncatchable haze. And I'm middle-aged, and my parents are elderly, and my eldest daughter is taller than my girlfriend—alright, wife—and the others are catching up fast. And my parents-in-law are always, and I mean always, there to help. And the songs we are writing are about things as a young man I'd never dreamed of writing about.

And you realise that life is not what you have but the memory of those things, and you realise, as your father's memories slowly slip away, that the blur is precious and that the memory is all you can take.

So to get married, today, is to put a little marker into my life, our lives, a memory we can all share together.

I can see a picture in my head of my little girls all grown up reminiscing about today, remembering how amazing their mother looked, so radiant, still so beautiful and young, talking about how their father was so happy to be with her, remembering their grandparents dancing, their wonderful uncles and aunts and cousins, the good food—and the food that Alma wouldn't touch—the feel of the wooden floors underfoot, the mirrors, the music and all our friends gathered together knowing that yes, we were sure we were ready and that really there was no reason to ask why.

'Love in the Middle Ages' never made it onto an album. We recorded it, we just never included it. I'm still not entirely sure why that is. Maybe I didn't need to anymore.

43

Blessed

I have been told often I am lucky. Sometimes the statement is framed like it's a birthright. 'You're born lucky.' I certainly feel very lucky. Back when one of my goddaughters was born her mother was so certain I could pass on this good luck blessing, she requested I spit on the new baby's head. And when her sister was born, I did the 'baptising' again. Who's to say it didn't work? They've both grown to be impressive young women.

It's not a life most people choose, with the difficulties of being self-employed, the doubts about your abilities (the creative person's lot) and the ever-present uncertainty of what will happen next. The flipside of that uncertainty is the sweetness of conjuring something that didn't previously exist, even if the sweetness is fleeting. It's the magic of serendipity, my constant companion of 'anything could happen'. It's not for everyone, but I feel incredibly blessed that I have been able to live that life and it's mostly worked, which means it's always worked 'cos nothing is perfect and 'mostly' is the very best you could hope for.

I was sitting in a hotel room in Perth in 1988, about to head off to a Do-Ré-Mi sound check when Keith, my manager, called to say, 'Pete Townshend—'

'WHAT—FROM THE WHO?'

'Yes,' Keith said patiently, 'wants you to sing the role of The Vixen on his latest project.'

'Oh wow!' It was a crazy out-of-the-blue proposition, to which I naturally said, 'YES PLEASE'.

The CEO at Virgin UK, Simon Draper, had played Pete Do-Ré-Mi's video of 'Adultery' apparently eliciting the response, 'I want her.'

His project was an adaptation of a 1968 novel by poet laureate (and Sylvia Plath's ex) Ted Hughes, into a musical rock opera. *The Iron Man* is a sci-fi fairy story of a metal giant who eats large-scale farm equipment, much to the distress of the local community who entrap the creature in a pit. The giant digs himself free, and ten-year-old Hogarth comes to the rescue to find him a home at the local scrap yard, which is where he is when the Earth is attacked by a space dragon, that the Iron Man must fight and defeat before it eats the world. A fierce battle is eventually resolved in happily-ever-after fashion and peace reigns.

It's not a plot I would have chosen to adapt as a rock opera, but that's also what I thought when I read *Wicked*, Gregory Maguire's epic backstory of the political intrigue and human rights abuses in Oz—so what would I know?

The original intention of a double album was abandoned in favour of a single album release, which was cheaper no doubt but sacrificed the 'making sense' part of the story. We recorded at Pete's studio Eel Pie in Twickenham; I sang a couple of songs but was never given the libretto to read so I never understood who The Vixen was or what she had to do with anything. I didn't mind being in the dark.

Between takes, Pete goofed around doing Mick Jagger impressions. We kept up some correspondence after the sessions but the proposed stage-show never eventuated and the reviews were tepid despite album credits for John Lee Hooker, Nina Simone, Pete Townshend and . . . Deborah Conway. There, on the CD in black and white. I sang with legends.

In London in 1990, during my year of Waiting For Virgin, I accidentally made friends with the composer Michael Nyman. My friend Cameron Allen (RIP) was staying with Michael in his rambling Queen's Park house. I walked over from my Portobello Road flat intending to meet Cameron, but he had been delayed. Michael was delightful company and we struck up a friendship over a four-hour wait with numerous cups of tea and conversation that ranged across all the finest creative pursuits and a few of the more carnal ones.

In the short term, this friendship got me a gig on the new Peter Greenaway film *Prospero's Books*, a sumptuous reimagining of *The Tempest*, which transpired to be about as dreamlike and opaque as a film could be. Michael invited me to sing the role of the goddess Juno that Annie Lennox had just turned down, a right-place-right-time moment that I didn't hesitate to say yes to. We recorded at Abbey Road with the London Symphony Orchestra, and I got to let my upper register head voice off the leash.

The scene location was a massive warehouse in Amsterdam. The divine Ute Lemper and Marie Angel played my fellow goddesses, all of us in giant Elizabethan collars and surrounded by hundreds of naked Dutch extras, men and woman, in body paint with genitals in contrasting colours to limbs, faces in contrasting colours to bodies. It was not dissimilar to a giant MTV rock video clip with lots of smoke and many moving (body) parts, though Sir John Gielgud, in the role of Prospero (fully dressed of course), was moving a lot less. At his advanced age, he required a cot for lie-downs between takes.

It's 2001, I'm behind the curtains waiting to be revealed in my wig and sequinned black frock, dressed as Patsy Cline and about to perform 'She's Got You'. It's a big moment in the show, the first number after interval, the audience need to be brought back from their foyer distractions and it's the opening notes of this song that have to do it. I stand tensed, thinking about how few shows I have the chance to play, how very blessed I am to be here at all, let alone to be given the task of filling the shoes of one of the twentieth century's greatest singers.

I am grateful, I am calm, I am not going to miss a moment, and this whole parade goes like the clappers. I am forty-one years old. I've just had my third child, another darling little girl barely a year old but I've just started getting hot flushes. My body is like a kettle that someone keeps flicking on. I heat to boiling point, before I turn off and cool down. Forty-one, premenopausal and on stage in a tight sparkling dress playing the part of a woman who was dead at thirty. But now it's me, and I am here and the only way to make it last is to be inside the moment for as long as it's going on, no matter how hot the moment gets.

I like to remind myself how fleeting is the time onstage, which of course is translatable to how fleeting is the time offstage too. The Adelaide run of *Always Patsy Cline* opened in the first week of September 2001. On 12 September, 2001, we played to a full house at Her Majesty's Theatre. Really, I just wanted to be at home, circling the wagons, holding my babies and their father tight. But the show had to go on. Probably there were many members of the audience who had to convince themselves to keep their arrangements that evening. They'd probably bought their tickets months before and had been looking forward to a night at the theatre, but who could possibly be in the mood for a musical in light of the day's events?

I felt for them, for all of us; the cast and musicians were in a strange place, too. A theatre built in 1913 is full of history. How many times would Her Majesty's curtains have lifted on performances during the wars of the twentieth century, performances where audiences were in mourning for fallen sons, husbands, fathers, brothers?

On 12 September, 2001, the audience needed no encouragement to be swept into the emotion of Patsy's tragic life and untimely death, and as I sang 'Crazy', the emotional outpouring we were struggling to give expression to burst forth into catharsis. We wept together for Patsy, for the men and woman who had perished that day and for their families, for America and the free world, for our lost innocence and our collective misunderstanding of humanity.

I've shared stages with Violent Femmes, Simple Minds, Culture Club, UB40, Midnight Oil, Sting, INXS, Madness, Barry White, Joan Armatrading, Boz Scaggs, Bob Dylan (a few times) and many, many more; but Leonard Cohen was personal.

In November 2011 at Rod Laver Arena we were Leonard Cohen's support act, waiting backstage to go on. The heavily tattooed, muscle-bound production manager snarled at us out of the side of his mouth, 'If you go over your allotted time limit, I'll kill you'; his regular gig was with Iron Maiden, he was just moonlighting for Leonard. He pointed out the oversized clock on the floor of the stage that would tell us when our thirty minutes was up. 'Dare go over,' he said, 'and face the consequences.' He was very tall with a chill in his voice.

Mr Zygier and I walked on stage and delivered a perfect set for the 14,000-strong crowd. They were on our side, they felt the relationship between the support act and the headline, and any resistance, sometimes encountered by support acts, was utterly absent. Then a conundrum. The last song normally finished with a guitar solo building to a harmonised vocal chant with an a cappella finish. If Willy played his solo we would go over our allotted time by two minutes, we would be killed. As we approached the end of the song we looked at each other and nodded—we knew we wouldn't get this moment again, so we plunged in, damn the death threat. The audience gave us a rapturous response.

Mr Iron Maiden was livid as we came off stage but, perhaps realising who he was employed by, decided not to rough us up and instead simply refused to look at us. We made for the kiosk in the foyer and signed squillions of copies of *Half Man Half Woman*. Then to the green room, where the great 'rabbi' himself, Leonard Cohen, rose and hugged me. It was beautiful, I felt blessed. Then our daughter spilt some of her glass of soda on his suit.

We wrote 'Blessed' as an homage, or a theft, or an exploratory journey of Cohen's song 'Hallelujah'. 'Hallelujah' casts King David as a bridge to G-d only to highlight his all-too-human inadequacies. The song has taken on the quality of a hymn for many people of faith and more remarkably for many more without.

Our song 'Blessed' shines a spotlight on the son of King David and Bathsheba (famous for her rooftop ablutions), King Solomon, who is widely thought to be the anonymous author of The Song of Songs and Ecclesiastes. Solomon was famously wise, wealthy, a great and ambitious builder and a man of enormous sexual appetites with upwards of 700 concubines. There are some interesting parallels to make between contemporary rock stars and ancient biblical kings.

'Blessed', *Everybody's Begging*, 2016

You fell into a trance one night
Saw the Lord in blazing light
And prayed to him to favour you with wisdom
But all the wisdom was a test
Like all the women you undressed
And rumours of your Holiness

Blessed? Were you blessed?
Blessed beyond the dust beyond the flesh

You took the beauties to your room
Your songs of love made them swoon
You worshipped at their altars you were shameless
You laid your head on every breast
Every word a new conquest
You cannot love and you cannot rest

Did it get you blessed? Did it get you blessed?
Blessed beyond the dust beyond the flesh

Poets aren't you all the same
Playing G-d at His own game
Creating out of nowhere out of nothing
The blank page is your nemesis
But the girl who moans against your chest
Lets you believe your press

Did it get you blessed? Did it get you blessed?
Blessed beyond the dust beyond the flesh

I loved you, thought I was the one
Sheba to your Solomon
You were my moon, you were my sun
Now I've seen what's left of your monuments
I read your lines in the testaments
I believed whatever you confessed
Thought I was blessed

Every breath just empty air
Every deed just disappears
The wise and foolish in the end are levelled
All our works a vain protest
Our drowning hearts, our souls possessed
The bad die just like the best

Were we blessed? Were we blessed?
Blessed beyond the dust beyond the flesh

Yet despite all of King Solomon's achievements he could still write this at the end of his life:

> When I surveyed all that my hands had done and what I had toiled to achieve, everything was meaningless, a chasing after the wind; nothing was gained under the sun.
>
> Ecclesiastes 2:11

Music performs a lot of different services and fills many needs. Musicians are background more than we are foreground, part of community more than we are under a solo spotlight, essential at times but also an indulgence. No one owns music, and each of us decides how central it is in our lives.

The serendipitous nature of my chosen profession has had me bumping up against all sorts of unexpected people performing in many forums, stretching my skills to encompass feats, triumphs and abject failures. The bumps and the blessings are inextricably linked. I am wiser for both.

44

Don't You Forget Me

When I was young older people would ask, 'When will you get a proper job?' Now people ask me, 'Are you still a musician?'

Once Do-Ré-Mi started gigging seriously, six nights a week for nine months a year, I was losing my voice with miserable regularity. An early singing teacher who had declined to teach me was worried about the possibility of nodules. These are small, hard growths that develop on vocal cords that are under stress for any number of reasons, but singing loudly every night in a smoky bar with substandard foldback (the speakers at the feet of performers, facing up at them so they can hear themselves) would be the ideal set of circumstances if you were looking to grow some. If you don't change your behaviour, nodules become serious and compromise the vocal cords.

It was time to take this in hand and get singing lessons. I found myself a teacher who taught me, crucially, exactly where the breath was supposed to originate. For optimum results, breath begins in the diaphragm and is sent upwards with the assistance of abdominal muscles, chest muscles, rib cage and lungs. The breath hits the vocal cords, the mucous membrane that stretches over the larynx, and they vibrate in a kind of wave formation.

Think of elastic bands parting at one end and opening at the other in rapid reaction to the air. The larynx adjusts the tension and length of the cords, which determines pitch and tone. The tongue, teeth and lips use the vocal resonances and shape them into recognisable sounds, then the chest and throat amplify the volume and stamp the individual style of the vocalist onto the sound. And it all happens in a nano-blink, before conscious thought.

Once I had that diaphragm trick under my belt, I stopped losing my voice. The bonus was that I could sing through a terrible cold.

The mechanics of singing waltz cheek-to-cheek with the romance of singing: opening your mouth wide or barely, pushing out air, forming notes, controlling those notes, sculpting melody, sound, from whisper to scream, guttural to matter-of-fact, primal to majestic, or sullen to anthemic. I learnt how to give emotional weight to certain phrases, deny it to others; to hold a note until I conjured an emotional frisson with the vibrating particles shimmering and dancing in the space between exiting my body and entering someone else's.

In the moments when everything's working together, you're tapping into an all-powerful force, something beyond your own physicality, even though that power resides entirely in your body: in your lungs, lips, limbs, with your head thrown back or spine curled down, mouth wide, arms in the air, or intimately caressing the microphone.

Equal amounts of vulnerability and invincibility are brought to bear, whether it's for an audience of one or for thousands in a great hall. Singing is a singular act of offering your agility, precision, tone, personality, emotional intelligence and essence, and if your performance finds its target, listeners will receive your offering of breath and generosity with goosebumps, tears, laughter, maybe collective silence, maybe thunderous applause.

And yet . . . I have spent at least as much time hating the sound of my own voice and cringing to hear myself played back as I have loved it. It's such an odd phenomenon, listening to an old recording and responding to it viscerally in the polar opposite way I responded to it the last time I heard it. That response will almost inevitably reverse again a year or two or ten later. It's ego and self-delusion and faulty memory, and is all too human.

My profession is obsessed with youth. Rock 'n' roll is primal, it's sexual, it's not just romance or courtship, it's procreation; it's lewd, crude, hot, horny, irresponsible, irrepressible, dirty, occasionally depraved and, crucially, it is acted out by young people for young people. Its oldest male exponents are still stripping to the waist, prancing like men a quarter of their age and are frequently rewarded (should they choose) with a line of women outside their stage doors.

For women it's different; not that there aren't plenty of older stateswomen still treading the boards and wailing into darkened auditoriums (including me) but the cougar thing will translate only so far. Suffice to say rock music is largely the domain of youth because, as a vehicle for sexual energy, youth is the most receptive to that underlying message. Let's lose control, let's define ourselves separately to our parents, let's make trouble, let's get fucked up and let's fuck.

The central quandary of plying a young person's trade in an old person's body, exacerbated by being female, is never far from the surface.

I have eschewed hair dye, a facelift and Botox and I'm giving ageing gracefully a red-hot go; I am grateful that I have managed to stay a child in the sandpit for all my working life and if my sandcastles are no longer priapic, so be it, I still love building them. But maintaining credibility, remaining relevant and contributing something that hasn't been said already either by someone else or worse, you, is a whole other tightrope walk with a vast swirling pool of disinterest beneath you; a balancing act that if you don't like, well, there are alternatives.

For better or worse I keep going, the holy grail of the perfect song, the perfect vocal performance perpetually just out of reach.

I have been abundantly lucky in finding a calling that has accommodated my curiosity, my ambitions, my good and bad habits. I have walked between raindrops for the most part and skated lightly on some precariously thin ice without breaking through to the deep, dark swirl beneath. I have wandered down broad, sunlit avenues of discovery curtailed only by my own imagination, and all my life I've been able to explore what was pulling me.

I like to think of myself as someone who does what they say they're going to do, even if it takes a long time. As I wrote in my diary back in 2019:

> I made some life plans to embark on in this, my 60th year. I'm going to learn to touch type, start learning a language,

probably Hebrew, and start writing something. A book? A play? A show?

Not sure, it is daunting but I'm told everyone has a book in them—it mightn't be a good one of course—that's the daunting part.

'Don't You Forget Me', *The Words of Men*, 2019

What can an old lady tell you
That you might want to know?
What can an old lady sing
If it's not Only The Beginning?
I give you a piece of my heart
What else to impart
On this well-worn path

Don't you forget me
You won't regret me
I'll still sing if you let me
Let's drink to getting old

It's easy to be seduced
By those sirens' calls
You gladly hand them your cock
But they want your balls
All I got is my fading soul
And rock 'n' roll
That takes its toll

Don't you forget me
You won't regret me
I'll still sing if you let me
Let's drink to getting old

The old and the withered
Were once the young and the strong
Make way make way
For the new youth to sing their song
I've moved off centre stage
Traded all that for wisdom or rage
Or a little of both

Don't you forget me
You won't regret me
I'll still sing if you let me
Let's drink to getting old

Let's make some heaven
In this place that feels like hell
Get over here baby
You know how to ring my bell
So it's you and me
Got our grandchildren on my knee
That's distinctly sexy

Don't you forget me
You won't regret me
I'll still sing if you let me
Let's drink to getting old

Acknowledgements

I have a lot of people to thank.

Starting way back:

To my life-long friends Jo Macdougall for introducing me to the joys of having a best friend and to Caro Wilson for expanding that circle and at the tender age of fourteen, introducing me to Joni Mitchell. To John Heselev, for suggesting that I put an ad in the paper. Dorland Bray, Helen Carter and Stephen Philip, with whom I shared the sometimes-glamorous, oft-times-not, stage, tour van, dressing room, rehearsal space, etc., for eight mostly fun years. And extra thanks to Helen for the recent reprise. The early supporters: Geoff Watson, and Roger Grierson, who stayed for the late support, too!

Keith Welsh for his unruffled insouciance, matched with his always being ready for business.

Martin Armiger (RIP) who introduced me to my first serious and extended recording sessions and became a good friend in the process.

Paul Hester (RIP), my co-adventurer for many years in many locations. You are very missed. As are you, Mark Sarfaty (RIP)—you would have liked this had you stuck around long enough.

Lydia Livingstone (RIP) and Linda Jackson who, it may be said, I had my only real proper job with (almost). Amanda Pelman, who managed to manage me; Dave Williams, a scholar and a gentleman; Paul Kelly, my co-traveller and dear friend; Michael Gudinski (RIP), with thanks for the hits and the authentic rock 'n' roll wild ride; Paul Goldman for going into swing for my golf handicap.

Warren Costello (RIP), Bill Page and Sarah Morgan, for the sanity in a sometimes crazy place.

Richard Pleasance and Peter Farnan, who had my back.

Pierre Baroni (RIP), Brett Hilder and Tony Mott, who had my front.

Frank Stivala, Deborah Murphy and Paul Mason, who are on my side.

John Clifforth for making me better.

Lidija for making me stronger.

Dan Rosen for being a mensch.

James Black, Gerry Hale, Cameron Reynolds & Mick Girasole for producer chops.

Rupert Pletzer (the Prince); Brett Doig the gentleman; masterer Ross Cockle; and Robin Mai, thanks for the overtime. Kenny and PBH—you really helped, and not just me. And all the crew I've worked with: Rob Barnham, Larry Ponting, Tiny, Sid, Dave, Andy, etc., etc., thank you!

Miranda Brown for being our publicist and so much more.

Jon Faine for the regular jousts and James Valentine for the ever-ready support.

Bob Weis for so many things even when we didn't see eye to eye.

Willy and I play a lot as a duo. There is also something incredibly exhilarating about hearing the crisp snare snap of an introductory fill, the promise that no musician will be left off this beat train; the rich chocolate of a double bass to the thinner syrup of an electric, the augmenting sweetness or vulgarity of keys, horns, strings and skins. Thank you to the very many soulful musicians I have played with: Dror Erez, Chris Wilson (RIP), Peter Jones (RIP), Bill McDonald, Al Harding (aka Big Al), Vika and Linda Bull, Renée Geyer (RIP), Hugh Benjamin, Michael den Elzen, Michael Barker, Tina Kopa, Helen Mountford, Hope Csutoros, Dougal Scott, Liz Corby, Roy Dodds, Martyn Swain, Jackie Orszaczky (RIP), Tony Floyd, Clayton Doley, Edmond Ammendola, Neil Finn, Nick Haywood, David Carr, Al Barden, Ben Hendry, Niko Schauble, Shannon Birchall, Andy Papadopoulos, Nick Tsiavos, Simon Starr, Clio Renner, Sam Anning, Kate Ceberano, Joe Camilleri, Rebecca Barnard, Clare Bowditch, Ruby Hunter (RIP), Katie Noonan, Sara Storer, Mia Dyson, Ella Hooper, Kate Miller-Heidke, Melinda Schneider, Abbe May, Anne McCue, Jade MacRae, Sally Seltmann, Dianna Corcoran, Laura Jean Englert, Elana Stone, Liz Stringer, Jonathan Zion, Stephen (Stretch) Teakle, Louis Gill, Matt Watson, Matt Earl, Mark Ferrie, Peter Luscombe, Glenn Richards, Monique diMattina, Daniel Farrugia.

. . . and I've worked with wonderful creators: Michael Nyman, Andrée Greenwell, Geoffrey Rush, Paul Grabowsky, John Nichols, Michael Kantor and George Dreyfus.

Gratitude to chief cyber nerd Mark O'Meara for launching us in cyber space and the Bitch listers, early adopters and fans who we watched grow up but who didn't get sick of us, Nicky Pelletier, Pez, Groube and XIii, etc., etc., with special honour to LJ, for getting me a special honour; massive thanks to all of you and everyone who has ever bought a concert ticket, a record or supported us in whatever way. Couldn't do it without you—well we could, but it would be lonely.

Thanks to my early readers, Barbara Hogarth for the detailed and honest feedback when the book was 210,000 words (I know how hard that is!) and Joanne Corrigan for persistence and the most trajectory-changing introduction you could have made.

Thanks, Ramona for all the good advice—that's when neighbours become good friends.

Thanks to Velly Slavin and Chabad House, for deepening my understanding.

To Alex McGregor, for going over old ground.

Enormous thank you to Malcolm Knox for your encouragement and taking the time to dive deep to show me a different perspective.

To my agent, Fiona Inglis, thank you for coming onboard.

To Jane Palfreyman and the enthusiastic Allen & Unwin tribe for the belief and the work—Samantha Kent and Sam Ryan, and freelance editors Ali Lavau and Jessica Friedmann.

Thanks to Geoffrey, Louise and Tully, all those early conversations were valuable.

To Shellie, who has been to a lot of the dark places I have been and can laugh with me. It's better to share.

To my darling, long-suffering mother, I'm sorry but it had to be done. I love you.

To Carl Conway (RIP) without whom I wouldn't be me. Thank you, love you, no hard feelings.

To Syd, Alma and Hettie, who have given me more life, joy, sorrow and inspiration than I could know what to do with. This book is for you, just so you know.

And to Mr Zygier, my first reader and my last reader. Thank you for going into the lion's den again and again. You are fearless and funny, and mostly you are right.

To the long list of those no longer with us, may your memories be a blessing.

Note

1 Joseph C. Self, 'The "My Sweet Lord"/"He's So Fine" Plagiarism Suit' http://www.abbeyrd.net/mysweet.htm